EMMA THOMPSON

CW01095731

Greeting the 500

GREETING THE 500
(An Idiot's Bet)

Jules Segal

First published in Great Britain in 2007 by Friday Books
An imprint of The Friday Project Limited
83 Victoria Street, London SW1H 0HW

www.thefridayproject.co.uk
www.fridaybooks.co.uk

Text and photographs © Jules Segal

ISBN 978-1-905548-590

British Library Cataloguing in Publication Data

A catalogue record for this book is available from the British Library

Cover and internal design by Snowbooks Design
www.snowbooksdesign.com

Typeset by Makar Publishing Production

Printed by MPG Books Ltd

The Publisher's policy is to use paper manufactured from sustainable sources

Foreword

If I'd been given one pound for every time I'd been asked to write a foreword for a book that centres around a 'bar bet', I'd have......oh about £3.00 now. Just enough for a pint actually, how appropriate.

Jules, the author of this book, informs me that the striking up of odd challenges whilst under the influence of something slightly stronger than a cherry cola, has become so common in this day and age, that the online encyclopaedia that goes by the name Wikipedia, actually has an entire entry dedicated to the Bar Bet.

It's here that I must hold my hands up and say that yes, I too have trampled down this boulevard of insanity, although I didn't get to meet any former Prime Ministers, Celebrity Chefs or England Opening Batsmen whilst transporting a fridge around the circumference of Ireland within a time limit.

Then again, I didn't have a crabby friend barracking me for most of my journey as it appears Jules did.

I also find myself as being in the privileged position of having had the first 'Celebrity' handshake with Jules as he strove to get to grips, quite literally, with 100 famous palms in his six month time limit and I'd like to think that he didn't wash his hand for months afterwards.

Whether he managed to track down another 99 subjects and was therefore spared the forfeit of having to place his arm up a cow's backside (I'll let him explain that one), you'll just have to read on, but I can do no more than raise my hat to the Jules Segals, the Dave Gormans and, yes why not, the Tony Hawks of this world, for making it an ever so slightly more interesting place.

Tony Hawks

To lil' Mo (not the one in EastEnders)
who's already brought me so much happiness.

Also to Michael, without whose help, friendship
and (most importantly) digital camera,
this never would have been possible.

PREFACE

According to the online encyclopaedic bible that is Wikipedia.com a **HANDSHAKE** can be defined as '...*a short ritual in which two people grasp their right or left hands, often accompanied by a brief shake. It is commonly done upon meeting, departing, offering congratulations, or completing an agreement. Its purpose is to demonstrate good will, and possibly originated as a gesture showing that the hand holds no weapon.*'

Meanwhile, a **PHOTOGRAPH** is described as '*a single image created using a record of light falling on a light-sensitive surface, usually photographic film...*'

A **CELEBRITY,** we are told, is '*a widely-recognised or famous person who commands a high degree of public and media attention...*'

And a **BAR BET** is '*a bet made between two patrons at a bar*'.

Oh, and just for your interest (or more accurately, mine) **SCARLETT JOHANSSON** is '*an American actress... who has been named the "sexiest" or "most beautiful" woman alive by several publications*' – including this one now.

Yes, well that last point is not exactly rocket science, is it, yet unlike the others it has no relevance whatsoever to this book. Anyway, why the hell am I banging on about ruddy dictionary definitions? Well, please permit me to further flesh out this atrophied and nonsensical

1

body of words with a brief explanation about who I am, who my friend Michael is, and what the bloody hell *Greeting the 500* is all about. It will all make sense in the end, I promise.

My name is Jules (Julian to my mother or members of Her Majesty's police force) and I live in London, which is a big shiny city at the southern end of a large island. This island is known by the name of England (oh, and Scotland and Wales). The London that I refer to is a city that is inhabited by many people from the four corners of the earth, all of whom live together in glorious Technicolor and harmony... most of the time.

And so the Lord looked at the City that he had made and he smiled and was happy-ish (possibly apart from that massive estate in Kidbrooke, which seems a little bit grim at the best of times).

I digress. In the past I have worked as a lawyer (I officially apologise), as a sports journalist and as a cashier in a betting shop. I no longer do any of these things. I now write film scripts from my bedroom, eat soup out of cans and scratch myself on the settee (although I don't think that's the correct biological term for it).

Michael is, I guess you could say, one of my best friends. He reminds me a great deal of Niccolo Machiavelli. This is not because he is an Italian statesman living in sixteenth century Florence. In fact he is a Greek-Cypriot (currently out of work) health inspector living in Cricklewood (or Krakow-Wood as we now refer to it because of the recent large influx of our Polish brethren to the area). No, the similarity lies in their somewhat cynical view of mankind and human nature, and that, my friends, lays the foundation to the little project that we came to know as *Greeting the 500*.

THE BET

I had six months from July 1 until December 31 to have my photograph taken while shaking the hands of 100 famous British individuals. These 100 individuals would all be taken from a list or 500 famous British individuals that Michael would compile.

There are only two stipulations that Michael must adhere to:

1. Each person on the list must be living (we deemed the alternative to be rather a sick idea).

2. Each person on the list must reside in the UK (so as to give me at least some chance of meeting them).

THE LIST OF 500

Jenny Agutter **Asad Ahmad** Caroline Aherne **Donna Air** Damon Albarn **Peter Alliss** Martin Amis **Clive Anderson** Toby Anstis **Nicole Appleton** Archbishop of Canterbury **Jeffrey Archer** Joan Armatrading **Leslie Ash** Jane Asher **Rick Astley** Rowan Atkinson **David Attenborough** Richard Attenborough **Alan Ayckbourn** Steve Backley **David Baddiel** Bill Bailey **David Bailey** Clare Balding **Zoe Ball** Cheryl Baker **Danny Baker** Tom Baker **Iain Banks** Jeff Banks **Sue Barker** Ronnie Barker **Sacha Baron Cohen** Michael Barrymore **Sanjeev Bhaskar** Helen Baxendale **Jeremy Beadle** Sean Bean **David Beckham** Victoria Beckham **Kate Beckinsale** David Bellamy **Floella Benjamin** Nigel Benn **Tony Benn** Cilla Black **Tony Blackburn** Cherie Blair **Tony Blair** Alan Bleasdale **Jennie Bond** Helena Bonham Carter **Ian Botham** Jim Bowen **Edith Bowman** Boy George **Geoff Boycott** Billy Bragg **Melvyn Bragg** Jo Brand **Richard Branson** Tim Brooke-Taylor **Derren Brown** Eric Bristow **Fern Briton** Michael Buerke **Julie Burchill** Kathy Burke **Darcey Bussell** Gary Bushell **Jenson Button** Darren Campbell **Naomi Campbell** Nicky Campbell **Will Carling** Jimmy Carr **Jasper Carrott** Willie Carson **Todd Carty** Craig Charles **Keith Chegwin** Linford Christie **Charlotte Church** Nicky Clarke **Jeremy Clarkson** Julian Clary **John Cleese** Martin Clunes **Sebastian Coe** Joan Collins **Robbie Coltrane** Sean Connery **Billy Connolly** Tom Conti **Jasper Conran** Terence Conran **Norman Cook** Steve Coogan **Jilly Cooper** Ronnie Corbett **Hugh Cornwell** Simon Cowell **Steve Cram** Mackenzie Crook **Barry Cryer** John Culshaw **Richard Curtis** Sophie Dahl **Lawrence Dallaglio** Paul Daniels **Jim Davidson** Alan

Davies **Barry Davies** Bobby Davro **Steve Davis** Peter Davidson **Darren Day** Cat Deeley **Angus Deayton** Jack Dee **Jermaine Defoe** Les Dennis **David Dickinson** David Dimbleby **Declan Donnelly** Greg Dyke **Sheena Easton** Eddie the Eagle **Noel Edmonds** Adrian Edmondson **Jonathan Edwards** Ben Elton **Tracy Emin** Harry Enfield **Chris Eubank** Chris Evans **Lisa Faulkner** Vanessa Feltz **Alex Ferguson** Helen Fielding **Ranulph Fiennes** Judy Finnigan **Colin Firth** Dexter Fletcher **Keith Flint** Andrew Flintoff **Keith Floyd** Carl Foggarty **Ben Fogle** Emma Forbes **Bruce Forsyth** Norman Foster **Dr Fox** Samantha Fox **Mark Lewis-Francis** John Francome **Martin Freeman** Anna Friel **Dawn French** Emma Freud **David Frost** Sadie Frost **Simon Fuller** Kirsty Gallacher **Liam Gallagher** Noel Gallagher **George Galloway** Leslie Garrett **Paul Gascoigne** Ricky Gervais **A. A. Gill** Trisha Goddard **Duncan Goodhew** Dave Gorman **Anthony Gormley** Damon Gough **Darren Gough** David Gower **Hugh Grant** Richard E. Grant **Leslie Grantham** Jimmy Greaves **Simon Groom** Sally Gunnell **William Hague** Eric Hall **Geri Halliwell** Christine Hamilton **Neil Hamilton** Nick Hancock **Ainsley Harriott** Keith Harris **Audley Harrison** Sara Cox **John Harvey-Jones** Max Hastings **Nigel Havers** Tony Hawks **Stephen Hawking** Barry Hearn **Stephen Hendry** Tim Henman **Lenny Henry** Sam Heuston **James Hewitt** Jimmy Hill **Damian Hirst** Ian Hislop **Amanda Holden** Noddy Holder **Eamonn Holmes** Kelly Holmes **Jools Holland** Bob Holness **Anthony Hopkins** Trevor Horn **Nick Hornby** Kate Humble **John Humphrys** Liz Hurley **Glenda Jackson** Colin Jackson **Marc Jacobs** Mick Jagger **David Jason** Lee Jasper **Elton John** Dom Joly **Aled Jones** Tom Jones **Vinnie Jones** Jordan **Boris Johnson** Digby Jones **Chris Kamara** Natasha Kaplinsky **Kerry Katona** Jay Kay **Peter Kay** Vernon Kay **Penelope Keith** Lorraine Kelly **Matthew Kelly** Martin Kemp **Ross Kemp** Felicity Kendall **Charles Kennedy** Nigel Kennedy **Patsy Kensit** Bill Kenwright **John Kettley** Richard Keys **Jodie Kidd** Robert Kilroy-Silk **Oona King** Neil Kinnock **Mervyn King** Keira Knightley **Cleo Laine** Frank Lampard **Lynda la Plante** Eddie Large **Hugh Laurie** Jude Law **Kate Lawler** John le Carré **Rusty Lee** Mike Leigh **Annie Lennox** John Leslie **Denise Lewis** Lennox Lewis **Victor Lewis-Smith** Robert Lindsay **Gary Lineker** Maureen Lipman **Ralf Little** Richard Littlejohn **Ken Livingstone** Lawrence Llewelyn-Bowen **Andrew Lloyd Webber** Rebecca Loos **Matt Lucas** Joanna Lumley **Des Lynam** Nicholas Lyndhurst **Humphrey Lyttleton** Ellen MacArthur **Cameron Mackintosh** Richard Madeley **John Major** Nigel Mansell **Michael Mansfield QC** Andrew Marr **Chris Martin** Bernard Matthews **Rick Mayall** Davina McCall **Paul McCartney** Stella McCartney **Ian McCaskill** Malcolm McClaren **John McCririck** Trevor McDonald **Alistair McGowan** Rory McGrath **Ewan McGregor** Ian McKellen **Paul McKenna** Linsey Dawn McKenzie **Colleen McLoughlin** Liz McClarnon **Andy McNab** Ant McPartlin **Alexander McQueen** Colin McRae **Sam Mendes** Paul Merton **Melinda Messenger** George Michael **Sienna**

5

Miller Bob Mills **Anthony Minghella** Miss Dynamite **Jimmy Mistry** Colin Montgomery **Patrick Moore** Piers Morgan **Chris Morris** Neil Morrissey **Bob Mortimer** Kate Moss **John Motson** Chris Moyles **Mystic Meg** Prince Naseem Hamed **Dennis Norden** Barry Norman **Richard O'Brien** Christian O'Connell **Des O'Connor** Bill Oddie **Martin Offiah** Paul O'Grady **Bruce Oldfield** Gary Oldman **Dermot O'Leary** Jamie Oliver **Kelly Osbourne** Ronnie O'Sullivan **Michael Owen** Michael Palin **Geoffrey Palmer** Tara Palmer-Tomkinson **Nick Park** Michael Parkinson **Tony Parsons** Nicholas Parsons **Joe Pasquale** Jeremy Paxman **Simon Pegg** Raj Persaud **Fiona Phillips** Matthew Pinsent **Courtney Pine** Billie Piper **Graham Poll** Eve Pollard **Su Pollard** Gail Porter **Ian Poulter** David Puttnam **Jason Queally** Caroline Quentin **Paula Radcliffe** Gordon Ramsay **Esther Rantzen** Simon Rattle **Claire Rayner** Steve Redgrave **Louise Redknapp** Vic Reeves **Tim Rice** Cliff Richard **Keith Richards** Wendy Richards **Miranda Richardson** Alan Rickman **Lisa Riley** Guy Ritchie **Shane Ritchie** William Roach **Anne Robinson** Tony Robinson **Linda Robson** Lisa Rogers **Wayne Rooney** Jonathan Ross **Nick Ross** Paul Ross **Patricia Routledge** Salman Rushdie **Steve Rider** Charles Saatchi **Rabbi Jonathan Sacks** Oliver Sacks **Iqbal Sacranie** Jennifer Saunders **Jimmy Saville** Julia Sawalha **Alexei Sayle** Phillip Schofield **Ridley Scott** Will Self **Brian Sewell** Pat Sharp **Suzanne Shaw** Alan Shearer **John Simpson** Rav Singh **Clive Sinclair** Frank Skinner **Carol Smillie** Paul Smith **Sheridan Smith** Zadie Smith **Peter Snow** Ringo Starr **Shakin' Stevens** Jessica Stevenson **Moira Stewart** Richard Stilgoe **Sting** Michaela Strachan **Peter Stringfellow** David Suchet **Alan Sugar** Suggs **David Sullivan** Meera Syal **Melanie Sykes** Jimmy Tarbuck **Lisa Tarbuck** Chris Tarrant **Bernie Taupin** Phil Taylor **Margaret Thatcher** Jamie Theakston **Louis Theroux** Daley Thompson **Emma Thompson** John Thomson **Alan Titchmarsh** Abi Titmuss **Ricky Tomlinson** Jane Torville **Sue Townsend** Philip Tuffnel **Anthea Turner** Denise Van Outen **Johnny Vaughan** Johnny Vegas **Terry Venables** John Virgo **Carol Vorderman** Rebekah Wade **Jessie Wallace** David Walliams **Julie Walters** Zoe Wanamaker **Dennis Waterman** Pete Waterman **Rachel Weisz** Irvine Welsh **Daniella Westbrook** Vivienne Westwood **Fatima Whitbread** Paul Whitehouse **June Whitfield** Ann Widdecombe **Jonny Wilkinson** Robbie Williams **A.N.Wilson** Quentin Wilson **Richard Wilson** Barbara Windsor **Claudia Winkleman** Michael Winner **Kate Winslet** Ray Winstone **Dale Winton** Ronnie Wood **Victoria Wood** Clive Woodward **Lord Woolf** Ian Wright **Alan Yentob** Thom Yorke **Kirsty Young**

A most eclectic roll call of names, I am sure you would agree. Yes, these happy few were to be my quarry (and by that I don't mean that I was going to excavate rubble from their crevices), it was they, and only they who held my fate in their hands... Quite literally.

Target - 100 handshakes in six months.

On being handed this list for the first time, there was some dissension in the ranks. Basically, I was convinced that not everyone on the list was actually British. However, as there only appeared to be one or two exceptions I told Mike that, like a bad case of intestinal gas, I'd let it pass. More worryingly, though, was my belief that some of those named above certainly lived abroad. I demanded Michael knock three or four people off my 100 meetings target to make up for this. He refused and so I decided not to return his replica Colt 45 cigarette lighter.

THE 'ANTI-STALKING CLAUSES'

1. **Every handshake with an individual from the list HAD TO BE AGREED TO IN ADVANCE BY THAT PERSON.**

In other words I had to contact them first, for example by letter or via their agent, before the handshake could take place and they then obviously had to agree to the meeting in advance. There was to be no lurking in the shadows outside the BBC or around the lavatories of the Groucho Club (as if I'd ever get in there anyway). I couldn't simply waltz up to any of them with a camera and an outstretched arm as they were exiting a stage door. This, Michael correctly deemed, would be far too easy for them to agree to. I concurred.

Furthermore, each of these famous individuals would agree to the meeting and the pointless photograph for purely altruistic purposes. They would receive nothing in return. No financial reward, no publicity, not even a peck on the cheek (which, come to think of it would probably be deemed as a negative not a positive, anyway) they would simply agree to it because they'd be informed that in so doing, they would be helping me in my quest.

2. **I was permitted to try and make contact with each individual from the list ONCE AND ONCE ONLY.**

This was obviously to prevent me being tarred with the 'stalky' brush. If I didn't hear back from them having sent my letter or if the letter had already been posted and I subsequently realised that I'd got the address wrong, it would be a case of spilled milk and no dishcloth.

THE FORFEITS

My common or garden bets with Michael, and there have been many of them over the years as you will discover, tend to have no more than a nominal amount of money at stake. As *Greeting the 500* appeared to be a bet on a slightly more grandiose scale, we decided to up the ante accordingly.

Below is a list of forfeits that one or other of us would be forced to endure. These forfeits were cumulative so obviously the better or worse I fared, the more numerous and unpalatable the tasks that lay ahead. They may appear slightly convoluted, but if you put your mind to it I am sure you'll get the gist of what is going on.

Number of Individuals met in 6 months	Forfeit
350+	Michael undertakes forfeits 1-7 (see below)
275-349	Michael undertakes forfeits 1-6
220-374	Michael undertakes forfeits 1-5
180-219	Michael undertakes forfeits 1-4
150-179	Michael undertakes forfeits 1-3
125-149	Michael undertakes forfeits 1 and 2
100-124	Michael undertakes forfeit 1
75-99	Jules undertakes forfeit 1
56-74	Jules undertakes forfeits 1 and 2
40-55	Jules undertakes forfeits 1-3
30-39	Jules undertakes forfeits 1-4
20-29	Jules undertakes forfeits 1-5
10-19	Jules undertakes forfeits 1-6
0-9	Jules undertakes forfeits 1-7

The forfeits

Forfeit 1: to purchase for the other party, a Sky Sports Football Season Ticket from termination of challenge until end of the Premiership Football Season.

Forfeit 2: to clean the flat of the other party once every two weeks for one year.

Forfeit 3: to stand at Oxford Circus for one eight-hour period holding a placard and bucket and asking people to donate to the RNIB.

Forfeit 4: to help a rural vet in checking on a cow's pregnancy situation (by sticking arm up rectum of said cow).

Forfeit 5: Michael to walk across hot coals, Jules to conquer vertigo by riding the UK's largest roller coaster.

Forfeit 6: to run next year's London Marathon (collecting for RNIB).

Forfeit 7: to swim naked off Brighton beach twice a week during month of February.

This agreement had been signed and witnessed and was legally binding.

So there you have it. Neither of us were expecting to have to do the naked swimming thing, which, with bodies such as ours (i.e. at either end of the Body Mass Index scale), would no doubt be a blessed relief to the inhabitants of Brighton. For Michael think hippo that has been rolled into a vat of honey and then a vat of hair, as for me, if I was any paler I would be translucent and, in addition, as another good friend mentions to me every time I wear shorts, 'That reminds me, I must get some new pipe-cleaners'.

THE CHARITY

The Royal National Institute of the Blind.

(Please give generously)

CHAPTER 1 – June

(The Background to the Bet)

Someone once said that there is a book in all of us. That's certainly true of my Auntie Vi (an invented relation for the purposes of this joke) who had open-colon surgery and ended up crapping out several pages of *A Surgeon's Guide to the Lower Intestine.*

Books come in all shapes and sizes but the offering that you are about to read (possibly a copy with jaundiced pages and egg-yolk on the cover, that you've just found in your timeshare apartment in Menorca) is quite patently about a bet. This bet concerned one skinny man, one large man and 500 – and I really baulk at using this word – 'Celebrities'.

I would imagine that if you *have* been generous enough to part with some of your milkshake money and have dashed out of your local Waterstone's with this tucked under you arm (or perhaps you even paid for it) it is possibly because you are one of the 32 million people in this country who seem to be afflicted with *celebretyus infatuationus* and the front cover seemed to grab your attention. Maybe you have an annual subscription to *heat* magazine, your ideal Sunday evening in involves watching Delia Smith take on Jordy Chandler in a televised '*Celebrity Tug-of-war*' and you once spotted Norman Wisdom eating a tuna sandwich in *Pret-a-Manger*.

For those of you who haven't got a ruddy clue what on earth I'm going on about, I suggest that you flip back a few pages and READ THE PREFACE where you will see 500 famous people named.

For the punctilious among you who have stuck to protocol by actually reading this book from page 1, you have now been fully briefed as to the details of the bet yet you may still have one question nagging away somewhere at the back of your mind like a hungry nit. 'HOW THE HELL did this bet come about?'

Thursday June 23rd 2005 – What's It All About (Alfred)
◇◇

I believe it was sunny.

According to Wikipedia, the San Antonio Spurs had just defeated the Detroit Pistons in Game 7 of the 2005 NBA Final, if that jogs your memory.

The location was The Crown public house in Cricklewood, London NW2, and Michael was screaming and spitting over his Jack Daniels, or should that be his 'Jack Daniels NO ICE! JESUS HOW MANY TIMES DO I HAVE TO TELL YOU?'

His furious words were booming around the room and pieces of his mother's home-made kleftikos were spraying from his mouth for two reasons. First, I'd got his drink order wrong and second, he was speaking.

Michael tends to have two moods: rage and lethargy.

Good friend? Yes. Exasperating? Definitely. More often than not, those who know him have learned to tip-toe on eggshells around his bad moods.

As far as my relationship with my good English-Greek-Cypriot buddy goes, if any topic of conversation is worth talking about, it's also one that's worth arguing about. For many years now, I've been of the opinion that Michael's constant desire to prove that he knows more than anyone else on a particular subject, even when he's as wide of the mark as an archer in a wind tunnel, is because he left school at an early age, and ever since then he's been paranoid that people will think he's thick.

Michael is certainly not thick. He is by no means a dribbling idiot. However, by the same token, there is little point in starting a discussion with him about the finer points of *Faust*, the second act of *La Traviata* or whether *Le Moulin de la Galette* was Renoir's finest work.

Michael is not a bad person for not knowing a great deal about these things, for I don't either and neither do a great many people in this day and age. He is, however, slightly tiresome when *pretending* to be an authority on them or indeed on anything else that he knows little about.

This happens quite often I have found.

He might, for example, be watching a news article on the depleted fish stock in the north Atlantic, only to start pontificating as though he were some sort of highly celebrated marine biologist.

Of course, everyone is allowed to have their opinion, yet it makes no difference how many times or how loudly they yell, 'LOOK, I KNOW ABOUT THE NORTH ATLANTIC, IT'S SOMEWHERE NEAR IRELAND ISN'T IT?', or how many swear words they use, or even how often they threaten physical violence against the person who thinks they are talking rubbish, they *are* still talking rubbish.

So you see, when Michael is at his belligerent worst and is (metaphorically) spouting excrement, the only way that he will ever back down is if you bet with him, for it is only in these instances, when a crumpled £5 note is at stake, that he will be bothered to get off his backside to find out the answer.

Before I detail our conversation that night in The Crown, let me first offer you a smidgeon more background information.

I currently live in an area of London named Belsize Park, (sometimes referred to rather crudely by certain people I know as Bell-end Park). This area derives its name from the Old English 'Bel Assize', which I believe has something to do with a 'pretty field', although I might be confused.

It is actually something of a curious little neighbourhood, wedged between several crack-estates in Kentish Town, the tourist Mecca of Camden Town, the la-di-dah tea rooms of Hampstead and Primrose

Hill and the... well actually there's absolutely nothing of stand-out interest about Swiss Cottage (although it does have at least TWO fine Chinese restaurants).

As for the locals of Belsize Park, well, many of them are Bohemian types and I say that without really knowing what Bohemian means, but it's a cliché that I have heard uttered on many occasions and I see no reason not to chuck it in here, or indeed to use a double negative while doing so.

I wouldn't be in the least bit surprised to find that there were a disproportionate amount of psychiatrists, celebrities and staunch left-wing, lentil-eating media types living in the locale. I'm not sure if there's any link between these three groups or indeed if they would overlap on one of those Venn Diagram things, but I do use the term 'Celebrity' loosely since, let's be honest about it, it's a crap one. It sticks in the craw and frankly sounds rather tiresome.

Anyway, I have no idea why so many actors, authors, pop-stars, footballers, artists, TV presenters and former hosts of *Supermarket Sweep* should choose to live in these co-ordinates, maybe it's because the delicatessens in Balham aren't up to scratch or because you can't get a decent bottle of Château Margaux in the off-licences of Hounslow; regardless, this seems to be where many end up.

I know that general conversation currently has numerous unwritten rules. Mentioning, for example, that you spotted Ewan McGregor coming out of the local newsagent or saw Frank Skinner in the curry house or almost ran over Jude Law as he was crossing Steeles Road, can be regarded as something of a social faux pas.

Despite the fact that at this moment in time some of the most popular TV programmes in this country are prefixed by the word 'Celebrity', it's generally regarded as bad form to tell your friends that you saw someone famous down your way. You do so at the risk of being labelled a name-dropper or a star-fornicator (or words to that effect). Your friends will invariably wear the face of someone who couldn't give a shiny shite.

As for me, I can honestly say – and this really isn't a case of me 'protesting too much' – that if I do ever spot anyone I recognize I rarely give them a second glance. In fact, the ONLY reason that I constantly inform Michael about these impromptu meetings is because I know it winds him up. I am not an avid reader of *Hello* magazine, I've never tuned in to 'Famous people on Skates' and I wouldn't know an *X-Factor* from a *Pop Idol* or an *Apprentice*. I tend to favour decade-old quiz shows on Challenge TV.

Michael, for his part, is even less bowled-over by those with well-known faces. If the TV programme doesn't involve American actors dressed up as aliens and boldly going somewhere, he really has no interest at all.

So let's get down to the nitty-gritty of the bet... the small chunks of bacon in the carbonara sauce if you like. In other words, how did this particular conversation come about in the first place?

Here is more or less what happened that night in The Crown and forgive me if my memory is as hazy as the B&H-smoke-filled air in the room that we were sitting in and apologies if the dialogue isn't 100 per cent accurate, but this was an evening of heavy drinking and sorrow-drowning for both of us. I had just had a major row with my girlfriend and Michael had just broken the miniature torch on his key-ring.

Me: 'You'll never guess who I walked past on my road this morning... Helena Bonham Carter. That must be the third or fourth time I've seen her. Interesting choice of clothes, I must say.'

Michael: 'Oh, shut the (expletive) up!'

Me: 'Come on Michael. I know how you like to listen to me name-dropping' (tongue firmly in cheek).

Michael: 'Yeah right!... couldn't give a toss... I worked in the theatre for three years... Shane Ritchie and me are like that' (he crosses his first and second fingers)

Me: 'Arthritis sufferers?'

Michael: '(expletive) off you (expletive)! Anyway, they're not interested in people like you and me!'

Me: 'Oh yes. They must hate being spotted in the street and have people approaching them and singing their praises, telling them how wonderful they are.'

– Decibels and Michael's blood pressure increase three notches –

Michael: 'THEY (EXPLETIVE) DO! I told you, when I used to walk out of the stage door on *Grease* and saw all these people waiting, I used to

15

get the right hump.'

Me: 'Errm, I don't think they were actually waiting for you.'

Michael: 'I'm going to punch you if you don't shut up. Look, I'm sick of you going on about someone famous you've seen, eating a doughnut on England's Lane on a Thursday afternoon. To be honest, you'd think they'd have better things to do, anyway.'

Me: 'Well, I only do it to get a reaction out of you... and by the way it was a Tuesday. Anyway, Michael, for goodness sake, how do you know that these people who are out in the midweek afternoon sunshine haven't spent all morning raising money for orphanages in Belize.'

Michael: 'Look, don't ARGUE with me. I KNOW these people.' (He doesn't.) 'I've worked The West End.' (I think I laughed out loud at that.) 'I'm telling you, the only thing that most of these people think about is feathering their own nests and singing their own praises. You *have* to be that way to get to the top... Oh Jesus, who put that on?...' (I believe a song from Erasure started playing at that point) '...Sure they'll be helpful or friendly if there's some money or good publicity at stake. Everything else is just a chore to them.'

Me: 'Michael, I've never heard such crap. Even from you. You're basically tarring every rich or successful or famous person with the same brush. Are you telling me that *none* of them remember their humble origins?'

Michael: 'Not by the time they've become successful. It's survival of the fittest in a strict Darwinian sense. They've had to become so cynical... pass me the lighter. Cheers... and so hardened to get to the top, that by the time they do, everything goes out of the window. It's only a certain breed of people who actually make it there.'

Me: 'Right, so if I wrote to 100 of them simply asking to meet them for 1 minute for absolutely no reason other than just to say 'Hello', not one would reply?'

Michael: 'YES! I've just said that!'

Me: 'What about if I wrote to 500?'

Michael: 'Look, you might get one or two replies, but they'd be the exception not the rule.'

Me: 'Yeah sure. You know celebrities so well.'

Michael: 'More than you. OK fine. If I gave you 500 names, how many of them do *you* think would give you a couple of minutes of their time for absolutely no reason whatsoever?'

Me: 'I dunno, if it was pretty easy for them to do so I'd say nearer 100.'

Michael: 'Hah! No (expletive) way. Right, I'll bet you.'

Me: 'Fine!'

Michael: 'Fine!'

Michael: 'Dick!'

And the rest, as they say, is history. You see I really did have little choice, since Michael was once again speaking with such authority about a random subject, as if the answer was totally black and white. I simply wanted to prove him wrong and before I knew what had happened, I was sat there shaking his clammy hand.

He did ask me the following morning whether I still wanted to go through with it and partly through bravado and partly through stupidity I shouted, 'Yeah, of course.' I didn't view this as so different to any particular bet that we had had in the past. Fair enough, I might have to take a little bit of time off work once or twice a week over the next six months, but bearing in mind what my day job actually consists of, I hardly considered that to be the end of the world.

So anyway, there you have it. A little taste of the characters of Michael and I. A small soupçon of our respective essences, which would probably be more palatable if you mopped them up with some bread, but if you still don't feel as though you've been fully briefed, here's a little more information about the two of us.

JULES
\\

Likes: Sherry trifle, *The Crystal Maze*, England (or GB or UK) winning at anything, sudoku in the bath, general knowledge quizzes, the city of Sydney, making a flush with the last card, drunkenly singing 'The Fairytale of New York' (usually occurs in early December), memories of that match on 13 May 1981, reading the column of Victor Lewis-Smith, the murder explanations on *Jonathan Creek*, being massaged anywhere other than back and shoulders, any film starring Joe Pesci, the sound of the rain, Cutty Sark whisky, using the word 'shyster', every living pore of Scarlett Johansson, the moment of relief after waking from a particularly vivid nightmare, finally dislodging the apple skin from between my teeth, sneezing, seeing ethnically different people sharing a joke.

Dislikes: Tomatoes, bunker shots, speed bumps, anything that is orange apart from oranges, finding blonde hair in my food (my hair is black), Frenchmen who love themselves (a majority of them, I have come to learn), four-wheel drive cars in London NW3, plane journeys, running up to a badly parked VW Polo only for a man to say 'Sorry, the ticket's already been issued', toe stubbing, noticing tubes in my roast beef, being put through to someone in Calcutta instead of London, any American sitcom that has someone's name as its title (a majority of them, I have come to learn), going clothes shopping with anyone female, mouth ulcers, everything about the London Underground but particularly the Northern Line, ironing a shirt, 'political correctness gone mad', anyone who uses the expression 'political correctness gone mad', macaroni cheese, any film starring Andie MacDowell, having to hold in flatulence, *Lady in Red* (song), any dog that is smaller than a loaf of bread, being told by a robot on the phone to 'listen to the following options', the name Julian, being woken by someone clanking crockery in the kitchen, icy pavements.

MICHAEL

Likes: Pizza, Sci-fi TV shows, shouting down the phone at people who work for utility companies.

Dislikes: Moving at anything other than a 'leisurely' pace, any food that's green (barring peas, he informs me), the current Mayor of London.

◇◇◇

'You're going to do what?'

My sister was the first member of my family to reply, when I announced details of the bet around the dinner table on this particularly Friday evening.

It wasn't the sentence 'You're going to do what?' that I recall so much, more the way she stressed the last word of it. It was as if I'd expressed an intention to butcher a group of meditating monks.

It is fair to say that certain members of my family, and when I say 'certain members' I mean those that are living, have grown a little exasperated with my recent *laissez-faire* attitude to life. What I am trying to say is that I am pretty lazy. In fact, ever since Iraq was invaded for a second time, I have tried to find alternative ways of earning a living than by working in an office.

By this, I don't mean that the second invasion of Iraq was the catalyst that made me want to try and understand man's inhumanity to man or to join Amnesty International to make the world a better place, or to try and find a just and lasting peace for the Middle East, I simply mean that it was in 2003 that I first decided that I was going to write a film script about a paranoid schizophrenic stand-up comedian.

Yes, In an attempt to plough my own furrow as both master and commander of my own leaky vessel, I even travelled to Australia in order to get the film written without any distractions.

It was, therefore, much to everyone's disappointment when our hero (a.k.a. me) returned to these shores some three months later, not so much clutching 150 pages of the most beautifully crafted, Oscar-worthy screenplay that had ever been conceived, but rather, holding 67 pages of half-baked nonsense and grinning away like Neville Chamberlain's idiot-savante brother.

I had simply written 'All work and no play, makes Julian regret becoming a trainee solicitor' 4013 times.

No-one in my family was greatly surprised by my failure to get the job done. No, what they *were* surprised about was my willingness to travel halfway round the globe, to a world of non-regular income, credit card abuse and general poverty, simply to, as my dad put it, 'piss about in the sunshine'.

Therefore, following my grand announcement that I was now going to try and shake hands with 500 of Britain's most famous individuals, not for any money, career-advancement or indeed purpose whatsoever, but purely because I'd made a bet with a friend about how successful I'd be, their responses ranged from sheer disbelief to... well no, just sheer disbelief actually.

Quite predictably I was soon bombarded with such inevitable questions as:

○ *'So how are you going to support yourself?'* – 'Don't worry, I'm not quitting my job.'

○ *'What good do you think will come of it?'* – 'None. Well, actually, having said that, I may get to touch Anna Friel.' (I meant her hand of course.)

○ *'How long are you going to spend doing it then?'* – 'I've got six months, from July 1 to New Year's Eve.'

○ *'Does this fish taste alright?'* – 'Yes.'

○ *'Are you actually going to see this through and finish something, unlike your film-script and your travel diaries?'* – 'You know I always finish my...' (I think I tailed off here).

○ *'Who are the people that you're trying to meet?'* – 'Michael's drawing up the list of 500 names.'

○ Etc., etc., *ad infinitum*, or at least *ad* it was time to go home.

So that was it. Father, stepmother, sister, brother-in-law, nephews and stepmother's family had been informed with, let's just say, a modest degree of support being shown back. I wondered how me mam (as I believe they say up North) would take the news...

Saturday June 25th 2005 – The Charity Aspect

I have never had a great deal of success with Katies. The reason I say this is because fate has somehow seen to it that on no less than three occasions in my life I have been seeing/dating/playing 'hide the bratwurst' with girls of this very name.

Generally, my courtships with Katies won't last more than two or three months because generally Katies (or the ones I go out with) see me as a git.

The Katie I was dating at this stage in my life was a pleasant enough young lady who hailed from Ealing. She had blonde hair, pale skin and a scratch on her Clio. Our eyes first met in the Pitcher and Piano on Dean Street and soon after that we became inseparable.

Yes, we were inseparable for the couple of hours we spend together every Wednesday and other Saturday in the June and early July of 2005.

I have absolutely no idea where she is now or what she is doing. Hopefully, she has become the director of a successful Hedge Fund or a chef but I have a hell of a lot to thank her for since if it wasn't for this snub-nosed little angel of delight, my project would not only have never got off the ground, but would in fact still be floundering like so many flat fish on the ocean floor.

'Jules I'm not really sure *why* you're doing this but I certainly respect your right to do it,' she said to me like some bottle-blonde Voltaire, 'but seeing as you *are* going to go through with it why not try to raise some money for charity in the process. I mean, after all, not only will it encourage more of these people to meet you if it's for a good cause, but it will prove Michael even less correct. You know, it'll prove just how many of these people are in fact quite selfless'.

Well, I really couldn't fault, or indeed understand, logic like that and I didn't see how the inclusion of a charity aspect into the bet would fly in the face of what had been agreed with Michael. After all, the object was to see how many of the 500 would be willing to meet me 'whilst gaining no personal benefit from doing so' and correct me if I'm wrong here, but raising money for others would not usually be classed as being of benefit to oneself (unless you're Arthur Fowler of course).

I gave Katie a kiss (plus change) to thank her for such a sound idea.

The more I thought about it the more it made sense. As far as I was concerned, there was an additional spin-off to be gained from trying to raise money for a good cause.

Permit me to be self-deprecatingly truthful for a moment. I am what the Irish would call 'a lazy wee fecker'. While countless friends of mine have run 27 miles to help children with Spina Bifida or have climbed Kilimanjaro to aid manufacturers of Odor-Eaters, I don't need to spell out the sum total of my charitable efforts over the course of the last 30-odd years (although I do recall buying a poppy in 1992).

So as you see, the additional spin-off to this raising money lark was that I would now finally have the chance both to purge my lazy, selfish soul and to act self-righteously all in one fell swoop.

I contacted the RNIB two days later.

Sunday June 26th 2005 – How the List of 500 Was Chosen

... or to put it another way, what are the criteria of 'fame'?

Having kissed goodbye to Katie for what proved to be the last time, my attention turned to more pressing matters, notably my lunch appointment with Krakow-wood's most churlish Greek-Cypriot night-club promoter (another of Michael's bow-strings).

'Michael, I know it's Sunday but you still can't classify a meal at 3.00 p.m. as being breakfast.'

'Look, shut up and stop whining. You sound like a punctured tyre. Just meet me outside the Docket in half an hour.'

To be honest I wasn't feeling very well. My sleep the night before had not so much been broken, more smashed to pieces, since *this* Katie held entire conversations in her sleep, as if haggling over the price of Jimmy Choo's latest sandals. Furthermore, the weather outside was wetter than the proverbial hooker's gusset and the prospect of meeting someone much bigger and more prone to physical confrontation than me in a heaving public house didn't fill me with much cheer.

I knew that I was guaranteed an argument with Laughing-boy, as I was convinced that the simple task I'd set him – compiling a list of 500 famous British people for me to try and contact – would not only be incomplete, but would probably so far only have the name of Sheridan Smith on it.

Sheridan Smith is, apart from Christina Ricci (and to a lesser extent Shirley Manson) the apple, banana and indeed whole bowl of fruit of Michael's eye.

For those of you not in the know, Sheridan Smith played Ralf Little's girlfriend Emma in *The Royle Family*; she also played Ralf Little's girlfriend Janet in *Two Pints of Lager and a Packet of Crisps* and so, suffice to say, Michael wishes he was Ralf Little.

Anyway... 2.45 p.m. Cricklewood High Street, The Beaten Docket Pub.

– Enter pursued by a bear... With a sore head –

'So let me get this right, Michael, you scream and swear at me the other night claiming that I'm a naive prat for thinking that these people might actually have some degree of altruism about them, we make a bet, I ask you to compile a list of 500 names and three days later your list is comprised of...'

'Yes, the Archbishop of Canterbury and Sting.'

'Right. Well, I commend you on your fine work. To be honest, I assumed that you would have only come up with Sheridan Smith by now.'

'Oh yeah, Sheridan Smith, of course. If she agrees to meet you, I'll definitely come along to that one. I know who her agent is, by the way, so I've got an address for you to write to if you like.'

'Yes, well thanks for your help, but I'd prefer it if you could just come up with another 497 names before July 1.'

'Alright I'm SORRY!...' he screamed, '... but I've had more important things on my plate over the last three days than compiling your ******g list!'

It turned out that the 'more important things' were buying some instant mash potato and watching *Will and Grace*... In one fell swoop I'd learned that while I had agreed with Michael to undertake this ludicrous challenge, he would not be taking it all that seriously, partly because he still didn't think I would go through with it all and partly because he couldn't be arsed to get involved. He was going to be, if you like, the *silent* partner of the operation (although not silent enough for my liking).

However, this whole list business did throw up one important question, one that I was frequently asked over the course of the next six months and one that I never did and still do not feel particularly well qualified to answer.

When Michael and I had been exchanging verbal blows in The Crown a few nights earlier, the conversation had centred around 'famous individuals' that I had spotted in the street. As I have mentioned already, I hate the term 'Celebrity' with its loose connotations and its capital 'C', but that's nothing compared to its hideously abbreviated form of 'Celeb' or 'Sleb'. As far as I'm concerned, 'Sleb' sounds as though it should be the surname of a Belorussian footballer.

I did not want to have to keep repeating the word 'Celebrity' for the next six months, since it was both inaccurate and inappropriate with regard to many of the people on my list. I could not, for example, imagine the Governor of the Bank of England dressing up in a leotard while pretending to be a cat on *Big Brother*, neither could I envisage the Chief Rabbi eating a kangaroo's scrotum in an Australian rainforest. Well, it wouldn't be kosher, would it? I preferred to think of these 500 as individuals of note in their professions.

I appreciate that I might be flying off at something of a tangent here, but the question remained as to how the list of 500 would be compiled. How famous did the people on the list have to be? Taking it one stage further, what are the criteria for fame? At what stage of an individual's personal achievements can they be said to have made it? How do we know when we have become famous?

To me the answer lies somewhere in a spectrum between achieving Warhol's '15 minutes' in the public eye and becoming Emperor of the Earth.

I am sure that certain scholars could answer that question more concisely than I could ever hope to. Perhaps I should ask the academics of Paisley University who even established a conference to analyse the concept of 'Celebrity Culture'. As far as the task that was entrusted to Michael was concerned, we wanted to steer well clear of the vacuous, coke-taking TV presenters and the oddballs from *Big Brother*, and for this reason I basically asked Michael to include EVERYONE.

I didn't only want to test the mettle of the footballer's wife sort, the sort who are famous by association and whose only discernible talent is to be able to recite verbatim the menu from The Ivy (what a bunch of Nobu-heads they are!), I wanted a veritable pot pourri of movers and shakers. I wanted people from all walks of life, politicians, lawyers, actors, athletes, architects, religious leaders, artists, authors, businessmen, singers and even businesswomen. If he so desired, I agreed eventually to let Michael chuck in the occasional vacuous, coke-taking TV-presenter and oddball from *Big Brother*.

Monday June 27th 2005 – Britney and The 'Been-Stalked'

I had my first conversation with an individual at the Royal National Institute for the Blind on this day. His name was Matt. Matt does not have ocular problems, he is the marketing and public relations director for the charity and despite sounding somewhat puzzled by my proposed quest, he was all in favour of it and promised to help me out in any way that he could.

My basic plan was this: I had decided that with every successful meeting I had, I would request that person to bring along some small memento, some trinket if you will, to our meeting and that these items would be auctioned off at a later date together with an autograph, with proceeds going to the RNIB.

In the meantime, Matt suggested that I send him the list of 500 names to see whether or not any of them were known beneficiaries to the RNIB already and if so, he mentioned that he might be able to facilitate some meetings. This was obviously of great help to me as it would reassure these Great Britons that I wasn't some sort of weird random stalker.

Ah yes, stalking. So why was it necessary to include the two 'Anti-Stalking Clauses' that I have already mentioned? Well, despite sounding as though it's a website dedicated to a political party in KwaZulu-Natal, encarta.com is actually amongst other things an online dictionary. Here is the website's definition of the verb 'to stalk':

4. transitive verb law harass somebody persistently: to harass somebody criminally by persistent, inappropriate, and unwanted attention, e.g. by constantly following, telephoning, e-mailing, or writing to him or her.

Jules Segal

I am well aware that many famous individuals have had their own stalker. For every Catherine Zeta-Jones there's a Dawnette Knight, for every Britney Spears there's a Masahiko Shizawa (OK, I've done a bit of research into this). These stalkers all share one common feature. They're nuts and by this, I don't mean that they all have similar testicles, I mean that they are all completely loop-dee-loop.

I give you as an example the case of Diana Napolis, a very normal social worker from Los Angeles. Very normal in every way apart from the fact that she stalked Steven Spielberg and his wife Kate Capshaw for several months, believing that they were in a satanic cult and were plotting to plant a microchip in her brain, which she dubbed a 'soul-catcher'.

You see. Completely barmy!

They were trying to implant it in her *arm*. (That's just a joke, by the way, before Mr S decides to sue me.)

Some might even believe that having a stalker should be viewed as an emblem of success, a sign that you are important enough and interesting enough to be obsessed over. I say that is bollocks. Any fool can have a stalker. Even I have had one – an ex (and no, it wasn't any of the Katies) who turned up at 3.00 a.m. because 'I just happened to be passing and I saw that your light was on'.

Well, in going about my foolish bet, although I could be regarded as mildly insane, I certainly didn't want to be regarded as a 'harasser', 'follower' or 'constant e-mailer'. Perish the thought that my name and face would be emblazoned across the front cover of the national Red-Tops with the headline: 'Is this Britain's Most Deranged Crackpot?' and it's for this reason that Michael and I came up with the 'Non-stalking Clause' in our bet.

As soon as it became clear that this might become an issue, in other words, having heard the line 'Oh, so you're going to be stalking celebrities are you?' for the umpteenth time, we decided that it was imperative to act.

Wednesday June 29th 2005 – The Three Ws

T-minus three days (milk, one sugar please).

26

When I first told my friend Paul about the project that I was about to undertake he seemed rather amused by it all, as he himself has created an entire website dedicated to the trivial and comical world of celebrity gossip. Anyway, he says to me, 'What I'd do if I were you would be to set up a weblog, so we can all check up on your progress and so you can plaster the photos on it and we can all have a good laugh at you'. Well, I'm certainly no computer whizz-geek, and it's fair to say that my entire knowledge of the world of IT could, in written form, just about fill the back of a Penny Black, (what an accommodating girl that Penny was) but I do know that a weblog, despite sounding more like the content's of a spider's lavatory, is in fact an online diary of sorts.

After much umming and erring and the odd spot of hmmming, it was decided by the two of us that the best website provider that I could utilise to host my rambling stream of conscious thought was called Typepad.com. This was chosen partly because it could store a great deal of data, had a nice layout and was very accessible to use, but mainly because it was the cheapest.

And so, from that day forward, even to the very present day, the awkward sounding www.greetingthe500.typepad.com came into being.

Thursday June 30th 2005 – The All-Important Letter

Picture the scene. You're Kate Moss and you are quietly, or perhaps loudly, munching your cornflakes of a Tuesday morning when a letter pops through your letterbox, presumably forwarded to you by your agent. This letter is from someone you have never heard of and who is asking if he can meet you for a couple of moments to shake your hand and then leave.

Let's face it, he might as well be asking you to translate *War and Peace* into Latvian; it's not going to happen. No, my strategy had to have a modicum of thought put into it, yet the one thing that *was* a certainty was that the first form of contact should be by means of a letter.

Below is the first draft that I came up with. This was before I deemed it necessary to alter it and to remove some of its more cringe-worthy lines.

Jules Segal

THE LETTER

Greeting the 500 – A Social Experiment

Dear …..,

I am aware that you are a very busy individual, but all I ask
is that you kindly read what I have to say before deciding
whether or not to act upon it or to crumple up this letter and
aim for the bin.

You will note an attached list of 500 names, all of whom have
received/will receive an identical letter to this one. My
request might seem a little peculiar, but I assure you that it
is totally genuine. Although you obviously have no idea who I
am, if you are able to check either of the websites:

www.greetingthe500.typepad.com or

www.justgiving.com/greetingthe500, this will provide you with a
little information about who I am and what I am doing.

In its simplest terms, my project, Greeting the 500, was a bet
that was issued to me by a friend. The consequences of losing
this bet, for either of us, are very serious. The only people
that can help me are (all of) you. My friend Michael has a
pretty dim view of the human race, not least of all well-
known individuals. Our recent conversation in a pub had him
pontificating, like some modern, latter-day George Orwell,
that once a person achieved success in his/her field, they
would raise themselves above the masses and, other than signing
autographs, would rarely help Joe Public unless they personally
benefited from doing so.

Having slightly more faith in mankind, I disagreed. We argued,
he shouted and swore and ultimately issued my challenge. I
have SIX MONTHS TO MEET AS MANY OF THESE 500 INDIVIDUALS AS
POSSIBLE. He drew up the list. 'Meet' means have my picture
taken shaking your hand, that is all. I will travel to meet
YOU, wherever you like. This will take no more than two minutes
of your time, whenever you like, in a six-month period (1st
July–31st December).

He believes that not more than 20 per cent (i.e. 100 people
maximum) will agree to this. The better or worse than 100

28

I achieve, the more unpleasant and numerous our forfeits
will be. Many of you are by now probably at letter-crumpling
stage, I just ask you to have mercy. The only thing to add,
and this is entirely optional, is that if you will kindly
agree to this 'meeting', could you possibly bring some small
memento, anything at all, that I could auction at the end of my
challenge, giving the money to the Royal National Institute for
the Blind. I repeat, that bit is optional and has no bearing on
my bet.

Well, that is it really. If you've got this far, (or your agent
has, before he/she KINDLY PASSES THIS ON TO YOU), I thank you,
and keep my fingers crossed that I might hear from you at the
address/email address or mobile phone number above.

Kind regards,

Julian Segal

There you have it. As you can see, another of my brainwaves was to include in each envelope, together with each letter, a complete list of the 500 names I was writing to.

There were two schools of thought behind this. First, it was hoped that if the recipient of my letter did fear that I was some sort of sweaty, heavy-breathing crank, they could merely ask some friend of theirs, who also featured on the list, whether they had received a similar letter (before presumably *both* deciding that I was some sort of sweaty, heavy-breathing crank).

Second, it was hoped that by reading through the list of 500 names and noting that they were in some rather illustrious company, they might be so flattered to have had their name stumble through Michael's subconscious that they would be certain to reply in the affirmative.

So did this tactic work and was my letterbox soon flapping away like the sole of tramp's boot? Well, you might be surprised by the results.

CHAPTER 2 – July

Replies received: Richard Littlejohn, Jeremy Clarkson, Tony Hawks, Tony Blair and Charles Kennedy.

Meetings achieved: Tony Hawks.

Friday July 1st 2005 – Are You Dave Gorman? NO!

I woke up on this morning in a terrible sweat. I'd had a vivid nightmare in which I had agreed to waste six months of my life in a totally pointless activity just to prove someone wrong. Why I had agreed to monitor the gestation period of a goat I have no idea, but if only my *actual* challenge were so simple.

I'd had a conversation with Matt at the RNIB on the previous afternoon. He had glanced at the list and pledged to do all he could to help facilitate some meetings. There *was* one minor hiccup though, in as much as I was asked to remove three individuals from my list of 500.

I was informed that Joanna Lumley, Michael Palin and ironically enough, Helena Bonham Carter, all undertook tireless work already for the charity and it was therefore deemed a little inappropriate for me to pester them with my annoying letter. The three were duly replaced with that respected triumvirate of Roger Moore, Joss Stone and Murray Walker.

On the plus side, however, I was informed that my first meeting had almost been arranged already – and this a day before the project had officially started and without me even having lifted a finger or licked the gum of an envelope. Talk about progress.

'Are you familiar with Tony Hawks?' Matt had asked me.

'Which one? The American skateboarder or the comedian?' I replied smugly. I am well aware that most people have heard of either one or the other, or occasionally neither, but rarely both.

'Oh dear, I do hope it was the comedian Tony on your list as I've already had a word with him and he's prepared to meet you.'

'Indeed it was. That's fantastic, thank you so much.'

We both agreed that I couldn't hope to meet a more ideal individual to mark my first 'greeting', since Tony himself has been known to indulge in the odd whimsical challenge himself. Such follies have included circumnavigating Ireland with a fridge in tow and taking on each member of the Moldovan national football team at a game of tennis (both of these arising from, surprise, surprise, the making of a drunken bet in a pub).

I read the hilarious *Around Ireland with a Fridge* several years ago and remembered telling Michael about it, which is no doubt why he mischievously elected to include this kindred spirit on my list in the first place.

Well, much to Tony's credit, and having struggled to plough his way through his own embarrassing undertakings while maintaining a few crumbs of dignity, I can only presume that he felt sorry for me which is why he had decided to help me. Either that or he owed Matt a favour.

While we are on the subject, I would just like to pay tribute to, and paraphrase, one of my favourite journalists, Victor Lewis-Smith, who I believe has been credited with the quote, 'Imitation is the sincerest form of being an untalented thieving bastard'.

The reason I mention this is as follows: although this whole project was only conceived following a night of too much familiarity with Jackie Daniels just over one week earlier, I had lost count of the number of times that someone I told about what I was soon to undertake replied, 'Gosh, that's a bit like something that Dave Gorman would do'. In fact, if anyone else flaming well says to me, 'Gosh, that's a bit like something that Dave Gorman would do', I will personally flay them alive and then shove a copy of *Are you Dave Gorman?* (written by Dave Gorman), down their Dave Gorman-mentioning cake-holes.

I can honestly say, hand on heart, that the first time I had ever heard of this man was just four days earlier, when a work colleague of mine, Lee, had said, 'Gosh, that's a bit like something that Dave Gorman would do.'

Having subsequently had his name mentioned to me on countless occasions I have looked into his activities and discovered that yes, like Tony Hawks before him and like my good self after him, he has been prone to tackling 'wacky adventures' following drunken bets, such as travelling the globe while looking for other people called Dave Gorman.

I also wondered whether he had had to put up with people saying, 'Gosh, that's a bit like something that Tony Hawks would do,' when he first announced *his* intentions.

I would therefore like to set the record straight. When deciding to take on this challenge, it wasn't a case of apery of either of these men, the former whose book I had not picked up in anger for about three years and the latter whom I had never heard of.

You might think that I doth protest too much and be-ith a bald-faced liar, in which case you are entitled to your opinion and frankly I couldn't really care, but the simple truth of the matter is that no-one should have a monopoly when it comes to acting out stupid wagers that were made in inebriated haste, be he Tony Hawks, me, Dave Gorman, Danny Wallace or even the brave Geoff Huish, a Welshman who actually cut off his own testicles after Wales beat England in a Five-Nations rugby match and returned to the pub carrying them in a bag (not to be recommended), as he had promised.

Sunday July 3rd 2005 - A Question of Logistics

◇◇

So, like the pilot and the Olympic sprinter, I was up and running. It was ten days since I had taken on this bet and a couple of days since I had started my own website. I had also finally put a picture of my face on the front page of it as directed by Typepad in an idiot-proof 'Insert picture here' way.

The picture was blurred as has been noted by the one or two individuals who had glanced at the site. I was happy about that since my anonymity would be, to some extent, preserved while I made a tit of myself.

Added to this was the fact that I have sometimes been a bit down on my looks and never been particularly comfortable with my face. I believe the French-speaking Vietnamese might call it a *Tête Offensive*.

Now I am not normally one who frightens all that easily. Slavering Rottweilers tend to spook me a little. Being on an aeroplane where a serious amount of turbulent wind outside the aircraft creates a similar effect inside of me, tends to ruffle my feathers (not to mention the back of my underwear), as does the image of a twitchy dictator or president who has a small, red, plastic button at arm's length, but other than that I am usually of a relatively sanguine and philosophical nature.

That wasn't the case on this particular Sunday in July.

No, at this time, my bowels were suffering from an irritable syndrome and I had been conducting elaborate gurgling symphonies from inside my gut. This was basically because I was of the opinion that:

1. I would completely fail in my task and end up having just two meetings and be deemed a failure by everyone who knew me, not to mention having to put up with Michael's smugness.

2. Everyone that I had told about my challenge so far might view it (and me) as stupid, pointless, desperate or sad.

3. I did not have the first idea how to find contact details for a single person on the entire list of 500.

4. I would waste what little money I didn't have on stamps and petrol and printing letters for absolutely no reason other than to prove a chunky Cypriot wrong and that by missing work I wouldn't be getting paid.

Furthermore, the covering letter that I was sending out to these 500 individuals also made me sound like something of a plum, so I decided to make several changes. The vomit-worthy 'A Social Experiment' phrase just had to go: it was stupid and redundant. An experiment, as far as I can make out, is supposed to be an academic exercise where empirical evidence enables one to draw conclusions from the findings that are on offer. Mine was not.

The line '...the only people that can help me are (all of) you...' sounded pathetic. Why on earth would they want to help? Why bother to try and give them a guilt trip? They didn't know me from Adam, and I am sure that in most cases they could not have given a damn if I was swinging from the chandelier.

The line '...some modern latter-day George Orwell' was oxymoronic.

Aside from all of that, the entire tone of the letter seemed so sycophantic and fawning that coupled with the faux intellectual 'A Social Experiment' heading, I believed it would be a minor miracle if *anyone* took me seriously.

As for the task of trying to find contact details for any of these people, I had at least compiled a short list of targets that I thought might bear fruit, such as newspapers, magazines, sports clubs, TV/film production companies, record labels, the Houses of Parliament, the BBC, radio stations and publishing houses.

I had also researched several websites that could be of use to me and discovered that agent's listings appear on www.spotlight.com, www. IMDB.com and www.contactanyceleb.com.

I thus retired to bed, to sleep (perchance to watch a bit of TV first), secure in the knowledge that at least I'd be able to get a *few* of my letters sent out over the next couple of days.

Tuesday July 5th 2005 – First Letters Sent

Another dictionary definition for you:

schadenfreude \SHAHD-n-froy-duh\, noun: *a malicious satisfaction in the misfortunes of others.*

35

I'm not sure if I was being overly sensitive because of too many late nights and a recent lack of vitamin B$_1$ intake (no veg), but the lack of sponsorship received to this point led me to believe that friends and family viewed my bizarre project as something of a joke. Some of the replies that I had received having sent out an email to a number of my friends as I sought sponsorship, appeared to back this point up.

They ranged from one school friend kindly telling me to 'P**s off!' without a hint of irony, another replying, 'Spending six months trying to shake the hands of celebrities. I can't think of a better way of spending your time' with a vast amount of irony and my mother (who I finally got round to telling) repeatedly calling me a 'star-plucker' or words to that effect.

Anyway, just as I was slumped at my desk, mild depression setting in, I noticed an advert on the TV in the corner of my bedroom which cheered me up no end. It had the sumptuous voice of Ella Fitzgerald claiming that fish in the sea, rivers running free and blossoms on a tree all knew how I felt. It was as if she was talking to me personally and at that very moment I felt myself well-up as though some higher power greater than any living thing was cloaking me in a warm embrace.

Unfortunately, it was just my halogen lamp that had tilted over.

Incidentally, I would also like to correct Ella on her assertion about the fishes since, and I don't think I am merely recounting a myth here, they are known to have very short memories and are unlikely to be lamenting the lack of sponsorship on their websites.

Anyway, let me recount my progress to this date.

Monday morning saw me dispatch the first of my letters. I thought it made sense to send the first batch to those who write for *The Sun*, *The Mirror* and *The Evening Standard*, as well as to Members of Parliament, since the addresses for all of these are pretty obtainable, *ipso facto*, the following of the 500 should have received/be receiving my letter over the next day or so: **Tony Benn, Tony Blair, Jeremy Clarkson, Sebastian Coe, George Galloway, A. A. Gill, William Hague, Boris Johnson, Charles Kennedy, Victor Lewis-Smith, Richard Littlejohn, John Major, Piers Morgan, Tony Parsons, Will Self, Brian Sewell, Margaret Thatcher, Rebecca Wade, A. N. Wilson, Quentin Wilson** and **Lord Woolf.**

On receiving an odd request from some strange nobody, who knew how they would react. I was aware that the above list of odd bedfellows only amounted to 21 of my 500 but I was of the opinion that 'softly softly catchee monkey' and more importantly, I'd run out of stamps.

Wednesday July 6th 2005 – Olympic Joy

I was at work; well, those pieces of data don't enter themselves into the company database, when I heard that this wonderful country of mine, indeed this wonderful city of mine, would be hosting the Olympics in 2012. It made me want to rush out and by a pair of Speedos and start training, but how could I inflict such a sight on the other patrons of the Swiss Cottage public swimming baths?

I also noticed the likes of Sebastian Coe, Kelly Holmes and 'Red' Ken Livingstone (well, it *was* a hot day) leading the celebrations and thought to myself that 'Yes, this sort of good news was going to make them all far more amenable to the idea of shaking hands with complete strangers'.

To cap off this brilliant news, I learned that not only had we won the right to host these games, we had done so at the expense of France, and, as they say, losing in this painful fashion by the narrowest of margins really could not have happened to a nicer country, I'm sure you'd agree.

Thursday July 7th 2005 – The Horror, The Horror

How quickly the cheers turned to tears following the actions of four subhuman pieces of detritus. May they spend eternity floating as turds on a fetid puddle of vomit. My diary entry from 07/07/2005 was as follows:

'*...As most of the globe is now well aware, my lovely City, the one that I was born in, grew up in, live in and work in, was hit by a series of terrorist strikes today. The first thing to say, quite obviously, is that*

I extend my sincere condolences to anyone who has been affected by this appalling and despicable tragedy. Frankly, this sick act made me evaluate a lot of things. In particular, I attempted to rationalise this project that I am currently working on with Michael, and whether or not, in the greater scheme of things, it has any merit or is particularly worthwhile. In short, it made me think 'What the hell am I doing with my life?'

I had a lengthy discussion with Michael, and while we agreed that quite clearly it has no merit whatsoever, we decided that the fact that money is being raised for charity is reason enough to carry on, and that no blood-thirsty wacko should be allowed to dictate what we do on a day-to-day basis.

That having been said, it is patently obvious that the last thing that any politician, newspaper editor, columnist, religious leader, indeed anyone on our list of 500, will want at the moment is to receive some daft letter from me asking to have my photo taken with them. It really goes without saying that most people probably have their mind on other things at the moment.

We have therefore decided that for the next two weeks there is little point in me writing to anyone and that I should recommence sending out my letters towards the end of July.

Michael has agreed to extend the time limit of our bet by two weeks and it will now end on January 14th 2006. This will also give me the opportunity of spending the next fortnight snuffling out the contact details of these 500 individuals'

As for the 21 already written to, by this stage, as my first week was just about slipping below the horizon, I had received just one reply... step forward Richard Littlejohn. I say reply, what I actually mean is that someone had organised for a stock postcard from *Sun* Newspapers to be sent to me. It read:

THE SUN

Thank you very much for taking the trouble to write to Richard Littlejohn.

The volume of mail received on a weekly basis means Richard is not always able to reply personally to every letter. However, he is grateful for your views - whether positive suggestions or criticism - and will consider the points you raise.

Once again, many thanks for writing.

Editor's Office.

That will be a 'No' then, I guess.

Friday July 15th 2005 - One Week Later…
◇◇

Having sent out the first 21 of my 500 letters at the beginning of the preceding working week some 12 days earlier, and having reached Friday evening of the following week, I can inform you that the flow of replies from these illuminati, glitterati, cognoscenti and anything else ending in -ti, through my letterbox, continued to resemble the flow of water through the Serengeti's mud-baked Mbalageti River during a particularly dry 'dry season'. No more than a trickle. One would, in fact, see a more noticeable trickle watching a man with a bad case of kidney stones urinating.

There was, however, a however, as on this fifteenth day of my challenge I ACTUALLY received my SECOND reply (much cheering and throwing of top hats in the air by posh people), and so I doffed my imaginary cap to Mr Jeremy Clarkson of *Top Gear* fame (and other car-related TV shows). I quote it directly:

THE SUN

Thank you very much for taking the trouble to write to Jeremy Clarkson.

The volume of mail received on a weekly basis means Jeremy is not always able to reply personally to every letter. However, he is grateful for your views - whether positive suggestions or criticism - and will consider all the points you raise.

Once again many thanks for writing.

Editor's Office

Now, this may sound familiar to you. It certainly sounded familiar to me and so I stored this 'card' of sorts, next to the identical one from Mr Littlejohn.

Anyway, I was delighted to hear that both Richard and Jeremy were both '*grateful for my views – whether positive suggestions or criticism*', which seemed slightly vague and a little bit strange in as much as I don't recall expressing any views. Well, I was equally glad that if nothing else, some office junior in Wapping was being kept relatively busy in sending out *Sun* postcards.

Marvellous.

Michael was indeed right. It looked as if I was going to fail his challenge miserably. Two 'No's' down, 498 to go...

Well, at least I had the Open to look forward to that weekend, or 'British Open Golf Championships' for those who prefer *Sex and the City*.

Tiger Woods, eh, what can you say? (Apart from it's a stupid place to go for a picnic.)

Hithankyow.

Tuesday July 19th 2005 – First Meeting Arranged

Who was it who once said that 'The darkest hour is the one just before dawn'? I'm not sure but presumably they've never been to Northern Finland in mid June.

Well, just as I was expressing my exasperation at the lack of positive replies received to this date, it appeared that my first 'Celebrity Meeting', sorry, my meeting with an 'Individual of Note in their Profession', would be taking place just a few days later, and in Wimbledon of all places.

Tony Hawks had informed Matt at the RNIB to inform me that a handshake could indeed take place outside Wimbledon train station if I turned up at 12.45 p.m. on Friday. I would therefore meet my spiritual father, provided that Marli (my boss) would let me take the time off work.

Well, what was the first thing I did on putting the phone down to Matt? It was to pick it up again to phone Michael so that I could crow about my great success. I mean at this rate, one meeting every 22 days, I would have accumulated a fantastic 8.95 handshakes by the end of my time limit. Come to think of it, that wouldn't be all that good would it?

Michael, quite predictably, was initially aloof and subsequently just plain rude.

He began by winding me up, telling me that the Tony Hawks on my list should have had an 'E' in the surname and was in fact meant to be the American skateboarder. After coming clean and laughing at me for rising to the bait, I recall our conversation went something a little like:

'Look at you. You're so saaaad. How excited are you that you're going to be meeting someone famous on Friday. By the way, can I come?'

'Why would you want to come, Michael?'

'Well, I'm not doing anything and, anyway, I thought we agreed that I was going to be your cameraman, taking the photos of the meetings.'

'Ummm, no Michael *you* agreed that, I simply asked to borrow your digital camera. Anyway, to answer your initial question I'm not excited that I'm meeting someone famous, I'm excited that my first meeting has now been arranged and I'm therefore one-hundredth of the way to proving that you're a cock.'

'Naaah it's not....' (I could almost hear the smirk) '...it's because you're going to be meeting someone famous.'

As he tailed off, saying something like '...blah, blah, blah, Shane Richie and me, blah, blah, working on *Grease* together...' I considered whether it was wise to present this babbling fool before Tony Hawks. I then considered that it was a case of no Michael, no borrowing of camera and that I was therefore somewhat snookered.

Wednesday July 20th 2005 – Mr Kennedy I Salute You
◇◇

Reading back over my earlier entries, I admit that some of my comments were a bit inaccurate. In no way would I wish to upset Holland, mobile phone companies, certain sections of the Northern Irish population, Dundee United or the Liberal Party.

I am talking about my likes and dislikes here, as alluded to earlier. I have no idea why I said that I dislike anything orange apart from oranges, for although I think the colour has something of a depressive quality about it (it conjures up images of a line of inmates heading for death row), I think that it was a little rash of me to make such a sweeping statement. So, aside from not having any problem whatsoever with any of the group mentioned above, I can also inform you that I quite like carrots too.

My appreciation of the Liberal Party had also slightly risen on this day but only because Mr Charles Kennedy MP, leader of the Liberal Democrats, and Member of Parliament for somewhere in Scotland I believe, a man who was one of the original recipients of the first 21 letters I posted, had sent me a most delightful reply.

Dear Julian,

Thank you for your letter regarding your campaign 'Greeting the 500'. Please accept my apologies for the delay in replying. Unfortunately, due to many diary and constituency commitments I will be unable to meet with you for a photograph.

I am sorry to give you what must be a disappointing response. However, I have enclosed a signed photograph as requested for your auction and may I take this opportunity to wish you the best of luck with your campaign.

Thanks once again for writing and best wishes.

OK, he is not able to meet me, but what a nice gesture. Bring back proportional representation I say (have we ever had it?).

(Incidentally, Mr Kennedy's constituency is actually Ross, Skye and Lochaber - I noticed it at the top of his letter.)

Friday July 22nd 2005 – A Reply from the PM (and Another from Jeremy)
◇◇

This particular day was a very productive one indeed for me – a very busy 24 hours. It was bulging, much like the scrotum of a man who has abstained from sex for 40 years. Anyway, I have decided to cut and splice this action into three 'fun size' bites.

First, I received a couple of replies in my pigeon-hole at my flat. 'Celebrity droppings' I guess you could call them. Now at this stage I would like to officially apologise to Jeremy Clarkson to whom I did a slight disservice previously.

Having received a stock postcard from the offices of *The Sun* newspaper, I suggested that Jeremy had not actually read my letter. Well, this was actually wholly inaccurate and unfair. I shall now walk through the streets of North London publicly flogging myself (I reckon I'm worth about £3.50).

A letter from Jeremy's personal assistant, Lucinda, read:

Dear Julian,

Many thanks for your letter of July 4th, it sounds like a most interesting bet you have with your friend and I would love to be able to help you. However, I am really sorry but I just can't. We get so many letters from people wanting just a few minutes of Jeremy's time and we have to say no. If we were to allow everyone who asked for a few minutes, in no time at all, Jeremy's day would be totally taken up and he would have no time at all to do all the work he does, so I am really sorry that we are not going to be able to help you win your bet, but hope the enclosed signed photograph will go some way to help.

With all best wishes…

So there you go. A debt of thanks was owed by me again. A signed photo enclosed with the letter.

I must say, I do greatly admire Jeremy Clarkson anyway, and I am not just saying that because the lots for my charity auction had suddenly doubled. No, being someone who always speaks my mind, even though

I sometimes offend others in the process, I've always had the utmost respect for like-minded straight-shooters. That's unless, of course, I disagree with what they are saying.

The other letter that I opened came from 10 Downing Street. It read:

Dear Mr. Segal,

The Prime Minister has asked me to thank you for your letter and recent enclosure. I regret that the many calls on Mr Blair's time will make it impossible for him to see you personally.

Yours sincerely...

It was signed by a Mr. 'Smith', and I'm sure that the mysterious Smith is indeed a legitimate member of the PM's inner sanctum as the reply came from 10 Downing Street's Direct Communications Unit.

On reading it, I wondered to myself how the *In*direct Unit might have replied, possibly a rock through my bedroom window with a note attached to it?

Well, not a huge surprise there to be honest as the Prime Minister probably had more important things on his plate such as, ummm, running the country. Neither could I truly be sure whether Tony did indeed instruct this shady cohort of his to thank me, although I shall stick with the mental picture I have of the PM chuckling over my strange letter while eating his boiled egg at breakfast.

Two more 'nays' then but at that particular moment in time I was incredibly relieved to have received *any* sort of response.

Friday July 22nd 2005 - Meeting 1 (Tony Hawks)

So how did it feel when one could FINALLY say on this late day in June - this glorious day of hazy sunshine (with a minor risk of scattered showers sweeping in from the West... best take a cardigan if you're going to be outdoors) - that all the hopes that had been welling up inside for the previous three weeks, would finally be realised and joy would spurt forth like so much pus from a lanced boil?

I HAD sent a letter to a man of not inconsiderable fame (apologies for the use of a double negative) and he WAS prepared to meet me for NO other reason than to shake my hand and to help me prove my friend WRONG.

To be honest, I felt quite sick that morning, not because I was chock full of nerves about meeting someone that I'd been more used to seeing on a TV screen or on the cover of a book, but because I'd eaten an anchovy pizza of dubious quality the night before.

Anyway, a huge amount of gratitude was owed to Tony Hawks who had got this particular ball rolling. I have mentioned elsewhere that this was a most appropriate member of my 500 to kick the whole thing off, since he himself was relatively familiar with these sort of curious experiments.

So would Tony be able to impart any wisdom as I sought to travel round *this* country with a dishwasher in tow instead of a fridge? (actually, come to think of it Michael *rarely* gets round to cleaning his crockery). Well, to be honest, I decided that I wasn't going to ask many questions. The central theme of my bet did NOT involve meeting famous people and indulging them in small talk or asking them annoying questions or singing their praises.

Nope, mine was a simple in and out procedure and therein lay the beauty of it. I wasn't going to labour them with any verbal jiggery-pokery. It would simply be a case of meeting, handshake, photo and then amscray. Obviously I'd be polite at all times, but I would let them take the lead. If they wanted to have a chat, fine, if they didn't, fine.

So, as for the meeting itself... I was conscious of a need to wake Michael – my photographer-in chief (well, until he found a job anyway) – in good time from his Behemoth meets Rip Van Winkle slumber. I did so at 10.15 a.m. and made my way over to pick him up

The journey down to Wimbledon itself was quite uneventful, apart from getting lost in Richmond Park and driving through the middle of it (it's OK, that's quite legal) for one and a half complete circuits. At least the landscape and deer made for a nice diversion, in every sense of the word.

On getting to Wimbledon, however, I had a blazing row with you know who, since he was desperate to buy a pack of cigarettes, not having had one for seven minutes. Not only were we pressed for time but I didn't particularly want Tony to meet us with Michael having a fag hanging out of his mouth like some hairy version of Marlene Dietrich. My co-betee, as is his wont, shouted and stamped his foot and swore endlessly and started to create a bit of a scene in the street and so for the greater good I relented.

I could see that as long as Michael would be tagging along to these meetings, my stress levels would soar. He was a source of acute embarrassment at the best of times because of his lack of social airs and graces, least of all when I was trying to be polite to the high and mighty of the UK.

Then it hit me. What the hell was I thinking?

'Actually, forget standing on ceremony with the individuals from the list who meet us,' I said to Michael as we walked down Wimbledon High Street. 'I've just had an epiphany', and the more I thought about it, the more sense it made. 'An a-what?' he replied.

'Look, it doesn't matter. You know what Michael, I've had a thought. When we meet Tony just be yourself. If you want to smoke, smoke. If you want to swear, curse until you're blue in the face'.

At this, he looked a little surprised not to say delighted.

Well, the reason that I'd given Michael *carte blanche* to act like a complete knobhead in front of Tony Hawks had suddenly become so obvious. I was the one, after all, who had insisted to Michael that all of these 500 people on his list were 'probably just ordinary people like us'. So why on earth was I worried about putting on act of false courtesy in front of them?

Surely famous people are sick to the back teeth of walking down the street only for members of the public to approach them with inane Cheshire-cat grins slapped across their faces simply waiting to act the sycophant. No, this was going to be different. Michael, a man with fewer social skills than a cuttlefish at a plankton wedding reception would, on this occasion, be given permission, nay encouraged to, how you say? 'Keep it Real'. It was my opinion that Tony might even warm to this refreshing approach. Either that or be rather frightened.

So we continued down the road and as we waited outside our prearranged meeting spot, my tension grew once again. It seemed as though this spot hadn't turned out to be the most serene location since this happened to be the last day of term for many schools. We were surrounded by hordes of kids screaming to each other across a busy High Road while conversations such as 'Oi Bev! Oi! Oi! Oi Bev! Oi Bev! What time you going to Tash's tonight?!' continued non-stop as we waited.

At approximately 12.50 p.m., Tony arrived with a Moldovan friend. I recognised him straight away and thought to myself that here before me was a man who, through his own endeavours, had afforded himself the luxury of being able to lead a most enjoyable lifestyle.

I thought this because he had a healthy tan. Perhaps he'd just returned from a month in Barbados where he'd been penning the intro' to his next book I mused. Maybe that will be me one day, I fleetingly thought for a moment (note to self – get agent) before crashing back to reality and into this surreal scene.

Tony introduced me to his Moldovan friend and asked where I wanted the picture taken. I looked to cameraman Michael for guidance, who I suppose to my relief, had not taken my previous instructions literally by replying, 'I couldn't give a f****g sh**' and instead directed us to the outside wall of W.H. Smiths.

On mentioning the charity auction, Tony seemed a little concerned that he hadn't brought anything suitable, as I'm not sure how much detail Matt had given him about the intricacies of my challenge (or lack of them), but I told him not to worry and that the pencil in his satchel would do (I thought that asking for his wristwatch might be a bit much).

Michael then made some crass comment to Tony about the pencil being a potential money-spinner as it still had his teeth marks in it (I knew his behaviour wouldn't last), before he signed an autograph on a sticker for us (to authenticate the pencil at the auction) and going on his merry way. I think he was genuinely surprised and a bit confused by the brevity of the whole meeting, but there was little else to say apart from to thank him for taking part in it.

As Michael and I strode back to my car, having given Tony ample time to disappear (we were worried that he might think we were following him), I could finally breath a sigh of relief that I was well and truly on my way.

Only 99 more needed.

Jules Segal

Friday July 22nd 2005 – Hooray for the 'Ham and High'

◇◇

'The papers, mate, that's what you want to use' was the sage counsel offered to me from the mouth of a stereotypical, chirpy-cockney taxi driver as we were driving from Baker Street to Ealing several days earlier. He had a fair point.

However unlikely it was that your Eltons and Rustys and Aleds were to grant me an audience, they were slightly more likely to do so if they'd at least heard about me or what I was doing rather than just by happening on my bizarre request in letter form.

It was for that reason I contacted a local newspaper (local both to me and to a number of the people on my list).

Well, they say that the best things come in threes, or am I getting buses and small packages confused? But having already been ably assisted by Matt at the RNIB, it appeared that another Matt was to prove a life-saver as I went about the business of trying to win my bet.

Matt mark II is a journalist on my local newspaper, *The Hampstead and Highgate Express*, and what a fine publication it is, I might add.

You can often see the '*Ham and High*'s' main headlines emblazoned on signs in garage forecourts and outside corner shops across my neighbourhood, headlines such as 'Stop blocking Fitzjohns Avenue with your effingg 4×4s!' or 'Camden Town drug dealer shot dead on Inverness Street – 27th this month'.

Anyway, having received my begging email, he contacted me to inform me that a piece on my challenge would duly be featuring in the next edition of the paper.

I gave a minor whoop of joy to myself before, in a rather upbeat frame of mind, I decided to compile another 30 letters to be sent out to the following high and mighty individuals: **Clive Anderson**, **Toby Anstis**, **Clare Balding**, **Edith Bowman**, **Melvyn Bragg**, **Nicky Campbell**, **Jimmy Carr**, **Craig Charles**, **Kirsty Gallacher**, **Eamonn Holmes**, **Jools Holland**, **John Humphrys**, **Vernon Kay**, **John Kettley**, **Des Lynam**, **Humphrey Lyttleton**, **John Motson**, **Chris Moyles**, **Christian O'Connell**, **Dermot O'Leary**, **Michael Parkinson**, **Raj Persaud**, **Courtney Pine**, **Jonathan Ross**, **Pat Sharp**, **Peter Snow**, **Suggs**, **Jamie Theakston**, **Johnny Vaughan** and **Ian Wright**.

By the way, Michael wanted me to point out that Nicky Campbell, who is named above, is one of the many people from the list of 500 who have eaten in his mother's fine Greek restaurant (Bacchus Greek Taverna) in Hampstead, NW London.

Right, plug done.

Monday July 25th 2005 - List Amendment
◇◇◇

People pass away all the time. In fact, I bet you that even as we speak, someone, somewhere in the world is dying right now. Amendments to my list for that reason were, therefore, always rather inevitable... but not for this reason surely...

Unbelievably, soon after I had finished my interview with Matt of the *Ham and High*, I was informed by him that Michael, in his infinite clumsiness, had actually included in the list one person who had died several years previously. How very embarrassing – I was most glad I hadn't sent that particular letter out.

That ex-Beatle was, of course, promptly removed from the list and replaced by the delightful Radio 1 DJ Sara Cox, a picture of whom actually adorns my bathroom wall and another of which I'd included on my website, somewhat illegally and in infringement of copyright laws I imagine.

I feared that there was absolutely no point in taking Michael to task over this, since I already knew what his reply would be.

'Well, Jules, You know that I struggled a bit to come up with the 500 names, and got a bit of help from Agos and Tom and Muss...'

'Yes.'

'...and Nicki and George and Kyoko and Karen...'

'Yes Michael, I know.'

'...and Seb and Regan and Sue...'

49

Jules Segal

'Michael, what's your point?'

'Well, one of *them* must have come up with George Harrison.'

Saturday July 30th 2005 – Hell is Round the Corner

◇◇

Like Annie Wilkes in the film *Misery*, I was depressed.

Although I didn't feel the sudden urge to smash someone's ankles in with a sledgehammer, I *was* in a very blue mood by the end of July. My progress had been so painfully slow that by this stage in the proceedings I seriously thought about giving up, but I really couldn't and it was all my fault for getting a charity involved.

How I wished I could just be back in my humdrum existence of rolling out of bed and rolling into work and then into a pub... then leaving the pub, going back to work for the rest of the morning and afternoon, then back to a pub again and then home to a drunkenly made omelette.

I recall that on this day, a lady named Cindy offered me some gentle words of encouragement. She mentioned that I had sad eyes. I think she said something like, 'Don't be discouraged, try to realise it's hard to take courage. In a world full of people, you can lose sight of it all and the darkness inside you can make you feel so small'.

Then she started banging on about showing my true colours or something. So I switched the radio off.

Of the 30 letters I'd sent out on the 22nd July, I had received somewhere between negative-one and one reply. To those that are mathematically challenged, that equates to none. I had always trusted the Royal Mail, but surely something was afoot.

It wasn't all bad news though. I'd recently attended one of the music pub quizzes that my friend Mark, who works for Radio 6, frequently organizes. It was there that, among quaffing Alpine Lagers, and incorrectly answering questions about Depeche Mode, I got chatting to a young lady by the name of Jude who also works for the Beeb.

She mentioned that she might be able to get me in touch with the BBC Radio 'press office', which I thought *might* be a good lead but I wouldn't be holding my breath. I'd already had so many people promising me this and that (and sometimes even a bit of the other).

'Sure I'll have a word with Guy Ritchie; Sacha (Baron Cohen) will definitely meet you', 'Yeah, my cousin works for Chelsea, Frank Lampard no problem'. You all know who you are. Even my sister, bless her, said she would have a word with Todd Carty's wife (who it turns out she vaguely knows). The thing I have learned however, and this applies generally in life, is that the only person who can really help you in these sort of situations is yourself (or possibly Max Clifford, although he didn't respond to my email).

The weekend ahead of me would therefore be spent in training for the London Marathon (see forfeits list). Following this and after much girding of loin, steeling of spirit, grasping of nettle, biting of bullet and thinking of cliché, I would be making a concerted effort to write to at least 100 more of the people on my list and by gum I wouldn't fail.

Then again, didn't Lady Macbeth say something similar?

In the meantime, I decided to undertake some of the long overdue housework that had been put off for a week or two while I had been busy sticking stamps to envelopes. In fact, my kitchen sink had started to become a bit like Denmark. There was something rotten in it.

CHAPTER 3 – August

Replies received: William Hague, Jimmy Carr, Michael Owen, Alan Shearer, Jonny Wilkinson, Dom Joly, Chris Morris, Ken Livingstone, Rowan Atkinson, John Motson, John Francome, Ricky Gervais, Jeffrey Archer and Patrick Moore.

Meetings achieved: Jimmy Carr and John Motson.

Monday August 1st 2005 – No More Questions

Since embarking ('barking' being the operative part) on my insane quest, and having mentioned the details of it to various individuals, I had literally tens of people asking me the same questions over and over again. After a certain amount of deliberation, I decided 'What the FAQ', I may as well lay these particular queries to rest for once and for all... With a peck on the cheek and a bedtime story. I therefore present to you the 'Frequently Asked Questions' page that featured somewhere in the darker recesses of my website:

Jules Segal

1. Hey Jules, what's your bet/challenge all about?

Look, if you actually have to ask this question having stumbled upon my website, where I have quite clearly explained the background of my bet on no less than FOUR occasions, then I assume that (i) either you have an IQ that's lower than the residue on the underside of an elastoplast in a swimming pool gutter, or (ii) you suffer from an acute form of attention deficit disorder, so stop drumming your finger's on the table and LISTEN!

Bet with friend in pub/500 celebrities/Meet as many of them as possible in six-month period/Forfeits to be undertaken by the loser.

2. It looks to me as if you are just desperate to meet famous people?

That is simply not true Mum. I am really not that fussed about the concept of celebrity, but having said that, I do admit to being quite intrigued to see which of the individuals that I have written to will respond, which of them will actually meet me and which will I not hear a peep from.

3. So is there anyone on the list of 500 that Michael drew up, that you would not want to meet or who you don't like?

Only two individuals, but I'd rather keep that to myself thanks.

4. But you can tell me, I won't tell anyone.

Look don't push it.

5. OK then, who on your list *would* you be keen to meet?

I guess my own personal heroes include Victor Lewis-Smith, Derren Brown, Simon Pegg, Julie Walters, Alan Davies, Kathy Burke, Jimmy Saville, Clare Balding, Jermaine Defoe, Keith Floyd and Hugh Cornwell.

I wouldn't complain about meeting some of the 'sorts' either, your Kate Beckinsales, Anna Friels or Michaela Strachans. And I suppose it would be something of a coup if I 'greeted' Tony Blair.

6. Yeah well unlucky, 10 Downing Street already replied, stating that he couldn't meet you. Anyway, remind me who Hugh Cornwell is again?

Lead singer of The Stranglers, you idiot.

7. Oh, OK, and Sheridan Smith?

I've already mentioned that somewhere. Michael has a minor obsession with her, but hopefully it's not got to the unhealthy stage yet.

8. So what's in it for you then? Why are you doing it?

Well, to be honest, my day job is hardly inspiring and I generally get home from work feeling really bitter and twisted. You know, like a kilo of lemons in a food processor. I simply wanted to do something a little bit exciting, just to spice up my life a little.

I would also dearly love to see Michael elbow deep in cow as a result of his cocksure attitude (See Forfeit 4).

9. By the way, I am struggling with my Chemistry thesis. Can you explain the difference between Boyle's Law and Newton's Law?

No, I was no good at 'subjects' at school.

10. Try this one then. Does Charles Dance?

I dunno, does Chris Waddle?

Monday August 1st 2005 – One for Sorrow Two for Joy

'I don't want to insert a lengthy post here', (as I believe Ron Jeremy said on a recent film set, and if you don't know who he is, I admire your innocent upbringing).

This was how I updated my diary on this blue-skied Monday afternoon. The reason being that I was at work, like most of the population, and it was therefore far more important for me to be entering the names of lawyers onto a company database in order to justify my derisory wage (just a joke, Mr C), than making facetious comments in an on-line journal that no-one was reading.

I did have some rather good news, however, as both William Hague MP and Jimmy Carr had agreed to a meeting. I was absolutely delighted and I obviously owed a huge debt of gratitude to both of these men, one who makes me laugh with his gibbering nonsense and the other who... well, I don't know a great deal about Jimmy Carr to be honest.

Anyway, this was the letter that I'd received from a lady named Kirsten, who is no doubt a diligent aide to the Member of Parliament for Richmond, North Yorkshire:

On behalf of Mr. Hague, I would like to thank you for your letter of 4th July concerning the challenge you have accepted.

Mr. Hague would be happy to meet you though, now that the House is in recess, I am afraid that it will not be possible to make any arrangements until the autumn. However, if you would not mind, I will make a note to contact you then in order to agree a suitable time to meet.

With kind regards…

So what could I say, fantastic. I had secured my first 'meeting' that was as a direct response to a letter sent by me to someone important who didn't view me as some sort of nutter. Following hot on the heels of this, an email from Katie:

Hi Jules, Jimmy (Carr) would like to help you out with your mission. If you could turn up to Xfm next weekend at 11 a.m. we can do the photo, etc.

Let me know . . .

So this day was truly a most pleasing one. There was I lying in bed the night before, tearfully casting aside my copy of *Harry Potter VI* after reading the harrowing final few chapters, unaware that all would feel so much better come the following evening.

Two positive replies without even having to resort to the Imperius Curse.

Tuesday August 3rd 2005 - Yahoo!
◇◇◇

Yahoo! is the raucous exclamation of delight, usually emanating from the mouth an excited American, although such explosions of joy can also sometimes take the form of 'Yee Haaw' and on occasions, the more patriotic 'Yoo Ess Ay! Yoo Ess Ay!).

Sorry, I am gabbling here.

Yahoo! also happens to be the name of a website-cum-search engine that had received a request from me.

In a nutshell, I contacted those responsible for the running of the 'Office Attachments' section of their website, a category that is clicked on by bored people at work who are looking for quirky stories, viral videos, computer-based games or just your usual stock photographs of giraffes on water-skis and the like. Anyway, I noticed that they had ear-marked a small corner of the 'Office Attachment' page to a section dedicated to 'interesting' websites and I had simply enquired as to whether or not they would like to feature mine.

I assure you that this was nothing whatsoever to do with me blowing my own trumpet (I prefer to play with my own organ), but I'm simply of the opinion that the more people that got to know about my project, aside from raising sponsorship money for the RNIB, the sooner those that were on my list would have actually heard about what I was doing, and would therefore hopefully be more inclined to grant me an audience. Anyway Yahoo! said yes, to which I gave out a very British 'Hurrah!'.

Thursday August 4th 2005 – The Snowball Effect

Admittedly, it was only a local newspaper (for local people), but I suppose it was a start. Katy from *The Barnet Press*, who had read Matt's column about my challenge in *The Hampstead and Highgate Express*, got in touch and asked if she could interview me for *her* weekly publication.

I therefore decided to take the entire afternoon off work the preceding day, to conduct this 15-minute interview over the phone.

A young photographer called Jazz had arranged to come round to Michael's before the interview, to take a few snaps of the two of us for the piece and before Jazz's arrival Michael was displaying an excitement and animation that I don't think I'd ever seen from him.

No really, I cannot stress that strongly enough.

He was like a puppy with a new rubber ball. Michael, unlike me, relished the idea of his face appearing in newspapers. Presumably, he assumed that it was only a short step from page 6 of *The Barnet Press*, to the front cover of *Vogue*.

Anyway, after a vast amount of wrangling and many harsh insults traded in the heat of battle, I finally persuaded him *not* to launch his modelling career by wearing his ridiculous Australian, leather cowboy hat for this particular shoot.

Anyway, Jazz arrived on time to a house that had recently been cleared of ashtrays from the floor, old fish and chip paper from the sofa and various other unsavoury objects from the bowl of the toilet. Pleasantries were then exchanged, photographs taken and Jazz soon departed.

So, while the man that I'd contacted from a national newspaper had, as of that time, not got back to me, I was buoyed by the news that a few hundred households in the outer London suburbs were being kept up to speed, on a weekly basis, about my limited success. It was only a short step to other exciting publications such as *The South Plumstead Echo* and *The Bromley Bugle*, I thought.

What with all of these photo opportunities, I decided to buy a lovely virginal white T-shirt that I subsequently had emblazoned with an advertisement for my website across the chest. This was done by some lovely people at Snappy Snaps.

When I returned home though, I was upset to learn that it had been printed somewhat haphazardly and I was thus forced to ask the kind souls at *The Ham and High* to doctor the picture of me wearing it, by removing the writing from the front of the T-shirt.

Snappy Snaps got my website address wrong you see, and while in theory I was well within my rights to storm back to the shop and get this error rectified for free, I was far too lazy and so instead, decided to buy a magic marker with which to make the necessary alteration myself.

Friday August 5th 2005 – G'day, Sport
<><><><><><><><><><><><><><><><><><><><><><><><><><><><><><><><><><><><><><><><><><><>

Michael Owen, Alan Shearer and Jonny Wilkinson – what can I say about these highly regarded sportsmen that hasn't already been said? Quite a lot actually, for it was on this morning that I received replies from all three of the said heroes. Sadly though, in this instance, the replies received (all negative) were without any of them actually having even seen my letter and no, they hadn't all recently become highly experienced in the ancient art of clairvoyancy.

Now don't get me wrong, I *had* got and *did* expect to get a number of negative responses to my requests for meetings, but I would have felt just a tad happier if those who were telling me that they wouldn't be able to meet me actually knew that they wouldn't be able to meet me or that they had been contacted at all.

In my initial email to the sports agency that deals with these three men, I had requested that my letters be passed on to each of them so that they could formulate a considered opinion on whether to meet me or not. Nevertheless, on this day I received a reply from one lady who worked for this organization.

It read:

Dear Jules,

Unfortunately, the players above will be unable to assist with your request as they have a huge backlog of outstanding charity and community commitments from last season, therefore we have been asked to limit any new enquiries for the time being. I am sure you will appreciate their position, in that they think it is only fair to undertake those elements they have already committed to undertake.

However, good luck with your challenge.

Kind regards...

Now obviously I do not in any way blame the good people of this agency (that I'd better not name) for this response, they are only obeying orders, it's just that when such high-profile individuals decide to 'limit new enquiries' they *may* inadvertently be overlooking those that are not only worthwhile, but would also take up no more than 30 seconds of their time... in other words mine.

I have to be totally honest here and admit that I now see this was one of the points that Michael was so ineloquently trying to raise in the Crown all those weeks ago.

Successful people, by dint of the fact that they *are* successful will, more often than not, be very busy. Sure, they'll stop and have a quick natter in the street with Joe and Mo public, but when it comes to actually *arranging* a meeting it is a different matter.

I reflected on such things and then for the first time, and with little over a month gone since starting the whole operation, I seriously considered the possibility that I wasn't only going to lose this bet, but that I was going to lose it heavily.

It was at that very moment that I suddenly remembered Sir Isaac Newton's Third Law of Physics. Remember? The one about every action having an equal and opposite reaction.

It seemed to follow that the more work I put into the whole thing and the quicker I sent out my letters, the sooner I'd receive replies. With that in mind, I rushed out of my front door and headed to the nearest post box. The likes of **Ken Livingstone**, **Paul Ross**, **Rav Singh**, **Eric Hall**, **Ann Widdecombe** and **Sara Cox** would all be aware of my intentions over the next day or so.

Friday August 5th – Without Me...

...is a song or 'track' (as I believe young people call them these days) by the American rap artist Eminem.

Eminem - a man with a particularly suitable name since he is a bit of a nut and is sometimes wrapped in a crispy shell (suit). Well, the only reason I mention him or more accurately, this track, is because the opening four words contained therein read: 'I've created a monster...'.

Having got in touch with Yahoo! who said they would promote my website from this Friday for one week on their 'Office Attachments' page, it appeared as though they had kept their side of the bargain and I spent much of this day in a slight state of shock.

Having checked my website 'hit' counter, a counter that over the last month had oscillated between four and ten hits on average per 24 hours, I noticed that on this day no fewer than 2 157 bored individuals had glanced at my website, and that was before lunchtime.

Maybe my website really *would* do the rounds, I considered. It could even end up as popular as the one containing dancing hamsters or the one showing the fat kid playing with a light-sabre or the email that EVERYONE had read where some girl had confessed to shampooing her hair with her boyfriend's own self-made product. Forget 'Wash'n' Go', try 'Wash 'n' Cum'.

As if all of that wasn't reason enough to go out to a local pub and buy crème-de-menthes all round, it appeared that as a result of this publicity, some total stranger had pledged a whole £1 to me on my sponsorship website.

All that AND a second Greeting to look forward to two days later. Heady times...

Sunday August 7th 2005 – Meeting 2 (Jimmy Carr)

Now I am not normally one who would wake up at 8.45 a.m. on a Sunday morning out of choice, but today was no normal Sunday morning, for it was the day of my second 'Meeting'. I would soon be shaking hands with the ubiquitous Jimmy Carr, a man whose star certainly appeared to be in the ascendancy.

The time of this extraordinary 'general' meeting: 11.00am.

The place: Leicester Square offices of Xfm.

Those in attendance: Jimmy Carr, Michael, myself.

Apologies: from me for having to bring Michael along.

Once again, I noted the urgency of the situation, for what could possibly be worse than having a prominent member of society kindly agreeing to meet you for absolutely no reason whatsoever, only for you to turn up late and waste their time. Michael was slightly more blasé about the whole affair.

You see, having raced round to Childs Hill to pick up my 'photographer', it soon became apparent that my urgency was matched only by Michael's desire to snatch an extra 45 minutes of kip. There he was, still flat out on his living-room sofa, drooling away and no doubt dreaming about Sheridan Smith or shepherd's pie.

After the inevitable brief argument and short drive into town, we entered the building in question and within five minutes were whisked upstairs by a friendly runner and into a sunlit open-plan office. The place seemed to be swimming in old newspapers, discarded CDs and DVDs. Magazines were strewn all over the place and there was a Playstation in the corner of the room. It was as though a hurricane had ripped through a Virgin Megastore.

I noticed through a glass window at the end of a corridor that my host was just finishing up his radio show, yet no sooner had Michael and I commenced a game of table-football, or 'babyfoot' as the French rather immaturely call it, than Jimmy approached, arm outstretched.

'Hold your horses, I've got to get the camera ready,' said Michael with all the grace of a Mongol invader.

Jimmy seemed rather bemused.

'So where's the camera crew?' he enquired.

'Ahaaa.'

I think that there had been a case of crossed wires somewhere along the way and so, while my panicking brain mulled the variety of possible responses that I could give to such a question, I eventually came up with the answer that I deemed to be the most suitable for this particular situation. Basically, I spun a complete lie.

'Aah right, yes, the camera crew. Well, I was in touch with Talkback Productions and while they are keen to start filming, they're not quite ready to do so yet. They'll probably join up with me further down the line.'

'Oh, OK', said a slightly baffled Jimmy before continuing, 'Yes, I know them quite well. Say hi to...' (I've forgotten the name he mentioned).

'Yes of course. No problem. Will do,' I bullshitted.

Michael then assembled myself and Jimmy, with all the authority of David Bailey's photography teacher, into what he considered to be the perfect spot in the office for the snap ('Has to be away from the window. No, not there', etc., etc.) before the picture was finally taken.

He then embarrassed me further by asking our subject for a photo of the two of them, which was agreed to, and taken by me and that was it. Job done.

The gracious Jimmy handed me an Xfm wall hanging and Xfm badges for my auction, and signed some stickers. He then made Michael and I both laugh heartily with some pithy observations, patted me on the back, compared my experiment with something that Dave Gorman might do and then departed to get on with his work.

'What was that cack about us being filmed?' asked Michael as the elevator descended.

'Just *that* Michael, just *that*. By the way, why the hell did you have to stick your oar in and get a photo of you and Jimmy?'

'Well, obviously, because I want everyone to think that these people that *WE* are going to meet are friends of mine.'

Euston, we have a problem.

Monday August 8th 2005 – On the Up and Up
<><><><><><><><><><><><><><><><><><><><><><><><><><><><><><><><><><><><><><><><><><><><><>

I was growing increasingly delighted that some of the 8500 people who had glanced at my website seemed to find what I was doing rather amusing, presumably because I was making an anus of myself, but on the other hand none of the rather embarrassing publicity seemed to have achieved the desired effect of garnering responses from any of the well-known individuals on my list.

Notwithstanding that fact, several extremely kind-spirited people had now pledged money to the RNIB on my sponsorship site and I had received 22 emails in three days. For example, Carl wanted me to know that he, like I, was extremely attracted to Scarlett Johansson (we are obviously two peas in a pod, Carl), Squirrel33 liked the site but wanted to correct my spelling, I assumed that Squirrel33 was a pseudonym created by my father, and Lilly B wanted to see a photo of Michael and to enquire whether he was single or not. No and Yes.

The only negative email received was from someone I actually knew – a former girlfriend of mine from several years back who amazingly enough seemed to have stumbled across my website totally innocently, much as a HEFTY COW might stumble across two lanes of the A35.

'Glad to see that you're not wasting your time in some childish endeavour', she wrote.

Then again she always was a little detached from reality. She only dumped me because of some stupid argument we'd had about music. I'd tried to convince her that 'Land of Make Believe' by *Bucks Fizz* was a work of genius and far better than anything Mozart ever achieved.

True story.

'Your writing stinks,' she continued, to which I recall replying 'Yes I know, but not as much as a dirty protester's.'

Tuesday August 9th 2005 – Desperately Seeking Replies

My hypochondria continued to rear its ugly head. It started on the Monday when I woke up in an awful state such as, say, Wyoming. Anyway, my head was all over the place. It was the sort of morning where your brain is in such disarray that you give yourself a toothpaste suppository and then brush your teeth with Anusol, so I decided to just sit around and eat raw vegetables.

It was also the usual affair with my letter box since I had received nary a single response to the last 20 letters sent out.

Perhaps there had been a problem with the Royal Mail, although I think he's been far too distracted by Camilla to interfere with my post (Hithankyo once again. I'm here all week).

So, at the tail end of the previous week, as I think I mentioned, I had been sending out various emails to the agents of some of the individuals on my list, simply asking them to please ensure that the letters would actually make it to their intended recipients.

On the whole, these agents had not been negative in their responses. This is because in most cases they had not actually been responding at all, but I decided to take their silence on the matter as an indication of grudging acceptance, although perhaps I was being a little naive there; time would tell.

That evening, I therefore thought it wise to print out another 26 of my letters which the following morning would be sent out to several stunning women, several merchants of humour and several more men from the world of sport.

So, in no particular order then: **Peter Alliss, Paul Gascoigne, Dawn French, Jennifer Saunders, Sienna Miller, Kate Winslet, Denise Van Outen, Patsy Kensit, Ewan McGregor, Sophie Dahl, Keira Knightley, Max Hastings, Bob Mortimer, Rowan Atkinson, Bill Bailey, Vic Reeves, Dom Joly, Lenny Henry, Chris Morris, Harry Enfield, Steve Backley, John Francome, David Gower, Richard Keys, Gary Lineker** and **Prince Naseem Hamed.**

I must say, that as these stacks of positive responses still obdurately refused to make an appearance through my letterbox, the more I considered that Michael's initial assumption was right.

How very depressing, outwitted by the Lord of the Fries.

Although I was unaware at this stage that my fortunes would subsequently pick up, I couldn't help but think that this really was quite a stupid thing to be doing. Once again I was more than prepared to give up the whole escapade, in other words giving it the full 'schizophrenic, stand-up comedian film-script' treatment, and I would have done but I just didn't think I would be able to face Matt or to let the RNIB down.

So why had I once again been so eager to pack the whole thing in? Well, it was partly because another absolutely amazing opportunity had suddenly come my way, for on this very sultry and still mid-summer's Tuesday, I received an email from a Mrs Mbwango.

It appeared that her late husband had acted as the *chargé d'affaires* (whatever that is), for the late Laurent Kabila, the former President of the Democratic Republic of the Congo.

I was informed that after Mr Kabila was overthrown '*a sum of monies totalling $6 000 000 US American*' was deposited in a bank in Congo, and Mrs Mbwango, viewing me (quite rightly) as '*a most trusted and loyal person to whom I am awaiting a verbal response in affirmative*' needed my help to get this money out of her country.

She was actually going to give me HALF OF IT! Can you believe that? All that she wanted was for me to send her my bank details. I therefore spoke to Michael and informed him that if he never heard from me again, it would be because I was happily building myself a palace on the outskirts of Kinshasa and it would be me that was having the last laugh.

Jules Segal

◇◇

I would just like to briefly recount some words that I heard in a song on the way in to work today. The 'track' in question was no collaboration between a president and an archangel as the title above might suggest, but by two fine stalwarts of the British music industry, Kate Bush and Peter Gabriel.

The only reason I mention this right now is because, as you may have noticed, I'd been feeling a little glum. The challenge that had been set for me by St Michael the Irate was starting to lean heavily in his favour. Forgetting the two weeks where I contacted no-one, I had been busting a stomach in trying to find contact details for these 500 individuals, yet in 27 days I had just two meetings (with one more lined up). If things continued at this leisurely rate, by the time that proceedings were concluded I would have had just 13.107 recurring meetings, and among other things, would be preparing to don some sturdy running shoes in search of a tin foil cape.

So, never did it seem more pertinent that, as I sat in a traffic jam on the Gray's Inn Road on this morning, while staring at my left eye in the rear-view mirror, a song with the title 'Don't Give Up' echoed around my car. Whether it's true that I have 'no fight left, or so it seems...' remains to be seen, but I had certainly been fortified by the kindly words of a number of people over the preceding few days, most of whom I had never even met, but who had taken the time to contact me.

I had well-wishers from as far afield as Rome and Southern Spain writing to my website and it was that more than anything which continued to bolster my spirits. Indeed, these complete strangers could have taught my so-called 'friends' a thing or two about being supportive, as my so-called 'friends' continued to label me as a 'publicity seeker', an 'insignificant little t**d who no-one would reply to' and 'a poor-man's Dave Gorman'.

The goodwill that these total strangers were showing me, however, was truly inspirational. It was so buoying to learn that the milk of human kindness had not totally dried up, even if the teat was starting to show a few stretch marks.

◇◇

Never ask for chips in an internet café. They'll probably bring you a plate of silicon.

I was sitting in an internet café in Baker Street, otherwise known as 'McDonald's with a computer', in order to update my website, since my home computer had, as of the night before, floated off to the great Comet in the sky.

Basically, it was dead.

Yet I had to update, because TRIUMPH! SUCCESS! No, I had not magically scheduled 98 meetings over the next two weeks, but I had finally received another reply, my first since August 5th. It was from the Mayor of LondON. The man whose title (i.e. Mayor of LondON), seems to adorn every advertisement, lamppost and flag in the capital at present, just in case we forget who he is. Goodness knows how we'd get by without him. Sadly, he didn't have any time to spare over the next five months. He was probably going to be too busy... actually I'll bite my tongue at this point.

Anyway, I was simply grateful that he or his PA actually got back to me. A reply was becoming as important to me as an actual meeting.

Meanwhile, I continued to be in discussion with several newspapers and magazines about the possibility of submitting an article about what I was doing, although there was no word from anyone on this point and to be honest I wasn't all that hopeful. For example, while speaking to someone on the newsdesk of one of the more well-known nationals the previous Friday morning, I was asked by some gruff journalist whether I believed that a story about some strange stalker was particularly newsworthy, to which I replied that first, I was no stalker (but let's not re-hash that old chestnut again) I was a creeper and, second, it was no less newsworthy than their usual fare of 'Glaswegian Man Finds Dead Mouse in Tin of Baked Beans'.

He disagreed.

I soon went cold on the idea of trying to get newspaper exposure since as Michael pointed out to me (while he was slurping on a pot-noodle, I recall), if news of what I was doing did see the light of the national newspapers, our bet might become invalidated. He argued that the people on the list would then have something to gain from meeting me – publicity. *They* would then be the ones who had met this 'wacky guy on some crazy adventure'. He was right. I couldn't think of a more upsetting way of being described. I suppose the truth hurts.

In the meantime, I was simply hoping that **Christine** and **Neil Hamilton, Dale Winton** and **Frank Lampard**, would all be contacted by *my* various *chargés d'affaires*, who had all promised to try and help me out by speaking to those from my list they actually knew.

Monday August 15th 2005 – Peanut Butter and Jam

Here is an extract from an email that was received by me from a kindly employee of PBJ Management – nothing to do with a Sunpat factory, it's an organisation that deals with many of the most amusing people in the country (and I don't mean it's an insane asylum, I mean they represent comedians... so actually quite similar come to think of it).

'Thank you for your interest in our clients regarding your bet, Greeting the 500. Unfortunately, our clients Dom Joly and Chris Morris are unable to meet up due to work commitments.'

Now I was most upset to learn that these two were unavailable as I'm a fan of both of them, particularly the 'maverick', 'renegade', 'loose cannon' – 'insert cliché here' – Chris Morris, who I forgot to mention on my personal list of heroes.

Come on, Julian, get a grip, this isn't about you bowing down to your idols, remember?

The only other thing of note that happened to me on this day was that I spotted Nicholas Parsons eating dinner in a Tapas Bar near where I live on Haverstock Hill, although on this occasion I elected not to approach as I didn't want to make the poor man choke on his battered squid. Besides, trying to explain the background of my challenge in less than 15 minutes was still an art that I had yet to master.

I therefore went home, poured myself a Red Bull and lighter-fluid and did the only other thing that I thought might improve my tally of meetings: I prepared another 13 letters.

These would shortly be winging their way to the lovely **Jenny Agutter, Richard Attenborough, David Attenborough, Jane Asher, Rick**

Astley, Joan Armatrading, Linford Christie, David Bellamy, Jeffrey Archer, Terence Conran, Jasper Conran, Tom Conti and **Jack Dee.**

Thursday August 18th 2005 - A Reply from Rowan
◇◇

So there you have it: a reply from another great British comedian.

I was, if I am honest, hoping to get a bit of relief from this portrayer of the bumbling vicar and sarcastic army captain since a quick glance at the scoreboard would show that I was making about as much progress as that of an 'asthmatic ant with heavy shopping', to use one of his lines.

Yes, I was seriously worried about my chances of success, while Michael my co-betee was growing more and more delirious with excitement at the prospect of watching over me as I scraped the hardened cack off his toilet bowl every fortnight for a year.

That said, I continued to have hope wherever I received any reply, even if it did arrive via the keyboard and printer of the agent of one of my targets. In any case, by reading the following, I am sure you will agree that at the very least, Rowan had certainly mulled over my request as outlined in my appalling begging letter, before instructing his agent to send me this response:

Dear Julian,

I am afraid that Rowan Atkinson has turned down your request on the premise that he doesn't feel that celebrities should be obliged to meet someone simply to disprove the cynicism of their friends.

Further to this is the ever present risk in the current climate of a scam, akin to Tom Cruise being squirted with water during an interview. Both the Tom Cruise incident and this request are in many ways indicative of the same problem: a cynicism and distrust of celebrity and putting the burden on the well-known individual to prove/disprove that attitude.

My apologies for getting back to you with a negative response.

Regards...

Jules Segal

Well, what could I say to such an eloquent and considered response?

When I considered that Rowan (or his agent) made the valid point that they had never heard of me and neither did they have any idea who I was or where I came from, it wasn't entirely surprising that they, like so many of these people I was writing to, viewed me as some sort of crank.

For all they knew, had Rowan agreed to a meeting as requested, he might have been patiently waiting outside a TV studio for me, only to see me stride up to him and spank him around the face with a haddock.

This, my friends, is how I am attempting to rationalise my rather poor return up to mid-August. If nothing else, it's a bloody good excuse. And you know who the real culprits are? The people who really buggered up my chances of making any headway in these early stages as I went about this sorry business? It was those imbecilic TV production companies who find it so hilarious to go up to film stars and pour orange juice over them while filming the whole sorry episode. Damn them!

And damn their britches! (Apart from Ali G; he's quite funny.)

Anyway, I sent the following email to Rowan's agent in response:

Hi Jxxxx and thanks for getting back to me. What an interesting reply.

First, could you please thank Rowan kindly for taking the time to consider my request. I really am grateful that he has given it such thought. When I find it hard enough to get a simple acknowledgement of receipt of my letter from some people, such a thorough answer as this is very refreshing.

Just to respond to his comments, first I would like to say that the individuals that I am contacting should feel absolutely NO 'obligation' whatsoever to meet me. They should agree to meet me for one reason and one reason alone – because they want to. If they don't, that is fine. I certainly won't think any less of them, particularly when they've had the good grace to ensure that I am replied to.

With regard your second paragraph, I think that Rowan has hit the nail squarely on the head there. In my opinion, one of the reasons that my quest is doomed to failure is because many of the recipients of my letter are highly suspicious of my motives.

For example, if, hypothetically speaking, I was having a number of these meetings every week and was getting a certain degree of media coverage, I am pretty sure that a number of others from my list would be a lot happier to meet me. In other words, they need convincing that I have no sinister motives, but am in fact quite genuine.

Unfortunately, I am in something of a vicious circle, since without meetings in the first place there WILL be no coverage, and no reassurance and in any case, strictly speaking, I am required to do this as anonymously as possible.

One thing that you can be sure of, however, is that I am no prankster. I am certainly not conceited enough to think that I have some divine right to take 'celebrities' down a peg or two. I have no desire to make anyone look foolish.

The makers of the programme that you refer to, have unfortunately fallen into the trap of mistaking crass and brainless TV for entertainment. Regrettably, this is commonplace nowadays, as you point out, and presumably that is why we have so many shows concerned with the likes of 'Celebrity Shoe Mending' or 'Placing 4 Teenagers in a Balloon over Iraq'.

Ultimately I am neither a 'cynic' nor 'distruster of celebrity', which is why I believed in the first place that many more individuals from my list of 500 would meet me than has actually been the case so far.

Anyway Jxxxxxx, thanks again for helping me out as you have. It's a shame that not all agents are as efficient as you.

And please thank Rowan once again for his honest reply.

Kind regards,

Julian

I think that said it all really, from my point of view anyway.

Monday August 22nd 2005 – I'm Loving Agents Instead

According to the ever-absorbing Wikipedia, on this day, a 4.1 kg (nine pound) meteorite crashed into the Dotito area of Zambezi Escarpment in Zimbabwe, leaving a 15 cm (six inch) crater.

That's equivalent to 4.1 bags of sugar, so imagine the crater that a *whole* can of cola would leave.

Forgive me Robbie Williams, wherever you are, but just as I was greatly impressed with the agent of Rowan Atkinson, who went out of her way to help me, it transpired that another extremely kind young lady had ridden to my aid. A little background: several weeks before this date, while lying on my couch, smelling my armpits and watching England thrash the Aussies in the Second Test, my mobile phone rang; I answered it and was greeted by a voice that I was sure I'd heard before.

Yes, it must be! It was! One of the most recognisable voices on British TV. Well, to the male half of the population anyway, and sorry I don't mean to be patronizing to the chicks.

'Hi Julian, it's John Motson here. Sorry I've only just got back to you but I've been on holiday... In principle I'm happy to meet you but could you possibly just clear it with my agent first?'

I thanked him kindly, put the phone down and smiled to myself. I could just as easily have been listening to a preview of a Third Round FA Cup tie from Ninian Park down my Nokia 62c. 'Hi, John Motson here, the conditions in Wales are a bit blustery at the moment etc.,...'

I just found it a little ironic, since this was a man whose voice, more than almost anyone else's from my list, would be instantly recognisable to me anyway, without any need for introductions. How UNBELIEVABLY kind of him I thought, to phone me up like that. No airs and graces whatsoever – an absolute gent.

John needed clarification from his agent since he was unsure as to whether the BBC might have a problem with the whole picture-taking thing and so I spoke with a delightful lady named Sara shortly afterwards. Despite sounding a little puzzled, she said that it sounded fine and that she would liaise with John to try and sort out a convenient date.

A little time went by and to be honest, I thought that I'd hear no more on this matter, yet a few days later, Sara the angel gets back to me and tells me that John would be happy to meet me on Tuesday 23 August.

Our quick chat raised a few other issues and she gave a brief word to the wise. It turned out that certain things that had been written on my website were slightly rankling some friends of hers who worked for another sports agency and she suggested that perhaps I ought to tone down my comments about agents.

Well, I certainly have no desire to offend anyone... apart from Michael (who is growing increasingly smug at my limited success so far: 'perhaps you should rename it Greeting the 5'), and so I would like to reiterate a couple of points that I have already made. First, I am WELL AWARE that every one of the 500 on my list already does a vast amount of work for good causes, receives hundreds of requests every day, and is incredibly busy. I hold absolutely nothing against anyone who will not meet me. I would not meet me. Second, I apportion no blame at all to the agents of those who decline to meet me, since their hands are tightly bound by the wishes of their clients.

I really can't say it any fairer than that.

Tuesday August 23rd – One Aye, One Nay

I would be the first to admit that I am to computer programming what Gengis Khan was to flower-arranging, yet miraculously, I actually managed to get my home computer operational once more, without having to telephone the AOL helpline in Calcutta. All it took was a serious rebooting of my computer across the room.

On this day I had my third meeting. It was with John Motson who proved to be incredibly generous both with his time and with the memento that he offered for my charity auction, but I will come to that in a moment as there was some other news concerning a meeting that was agreed to today.

We were on our way to BBC TV Centre – Michael and I – to meet Motty and were deep in argument in a traffic jam on the Westway. If you are growing slightly weary about hearing how frequently the two of us are at loggerheads, I assure you that it is not in the least bit contrived and is all completely true. I basically regard Michael as the incredibly crabby brother I never had.

Anyway, on this occasion we were discussing Michael's desire to have his photo taken with John Motson after me, and my desire for Michael to shut his mouth and try and last a day without shaming me. Well, just as I thought my passenger was about to combust with rage my phone rang.

'Hello, is that Jules?' said a voice with a strong West Country lilt.

'Speaking,' I said while glaring at Michael who was still mid rant.

'John Francome here, yeah I'll meet you, no problem, no problem at all. It's as easy as pie. Are you going to be near Newbury next Saturday?'

'Errm, well, I'm not really sure, John. I wasn't planning too, but I...'

'How about Goodwood the following Wednesday?'

'Well, I don't see any reason why...'

'Newmarket. Can you make Newmarket on September 3?'

And before the poor man was forced to flick through his entire diary for the whole year, I replied that I'd be delighted to meet him at the HQ of British horse-racing on that date and thanked him ever so much for phoning me in person.

'No problem at all. Easy to sort out. Try and get there before the racing starts and it'll be simple to arrange. See you then.'

Once again I was taken aback and delighted in equal measures. John Francome, aside from being one of the country's most successful ever jockeys, is someone that I have always had time for. A bit of a maverick. A bit of a bad lad but in a good way, if that makes sense.

So, horse-racing at Newmarket in a few weeks. I thought it a good idea to spend the interim period trying to pick up some tips from my friends who are in the know. I don't mean the old 'yeah, don't chop wood in a dinghy' type of tip, I mean whispers from the world of horse-racing. After all, with all this time off work I needed to make money fast, and obviously the best way to do that is to gamble.

The other reply that I received was an email from a lady called Lisa (a big thank you to her too), who acts as the agent of Ricky Gervais. She regretted to inform me that since Ricky was totally inundated with work at the time, he would not be able to meet me. This was one that I was certainly prepared for. Being one of the hottest properties in comedy, it wasn't altogether surprising that he had slightly bigger fish to fry.

Tuesday August 23rd – Greeting 3 (John Motson)

It's official. Motty is even more of a hero of mine now.

In addition to being an icon in the world of football commentary, and telephoning me directly when receiving my letter, he was an absolute delight in person.

Our meeting took place in the bright and airy entrance of the BBC building in White City. It was a modern looking place, all plate-glass and chrome, like some sort of themed bar in Kew Gardens. There also appeared to be a large number of security gates and personnel to manoeuvre, although why so much security was needed, I couldn't say. The only people that seemed to be wandering around were a group of South African tourists, a gaggle of school-children and teacher, a wheezing Cypriot and a pasty, prematurely greying Englishman.

I was slightly hot and bothered by the time we turned up, partly because today was hot and Michael was bothering me (having rolled out of bed an hour before the planned meeting) and partly because parking a car in the new Mega-City under construction on the other side of Wood Lane proved both time-consuming and treacherous. I even added a new dent to the collection of war-wounds that currently scar my VW.

My mood soon lightened though, as John turned up and immediately on so doing, extracted his 'auctionable memento' out of a bag. 'This,' said John, 'is my favourite tie that I wear on *Match of the Day*'.

Solid gold! (Not the tie, but my opinion of John and this gift.) He apologised that several autographed pictures were missing from the carrier bag and that his wife had forgotten to pack them or something, but I am sure that his wife is lovely anyway, and I am sure that John thinks she's lovely too.

It should, though, be pointed out that each letter I sent out to these 500, stated that the bringing of these mementos, while very generous, was entirely optional and had no bearing on my bet with Michael. The all important thing to me was the photo and the clasping of palms.

The picture in this case was then duly taken, despite protestations from Michael about standing away from the window, such protestations largely being ignored because nowhere was away from a window in that place.

And that was it, a brief meeting, a handshake, a photograph and like Keyser Soze <pfffftt> we were gone.

Very much so, I fancy...

'So you decided *not* to ask John if you could have a photo too,' I enquired with relief as we made our way home. '...Thanks, Mike. It would have just been a bit awkward.'

'Bollocks it would!' he retorted. 'The only reason I didn't ask was because he looked a bit scared of me.'

That John Motson, a very perceptive man, I've always thought.

Thursday August 25th – Quarter Hounder

At this stage in proceedings I had hounded over one-quarter of the 500 people on my list, since by the end of August I had posted out the 133rd of my 500 letters. Added to this good news was the fact that I now had only 367 stamps to buy and I hadn't even yet succumbed to the awful ailment sometimes known as envelope licker's tongue.

As I was in need of a little divine intervention in my quest, these most recent letters (or perhaps more appropriately epistles) included those that were dispatched to various faith leaders, such as the Archbishop of Canterbury **Rowan Williams**, Chief Rabbi **Jonathan Sacks** and the Secetary General of the British Council of Muslims, **Sir Iqbal Sacranie**.

Rather incongruously, I also sent them out to a jazz singer, an Olympic gold-medal winning swimmer, an Oscar-winning animator, a night-club owner, an astronomer, a chef, a fashion-designer, a... oh never mind, here's the full list: **Rowan Williams, Jonathan Sacks, Iqbal Sacranie, Cleo Laine, Duncan Goodhew, Nick Park, Peter Stringfellow, Patrick Moore, Gordon Ramsay, Paul Smith, Fiona Phillips, Charles Saatchi, Tim Rice, Bill Kenwright, Andrew Lloyd-Webber, Carol Vordeman, Daley Thompson, Kate Humble, Ben Fogle, Lorraine Kelly, Dave Gorman** (spiritual father it appears), **Frank Skinner, David Baddiel, Philip Schofield, Iain Banks, Frank Lampard, Floella Benjamin, Ian Hislop, Chris Eubank, Cherie Blair, Will Carling, Julie Burchill, Assad Ahmed, Digby Jones, Geoff Boycott, Fern Briton** and **Darren Campbell**.

I also received some help from an unexpected quarter thanks to a good friend of mine, James, who happens to be a resident DJ on Xfm, as he kindly agreed to mention my challenge on his radio show. I wasn't sure if this broadcast would make any difference to my progress or facilitate any meetings, but I was hopeful that perhaps one his regular listeners, when they weren't discussing 'breakbeats', 'mash ups', 'post-progressive ambient trance' or any other term that I don't understand, might be able to point me in the direction of Keith Chegwin.

Monday August 29th 2005– A Sagittarian Accord

Well, this had been a lovely bank holiday weekend, the sun was shining, Notting Hill was partying, Australian cricketers were cursing and the pub across the road from me was blaring out 'Hard House' music until 4.00 a.m. every night.

Basically no-one had an excuse not to be either pickling their innards with rum at a friend's barbecue, basting themselves in factor 45 on Brighton beach, or swearing in a bunker on a golf course.

The reason I mention this is because as I tuned in to update my website on this Monday evening, I noticed that almost 3500 people had looked at it over the Bank Holiday weekend.

It seemed that either Britain had, unbeknown to me, suddenly become a nation of porphyria sufferers, or other sun allergy type illnesses (apologies to anyone who is) or else perhaps my site had received some form of publicity in Peru.

In addition to soon meeting John Francome at Newmarket, where I would be surrounded by more horses than you would find in Paris's largest butcher's shop, I would also be meeting Jeffrey Archer in the coming week, since I'd received an email from his friendly PA, Alison, who kindly mentioned that he would be more than happy to indulge my request of an audience with him.

I must say, these first few subjects that I met were not only extremely generous with their time, they were also rather brave – the Davy Crockett-like pioneers of my challenge. They benefited in no way by meeting me, no publicity, no picture in *Hello*, yet they were continuing to making me so very happy since they continued to disprove Michael and his cynical faith in mankind.

On the subject of golf courses, I noted with some regret that I wasn't invited to Celtic Manor on this particular weekend where British

'Celebrities' took on their US counterparts in a 'Two-Day Golfing Extravaganza'. Quite apart from being able to watch this alternative (Sean) Ryder-Cup, I would also have been able to tick Ant, Dec, Chris Evans, Ian Wright, Robbie Williams, Jodie Kidd and Colin Montgomerie off my list.

Instead, I attended a Greek Orthodox church where I bumped into Michael while he was cramming a plate of lamb into his face, at the christening of his niece. He was unhappy with me because a mutual friend of ours who recently glanced at my website told him that I had been liberally sprinkling it with insults about him. I hadn't been worried about Michael ever reading them, since he's too lazy to read. However, I vowed to make no more pejorative comments about him. After all he too is only human, if you prick him will he not burst?

Wednesday August 31st 2005 – The Moore the Merrier

It is not every morning that one is woken by the voice of one of the most famous singers ever to have lived, yet at 8.47 a.m., on this very morning, and while I was driving what appeared to be some form of Sherman Tank through Windsor Safari Park, I was roused from my Dali-esque dream by the dulcet tones of Elton John on my mobile phone.

He wasn't actually on the other end of the line, it's just that my ringtone is *Rocket Man*.

On the end of the line, rather appropriately (because of the rocket reference), was the famous astronomer and highly accomplished xylophonist Patrick Moore. Sadly, however, I was unable to find the damn thing before he rang off (my phone was subsequently discovered in my waste-paper bin), yet Sir Patrick had kindly left a message stating that he would be happy to welcome me the following week, provided that I could make my way down to Sussex. I subsequently phoned him back, apologised for the sluggish hours that I kept, and thanked him warmly for being so amenable.

'So I have your address, Sir Patrick,' I said, 'but is your house easy to find when I get there?'

'Oh yes, very easy,' he replied. 'It's the one with the observatory in the garden.'

Oh yeah.

CHAPTER 4 – September

Friday September 2nd 2005 – Greeting 4 (Jeffrey Archer)

Driving through central London on a Friday afternoon is not particularly enjoyable at the best of times, but when you're pressed for time and St Johns Wood tube station has been closed, causing traffic jams in that area, your passenger is sulking because he hasn't eaten for three minutes, you get stuck behind a dustcart in Paddington and then you accidentally stray into Red Kenneth's congestion-tax zone, you know it isn't going to be your day.

Well, how wrong I was.

For his part, Michael was having a whale of time as we traversed central London. With his head out of the window, he was clicking away at his camera like a man possessed, just to 'make sure that the 'Vista Setting' and contrast buttons work properly, you fool'.

'Look, a man walking along the top of a wall,' said Michael enthusiastically before snapping away.

'Look, a group of Japanese tourists taking photos of Big Ben.' They were instantly snapped back.

I did, however, lose my rag a bit when he took no less than three photos of the MI5 building as we drove past it on the south side of the Thames.

'For crying out loud, Michael. What the HELL ARE YOU DOING?'

'WHAT?'

'Well, do you think it's wise, just two weeks after the worst atrocities to have hit London during peace time, for a Mediterranean looking man to be hanging out of a car window and photographing the nerve-centre of the British Intelligence service?'

He mulled this over for a second before delivering his considered response .... 'Oh, SHUT UP, you tart!'.

Jeffrey Archer resides in a building overlooking the Thames, not far from Parliament. I found a place to park and we approached our target, Michael lagging behind and mumbling something about a lack of cigarettes and a petrol station he had spotted.

As we got nearer, I noticed that a camera crew was filming someone on a patch of grass in front of us. Well, blow me down, if the subject didn't turn out to be a man who only recently was one of the most recognisable individuals on the planet.

It was John Merrick.

No, it was not.

Former British Prime Minister John Major was standing on a small verge by the Thames, in the shadow of Jeffrey Archer's apartment, patiently answering questions being put to him by a female reporter.

I know that in theory I wasn't supposed to approach anyone from my list without having attempted to contact them beforehand. However, in practice, I *had* attempted to contact this man. In fact, his letter was among the very first that I had sent out – he just simply hadn't got around to replying yet. Well, in order to garner a second and unexpected handshake for the day, I approached one of Mr Major's aides on the sidelines, who despite not having the slightest inkling as to who I was and what I was blathering on about, '500 celebrities... RNIB... received my letter... photograph,' listened to my plea and said that he would see what he could do.

In the meantime, Michael and I entered the apartment building of Jeffrey Archer despite being ten minutes early. I know that he's had his critics in the past, as have most of us probably, but when he turned up he truly was as nice as pie to us.

Thrusting out a welcoming hand, we exchanged pleasantries before Jeffrey asked where we would like the picture taken. Michael, who seemed to be sweating, announced that we should go outside as it was a warm day, and the photograph was subsequently taken no less than 15 metres away from where John Major was being interviewed.

'Excellent,' I thought to myself, this might convince the former PM to indulge my request. He will see that I am no random freak. I am having my photo taken right next to him while shaking hands with the Baron of Weston-super-Mare, and while wearing a white T-shirt covered in magic marker ink.

As we made our way back inside to gather the auctionable memento, and my cack-footed friend embarrassingly managed to kick over a metal bollard that formed part of the structure of the building, talk turned to John Major. Jeffrey seemed surprised to learn than he'd never got back to me, as he considered the former PM to be a really good sport. Well, the reason for this lack of a response would soon become clear...

Up in Jeffrey's stunning apartment, the foyer of which reminded me a little of an exhibition of the British Museum (numerous lovely antiquities and curios), we were generously given a book for the RNIB auction, which our host signed in front of us. We then waited by ourselves while an assistant of his went off to fetch Michael and I a can of cola to take on our way. Michael took the opportunity to take a snapshot of a lovely sunny view along the Thames, through the window of this penthouse apartment.

Jules Segal

'I'm such a superb photographer,' he said modestly, informing me how he managed to frame the London Eye in the background.

Maybe so, I thought to myself, but I don't think you'll be joining me on these little outings for much longer.

Friday September 2nd 2005 – Greeting 5 (John Major)

Back outside, the filming of John Major was completed. It was a wrap. I glanced hopefully at his assistant who looked at another assistant who went over to have a word with the former Prime Minister.

Within a few moments, and to his huge credit, Mr Major approached me together with his entourage. As he drew near, I thought that I would break the ice and show him that this meeting wasn't totally random, by asking if he remembered receiving my letter.

On this occasion, however, I think the ice was broken a little too early, as I ended up shouting my question to him when he was still several meters away. He looked slightly concerned as he approached, replied in the negative and asked where I had sent it to.

'Errm, I wrote to you at the House of Commons,' I stammered.

Mr Major smiled. 'Aah, well, I haven't been working from there for some time I'm afraid. I stood down in 2001.'

Cue one humiliated young man in a cryptically messaged T-shirt staring down at his black leather Matalan shoes.

You see, my friends, all of my cogitating and hypothesising and analysing of statistics over the past few days about the number of replies that I had received so far, failed to take into account one constant – namely, my own bare-faced stupidity and general tittishness.

If knowledge is 'king', then accurate research is almost certainly 'prince regent'. Nonetheless, Mr Major generously shook my hand, despite being somewhat unsure as to why I was showing him so much appreciation. For this I thank him greatly. However, I decided not to ask him whether he had anything, 'be it a piece of fluff or a Ferrari' (see my begging letter template) for the charity auction as I believed that this would have been a bridge too far. A bridge over the river Total Bemusement perhaps.

On our way home, and on a similar subject, I discussed with Michael the statistics that I had compiled over the last few days. 'Why is it, do you think,' I enquired, 'that unlike with the famous males that I've approached, I am having such a particularly bad response from the females that I've written to? Not one reply from 27 letters sent to the fairer sex.'

'Perhaps they've seen a photo of you on your website,' was his painfully blunt reply.

Saturday September 3rd 2005 – Postponement

The drive up to Newmarket to meet John Francome was one of the most unpleasant experiences that I have ever been forced to endure. My passenger was complaining and whingeing the entire way because he'd been forced to wake up at the ludicrous hour of 8.30 a.m. on a Saturday morning in order to get to the racetrack on time.

He took out his frustration by constantly swearing whilst pressing the camera's button with 11 000 pounds per square inch of pressure and taking hundreds of photos of the A11. After each photograph was taken, he'd let out a loud expletive for no other reason than to show the world what sort of mood he was in.

Who could possibly have foreseen that this small digital box, fabricated in some large factory in the heartland of Japan, would end its days as a stress ball for an angry man in Cambridgeshire.

The journey back to London was even worse. This was because John Francome hadn't actually been at Newmarket and that I had, as my Cypriot sidekick informed me, 'Wasted his entire bloody day!'. Yes, it was a day that he could have spent far more constructively crashed out on his living room sofa.

'This is the last bloody one of these that I come on!' he announced, much to my relief as we sped past Saffron Walden.

'Do you promise, Michael?'

The temporary postponement of this 'greeting' wasn't caused by some unforeseen 'Act of God' but rather by a deliberate 'Act of John Toshack'. The manager of the Welsh National football side had called up Swansea City's Sam Ricketts to play at left-back for Wales against England in the World Cup qualifier that was played in the afternoon.

This call-up was great news in John Francome's household as he is Sam Ricketts' uncle and quite understandably wanted to see his nephew in international action for the very first time, down in Cardiff. He was extremely apologetic when I contacted him, but I quite understood, and he assured me that our meeting would still go ahead at a future date.

As for this weekend, well, I learned quite a few interesting lessons myself, namely:

O England *are* better off sticking to the 4-4-2 formation (final score: Wales 0, England 1).

O The constant airing of the TV advert for the sweets known as 'Skittles', where an old lady raps about being 'a bad grandma' to her grandson, despite being shown with such annoying frequency, should not encourage you to throw your remote control at the TV set. It is likely to break.

O Never row over the phone with the pizza delivery people (anything can be hidden under a layer of melted cheese). The argument will ultimately leave you with a nasty taste in your mouth.

O Broken glass on a bathroom floor will one day come back to haunt you.

Wednesday September 7th 2005 – Greeting 6
(Patrick Moore)

What a green and pleasant land I live in, I mused (like Brent) as I made my way to the sunny South Coast, past such exotically titled hamlets as Woolbending, Liphook, Cocking and Hurtsmore (no wonder it hurtsmore if you've been cocking).

OK, so our national football team is substandard from time to time, but after soaking up the beauty of small country villages such as Midhurst, which has been only fractionally buggered-up by the eyesore of a Tesco Metro, and Chichester (famous for quaint tea-rooms and Sir Francis, as I've been led to believe), I have decided that I love my country and that except for Sydney, Singapore or a Paris devoid of Parisians I could never live anywhere else.

I was on my way to meet the country's foremost astronomer, Sir Patrick Moore, who apologised for his immobility – well, he is an octogenarian – and the fact that I would have to make the short trip around the M25, down the A3, and along the A286 to greet him.

As he had described, his front garden did indeed have an observatory in it. In fact, to be more accurate, it actually contained more telescopes than you could shake a 25 inch polymethylmethacrylate ocular stargazing device at... possibly one for every star.

Sir Patrick, who insisted that I simply call him Patrick, was a most welcoming host. As soon as he saw my weakened and feverish state fresh from the lengthy journey, he uttered, 'What can I get you? Tea? Coffee? Fruit Juice? Brandy?'

I considered the long drive home ahead of me and always being one who is concerned about his health, opted for a brandy (single).

'Don't be deceived by my frail condition,' he said to me as we sat in a study that rivalled the Bodlian Library for its collection of books, 'I only stopped playing cricket a few years ago. Bad leg, you see.'

So while I attempted to drink my brandy, a curious little number that had the consistency of molasses and a taste that was a bit potent for my delicate palette, I learned that this noble old chap had been more active in his 80s than I had been in my entire life.

Conversation turned to peacocks, before rather incongruously switching to the United Kingdom Independence Party or UKIP, a party that I confess to knowing little about, but one that Sir Patrick happens to be an eminent member of.

'Oh yes, isn't that something to do with Robert Kilroy-Silk?' I innocently enquired. 'He's also on my list,' to which my host almost spat out his drink while giving me the iciest of glares.

'He LEFT UKIP!' I was informed (in slightly more colourful language than that).

'Oh, OK.'

As I shuffled slightly in my seat, I changed the subject and suggested that we take the photograph and this was duly completed with the help of a friend of Patrick's who, fortunately enough, happened to be there. Just as well really, since Michael, true to his word, had decided to boycott my meetings. I must admit that I wasn't altogether unhappy about his decision.

As I was leaving, I was offered a lovely book on astronomy for the auction, before Patrick signed a sticker and saw me on my way with a cheery wave.

'By the way, this charity that you're raising money for, is it a British-based one?'

I was slightly confused by the question and wondered whether it was linked to our brief discussion about party politics earlier, but I answered in the affirmative and departed.

A hearty pub lunch followed *tout seul* (and with no alcohol), before I felt adequately fortified to suffer the long journey home.

As I made my way back home, I drove past a landmark called the Devil's Punch Bowl, just off the A3 near Hindhead, which intrigued me and I wondered if it had ever been filled with funny-tasting brandy. I subsequently found out what exactly it is anyway, and am rather upset that apparently I drove past one of the 'Seven Wonders of England' without so much as a cursory glance.

Thursday September 8th 2005 - Double Whammy
◇◇◇

Two more 'sorry but it won't be possible'(s) arrived, one from Jonathan Sacks and one from Nick Park. Once again, two names one wouldn't usually hear in the same sentence – the Chief Rabbi and the Oscar winning 'stop motion' animator – but there you go, they both replied on the same day.

The Chief Rabbi regretted that time would not permit him to meet me, to which I was going to reply that I would have a word with 'time', and get him to buck his ideas up but I don't think that sarcasm would have cut much ice with this holy man.

As for Nick Park, a kindly young lady from Aardman Animations emailed me to tell me that a meeting with him might be difficult as Nick is away on a promotional tour for the new film at the moment until the end of the year.

Damn *The Curse of the Were-Rabbit* (do you see what I've done there?).

Well, that having been said, there was still a glimmer of hope as the door was left ever so slightly ajar for me. Angie said that I *might* be able to meet Nick at one of the premieres, while not really giving me much of a clue as to where they were, when they were and how I should go about getting past the thousands of people, the police, the security barriers, and the security guards.

So two 'no's then.

Friday September 9th 2005 – Ashes to Ashes

Some years ago, my mother said, to get things done, I'd better not mess with this guy called Tom (a friend of the family who held some rank in the army... I think he was a Colonel).

I mention this because on hot September days, when there is a fantastic game of cricket to be watched and glasses of Pimms to be supped from, the last thing I felt like doing was going in to work to enter the name of the Senior Vice-President of the Daimler Chrysler Corporation into our company database.

The second to last thing I felt like doing was sending out letters to people that I didn't know and who didn't know me, asking if I could meet them and then updating an internet-based diary while trying to avoid the gaze of my boss. I would much rather have been having a swim or trying to master the piano solo from Coldplay's *Clocks*.

Yours,

Slothful of Belsize Park.

Actually, I'd better stop mentioning the name of my neighbourhood left, right and centre since I'd hate to give it a bad name or offend the liberal cognoscenti who live around there. See, in order to get ahead in my neck of the woods you have to constantly criticise anything to do with America, while reading the Guardian, eating your muesli and scolding your daughter Cressida. Under no circumstances must you bunk off work to watch the Ashes.

Jules Segal

I was, however, able to undertake *some* constructive activities on this day, however, as I was mostly sending my letters to EastEnders actors **Shane Ritchie** (Michael's *best friend*, blah, blah, blah), **Barbara Windsor**, **Jessie Wallace** and **Wendy Richards**, football referee **Graham Poll**, golfer **Colin Montgomery**, tennis player **Tim Henman**, Governor of the Bank of England **Mervyn King**, comedian **David Walliams** and theatrical producer **Bill Kenwright**.

Saturday September 10th 2005 – The Archbishop of Mirth

◇◇◇

Without a shadow of a doubt the finest, most amusing and beautifully crafted rejection letter that I've received since starting this project was sent to me, somewhat unexpectedly, from Lambeth Palace.

My respect for the Archbishop of Canterbury shot through the roof; not that I didn't have a high opinion of him anyway, or indeed a low one. Truth be told, I didn't know a great deal about Dr Rowan Williams before I wrote to him.

As I alluded to, I wouldn't be meeting Dr Williams, since, as the letter penned by his Lay Assistant Andrew Nunn understandably pointed out, the Primate and leader of the Church of England is not in the habit of helping complete strangers to win bets made in a pub.

I do hope I will be forgiven for detailing part of the letter, yet it was so nicely written and made such valid points, that I really do feel obliged to share it:

… He is sorry of course that by declining you may be subject to a forfeit, but since whether he accepts or declines, someone *(either Michael or I)* may have to take up bovine gynaecology he's in a no-win situation and somehow will have to learn to live with it.

He hopes that you will contribute to the RNIB the money you won't have to spend travelling to see him, indeed all the money you will save if lots of people turn you down. I am sure then that the warm inner glow you will feel will sustain you off the beach at Brighton *(see forfeit 7)*.

Very droll indeed.

I will most certainly agree to his wish and donate to the RNIB the petrol money that I would have spent driving to Lambeth. That worked out to be 27p.

Monday September 12th 2005 – Dave Who?

Today I received a reply from an agency by the name of Avalon, which is also the name of a legendary island that was famed for its delicious apples. (There is no joke in there, I just wanted to tell you that.) They represent a comedian and author who you might have heard of – Dave Gorman.

For anyone who skipped the first three chapters of this book or who borrowed a copy from a friend who's torn them out, possibly to plug a leak in a Zanussi Universal Compression Flexible Wastepipe, Dave Gorman is a man who… . Oh, I can't be bothered to go through all that again. Look him up on Wikipedia.

By the way, for the technically dumb-arsed and my mother, the 'Wikipedia' that I keep referring to is an online encyclopaedia that you can click on (click meaning to press the button on the mouse; the mouse being that thing you push around the table).

Basically, he is a man that has become involved in odd projects, similar to this one, following inebriated wagers. He, like Tony Hawks, has trod this path before me.

However, they are both rich and successful and famous and hence on my list, whereas I am presently eating a bowl of spaghetti hoops with plastic cutlery in my bedroom.

Having heard so much about him over the last few months, I was particularly keen to 'greet' the man, yet, unfortunately, the email that I received from Hannah, his kindly agent, read:

Thank you for your letter for Dave Gorman. Unfortunately Dave has just started a six-month tour in the States and so will be unable to help with this project.

However, best of luck with everything…

Talk about 'Gutted from Ilford'. I'd like to think that had he been here, he would have been up for it but obviously the small matter of 3 360 miles of water between us was an insurmountable problem since I wasn't only heavily in debt, but also a weak swimmer.

Oh well, that's how the chocolate Hob-Nob collapses into small fragments.

Tuesday September 13th 2005 – One More For the Collection
<><><><><><><><><><><><><><><><><><><><><><><><><><><><><><><><><><><><><><><><><><><><><><><><><><><><><><><><><>

Thousands of people continued to log on to my website for some inexplicable reason and I was still getting a hundred or so emails every week. A girl of 18 asked me out on a date (no picture and bordering on the illegal), a man claimed he laughed so hard at something that he nearly 'shat himself' and, generally, people were almost universally positive about what I was doing.

I found this astonishing.

Meanwhile, I was now indebted to yet another of my listees, this time Gary Lineker who had become the latest individual from my list to agree to my request for a meeting.

It seemed a bit of a shame that I didn't confine my original list of 500 people to politicians and *Match of the Day* employees, as I had an amazing response from this small subset of the populace.

Well, what could I say, I was both honoured and delighted that the footballer who has scored the most goals ever for the England national side (although correct me if I'm wrong on that) and a man that I used to watch in awe from the Paxton Stand as he slotted goals in week after week, had kept a few minutes spare on October 22 in order to help me out.

I had a feeling that Motty (who was kind enough to meet me a few weeks earlier), may have had something to do with this, and may have had a word in Gary's ear. No jokes there please..

So many thanks to Mr Lineker. For my part, I will ensure that Michael continues to almost single-handedly keep Walkers Crisps in business. He did actually munch his way through six bags in one sitting last week. Fact.

Finally, I had better respond to a theme that had cropped up in a number of emails recently received. A number of individuals seemed confused about certain words, phrases or expressions that I would habitually pepper my writing with.

Permit me to give you an example: The first two lines from my 9 September entry confused the likes of Daphne333, Cockerhoop and my sister (who claimed that she didn't remember any Tom). This was simply an unamusing link between the song *Ashes to Ashes* by David Bowie and the cricket match that I was watching.

Therefore in future, if you read something that I have written and you don't have a ruddy clue what I am on about, the chances are that I'm quoting some random song, book, film or TV programme. I am not going to explain every reference, just live with it, relax, be at one with your ignorance and move on.

Elsewhere on this day and I spotted both the comedian Matt Lucas, who was apologising to a cab driver on England's Lane, while carrying heavy baggage and the French footballer Robert Pires parking his car in a disabled space in Belsize village (maybe that's why Arsenal were struggling), all within the space of 45 minutes.

I'm not in any way crowing about seeing these two men swanning around (two birds in this sentence is worth three in the bush). You don't have to be eagle-eyed to spot actors and sportsmen in this area of London. I simply use this as an example, to highlight the origins of my bet with Michael and how our initial discussion came about while we were down at The Crown in Cricklewood a couple of months earlier.

Friday September 16th 2005 – A Woman at Last!

Well, it had only taken 77 days, but finally I had my first response from one of the females on my list. More of that in a moment.

First, I would just like to refer to a comment that a lady named Rema posted on my website on this day. In it, she mentioned the astronomer Patrick Moore and suggested that he was a real 'star' for agreeing to meet me. Well, thanks, Rema, but I'll do the jokes around here if you don't mind.

I was now over one-third of the way through my project. If my meetings, both those carried out and those in the pipeline, were to carry on at a similar rate, I could hope to have achieved about 30 in total by the time it all ended on January 14. This would mean that I wouldn't have to run 27 miles or streak off the south coast or indeed ride a rollercoaster, but I would still be forced to reach into a cow's bum. On the down side, I wouldn't have collected quite as many gifts for my auction as I'd have liked. And Michael would be smugger than ever.

So back to the most recent reply.

Endemol kindly passed my letter on to the agent of BBC science and nature presenter Kate Humble, a lady who Michael is quite familiar with, since his waking-up time tends to coincide with the daily airing of *Animal Park* (BBC1 mid-afternoon), where Kate and her male co-presenter Ben Fogle, catch up with the goings-on at Longleat Safari Park.

Cutting to the chase, Kate's agent Katie (ooh, I best not go out with her) regretted to inform me that a meeting would not be possible since her client had an incredibly busy schedule and would be filming abroad over the following few months. More importantly, as Michael had predicted a few days earlier, she had seen my photograph on my website and had baulked at the idea of coming into close proximity with me.

Actually that last bit isn't true, but nevertheless, I appeared once again, to have been stymied by overseas travel.

As I recall, on receiving this reply I instantly posted two photos up on my website. One picture was of a snow leopard, an endangered species, which was meant to symbolise both Kate Humble's work with wildlife and the fragile nature and state of flux that exists in many of the precious ecosystems of our planet. The other was of Scarlett Johansson, because she's got nice boobs.

Monday September 19th 2005 – My Beautiful Neighbourhood

Leafing through my Kate Moss-filled Sunday newspapers, I couldn't help but sympathise with the 500 people on my list who must all lead their life in the gaze of the public to such an extent.

Imagine never being able to nip to the corner-shop on a Sunday morning dressed like Coco the Clown's scruffy brother after he has rummaged around a car-boot sale in Alperton. Or never being able to swear at a traffic warden (although in no way touch them as that is very much illegal – Section 20 Offences Against the Person Act 1861).

If Frank Skinner were to walk to his corner-shop attired that way on a Sunday morning, I may well spot him from my bathroom window, as his local corner-shop is also happens to be mine. Or, to give it its full name, HAVERSTOCK MARKET – Foods – Off-licence – Grocery – Open 7 Days.

Yes, of all the individuals from my list, Frank would have been the easiest to meet since he lives the closest of any them to me; at the end of my road in fact.

However that is neither here nor there, since I had just received another reply from Avalon Management (how d'you like *them* apples, eh?).

Jon wrote:

Unfortunately Frank is unable to help you on this occasion but he sends his best wishes…

Meanwhile, I noticed that Kate Moss's boyfriend was also in the Sunday papers once again. At this stage I was thinking about starting my own pop-group based on his. I was going to call mine Myprojectsa-shambles.

Tuesday September 20th 2005 – Bill and Dave Help Out

It had just gone 11.20 on Tuesday morning and I had been in work no more than ten minutes. I was still asleep only 90 minutes prior to this, and was disturbed by a particularly vivid dream where I was standing by the lake in Kenwood, minding my own business, when a duck with a sharply chiselled beak and white pupils flew out of the water and started to go berserk at me. I woke up, heart pounding, to find that my pillow had ripped and my bedroom had a new carpet of feathers. Weird, no?

While checking my emails I spotted one whose subject simply read 'David Gower'.

It turned out to have actually been penned, or fingered I guess, by the cricket legend himself. He mentioned that he would be in town on the Thursday of this week and suggested an appropriate meeting place. What a complete and utter gent!

You see this is how it was meant to work. Motty is kind enough to meet me a couple of weeks ago. He mentions my name to Gary Lineker who generously spares me some of his time. Gary then gives the nod to David Gower, who does likewise.

I am only *guessing* this is how it went, of course. Perhaps Rory McGrath or Jonathan Ross next, who knows?

The day got even better, as later that afternoon I had a chat with Bill Kenwright, the theatre impresario and Chairman of Everton Football Club.

Having just returned to my desk from lunch, £4 all-you-can-eat Chinese takeaway in hand, my mobile phone rang.

'Hello, is that Julian, the mad person who wrote to me?' chuckled Bill, and indeed, for the first 30 seconds of our conversation, I did have to persuade him that I wasn't actually clinically insane.

In fact, Bill spent most of the conversation chuckling, as I briefed him on what I was doing, who had replied to me and how it was all going. He cordially invited me to contact his PA Emma to arrange a date to meet him before wishing me luck. I, in return, wished his team luck for that evening's game against Arsenal. I fear they needed it.

What an unbelievably genial man.

On the downside, my *egg foo yung* got cold.

Wednesday September 21st 2005 – A Date at Number 10

'Well, that's good', I thought to myself when I left work yesterday. It had been almost two weeks since I met Patrick Moore and there had been a worrying little hiatus in my progress, then three meetings arranged in one day.

You see, I forgot to mention, largely because I was in a state of complete shock at the time, that I had been invited to Number 10 Downing Street to meet Cherie Blair.

So from waking up a day earlier with loads of feathers scattered around my bedroom floor, I went to bed with one in my cap.

Yes, at about 4.40p.m. the previous afternoon, as I was web-surfing through Wilkipedia at work, educating myself about 'Samuel Taylor Coleridge', the 'Country of Namibia' and 'People who were Born in 1971', the charming Sue (Cherie's PA) telephoned my mobile to mention that Cherie, who already supports the RNIB, would love to help me out.

If that didn't send my head spinning slightly, on being told that rather than meet at her barristers chambers, I should turn up to Number 10 in early October with photo ID, my poor noggin almost detached from its shoulders and bored a hole through the ceiling.

Once again I found myself hugely indebted to someone, who on this occasion happened to be the wife of the Prime Minister. Who knows, maybe even the big man himself would turn up? (And I don't mean Peter Crouch).

Thursday September 22nd 2005 – Strange Days, Here We Come

The Smiths (nearly).

Yesterday was the most surreal one in, oh I don't know, three weeks. First Michael – remember him – actually got a job. Yeah, I know.

I have often pitched that old *bon mot* at him, 'Michael you know you should be on stage... sweeping it,' to which his reply is usually two-worded and seven-lettered. But there is actually a scintilla of irony in saying this to him, as the last time he did actually have a job, it involved him propelling his carcass and large pieces of scenery, around the stages of various West End Theatres.

Now it seemed as though Michael would once again be treading the boards, and hopefully not cracking them, as the Garrick theatre offered him a six-month contract. My faith in humanity had been fully restored with this news that even those with his temperament could find employment in 'Theatreland'. Let's just hope that they don't ask him to pick up the Garrick litter as he might go looking for a disgraced pop star.

So, as we prepared to celebrate this momentous event last night, sadly I was forced to call off our trip to the pub, as my DJ friend James, who did some of the music for Guy Richie's new film *Revolver*, rang me at the 11th hour (actually it was about 4.45 p.m.) to ask if I wanted to attend the film's premiere.

Having never been to one, I gratefully accepted, pondering who I might be able to cross of my list of 500. Guy Richie for a start, maybe some others. I stopped short of wearing my *Greeting the 500* T-shirt as I was told that dress was to be smart.

Well, that turned out to be the wrong decision, since when I turned up I noticed that a number of the people in our group hadn't exactly taken this advice literally. Nonetheless, we trod the red carpet, to the murmurs of 'who are *they*?' from the watching hordes, and entered the Odeon Leicester Square.

Having watched the, dare I say it, slightly confusing film, we then went to a party in a bar nearby. It was there that, overcome by cowardice, I failed to have my photo taken shaking hands with Guy Richie, Dexter Fletcher or Sting, was sworn at by a drunken man as I awaited my mojito, broke my watch strap and bumped into someone from school who pretended not to know me.

On the plus side, I avoided watching my football team getting humiliated.

Friday September 23rd 2005 – Greeting 7 (David Gower)

I met this legend of English Cricket despite not being in the finest of fettle.

I had recently taken a meal with a friend of mine in an Italian restaurant and believe that I might have eaten something that disagreed with me. I was going to start the meal with a Tricolor salad, as I'd heard there's a lot of fibre in a flag, but instead I went for some sort of 'farmhouse paté' that looked fit for a bucket. Judging by the state of the mess on my plate, the 'farm' in question must have been some corrugated iron-roofed hut in central Armenia. When I received the paté, it dawned on me that the waiter may have just as easily emerged from the toilets as from the kitchen.

It turned out that my hypothesis was wrong, since I was subsequently informed by Dr Brassey that my dizziness and general malaise was caused not by food poisoning but by an infection of the inner ear.

Anyway, back to the meeting and this September morning saw me drive to the Bond Street area of London. On my way, the thought did actually cross my mind that the email sent to me and purporting to be from the former England cricket captain, may have been a hoax, as my email address was posted on my website for anyone to use. This worried me but I counted to ten and it passed.

I'm not sure what the collective noun for a group of traffic wardens is, perhaps a squadron, but as I waited outside the offices of Hugo Boss, they started to hover near my car. I was therefore forced to scurry to and fro every 30 seconds between the office and my battered Polo, by the end of which time I felt my eyelid start to flutter with anxiety.

Eventually, inside the building, I caught up with a lady called Jude who told me that David was running a little late but was indeed on his way and so I skulked in the foyer and within a few minutes, the dapper David *did* turn up with his elegant wife in tow. He approached me with an outstretched arm and apologised for the delay. We had a brief chat and the lovely Mrs G. took a couple of snapshots of us.

I was encouraged to 'smile' in the second photo but I mumbled something about my unphotogenic face and how when I smile, I resemble an albino raisin; I think the message was understood as she didn't labour the point.

David assured me that a little gift would be sent to me in the post in the near future and so I thanked them both, made a passing comment about 'those bastard traffic wardens' and hurried off.

Sunday September 25th 2005 – Mean Streets

I would just like to raise a quick point about the photo taken of myself and David Gower that you might spot somewhere in this book. Please note my new apparel, which I personally believe is just the ticket. Although it had a hood, I had vowed never to hide under it, like so many of our angst-ridden youth. I am sure you will agree that the colour offsets my pallid complexion. I got sick of the old white *Greeting the 500* T-shirt; more to the point, winter was on its way and brown hides gravy stains.

Saturday night in my corner of London has become a very depressing affair. Woe betide anyone who walks past the Queen's Crescent Estate in Kentish Town once the stars come out, since sadly opium has become the religion of the masses there.

As I walked up towards Hampstead, a young urchin in a Burberry cap, who looked as though he should have been at home eating rusks and watching the *Tweenies*, aggressively asked to look at my mobile phone... like some sort of foetus with an attitude. I'm not ashamed to say that I ran. I knew that his little legs wouldn't keep up with mine.

...And what of Hampstead itself when I arrived? Surely never have so many 16-year-old girls, in so much make-up and wearing so few warm clothes, congregated in one place. I would never let my daughter out like that. Not that I have one, as I'm not married and at this point in my life, hadn't even been in a relationship for nearly two months (not including the one I had with an animated female bounty hunter who runs around raiding tombs).

This weekend I burst through the 200 letters sent barrier, my most recent dispatches directed towards **Ant McPartlin, Declan Donnelly, Cheryl Baker, Danny Baker, Ralph Little, Sheridan Smith, Zoe Ball, Jeremy Beadle, Trevor McDonald, Tony Blackburn, Michael Buerke, Cat Deeley, Noel Edmonds, Kate Lawler, Jonathan Edwards, Denise Lewis, Lawrence Llewelyn-Bowen, Judy Finnegan, Richard Madeley, Trisha Goddard, Bruce Forsyth, Davina McCall, Melinda Messenger, Sam Fox, Des O'Connor, Melanie Sykes, Ian McCaskill, Lisa Rogers, Anne Robinson, Gail Porter, Steve Rider, Bill Oddie, Tony Robinson, Chris Tarrant, Abi Titmuss, Carol Smillie** and **Dale Winton**.

In addition, I decided that I should finally tackle those within the music industry. I know very little about music. I used to think that MC Hammer was a Scottish carpenter and that Billy Idol was a name for a lazy goat, but I do know that musicians are notoriously hard to get hold of since they are often out of the country and have thousands writing to them, all of whose letters have to be sifted through by their respective record companies. I therefore also wrote to **Damon Albarn, Liam Gallagher, Noel Gallagher, Billy Bragg, Annie Lennox, Charlotte Church, Victoria Beckham, Cliff Richard, Mick Jagger, Elton John, Geri Halliwell, Paul McCartney, Liz McClarnon, Robbie Williams, Joss Stone, Sheena Easton** and **George Michael**.

I decided that if I did actually hear back from any of that lot, I would eat not only my hat but indeed the entire wardrobe. To make matters worse, it appeared that Michael, who drew up the list of 500, didn't stick to the rules that were stipulated in the terms of our bet, since I had discovered that at least a couple of the names mentioned above reside in America, and would therefore be nigh on impossible to meet.

This might well be brought up at a later date.

Tuesday September 27th 2005 – Now That's How You Write

I was both happy and furious.

I was happy that my meeting with Bill Kenwright had been scheduled for the Friday of this week, where in order to spare him any pain, no discussions would take place about the fortunes of a certain Merseyside football club that he owns and who were not doing too well at that time.

I was also happy because I had just received a letter from one of my favourite authors, Iain Banks. I find his books thoroughly absorbing. I'm sure he could teach me a trick or nine.

Truth be told, I'm not a massive reader... I am 5ft 9. (Apologies for that one.)

No, I'm not a massive reader, but one author I certainly have time for is the aforementioned Scotsman, and I think Michael was aware of this when he compiled the list. I have for a long time tried to cajole young Michael into reading cracking little books like *The Wasp Factory* and *The Crow Road*, but I suppose first he'd have to learn to read. Just a joke (he's threatening to sue now as well).

Anyway, Iain kindly wrote to me and stated that although he was happy to help, he wasn't expecting to make it to London before the end of the year, but he would be happy to meet me in Edinburgh.

Well, *prima facie*, this seemed quite an arduous journey for me, but as luck would have it my flatmate at the time was leaving me to seek her fortune in 'Auld Reekie' and had invited me to stay in her newly rented accommodation, and to give me a guided tour of the City anytime I liked - as long as it was in November.

So why was I full of ire? Well, having tried to pay Ken's Congestion Tax that day for having the audacity to actually drive around on a road in central London, I was told by the congestion operator that my payment had been rejected.

After phoning some poor helpless women at my bank and spending a considerable length of time screaming and swearing at her and watching tiny pieces of gob fly from my bottom lip, I finally let her get a word in edgeways to tell me that my account had only been frozen because some absolute anus has been using my cloned bankcard fraudulently. For example, on 23rd September, someone paid for £389 worth of goods with my card at Argos, so he was obviously a man of impeccable taste. Police were said to be combing the Croydon area. (Just a joke by the way, for any Croydonian who may be reading.).

I can also tell you that this nasty little thief had a T-Mobile, shopped at a hardware store in Ilford, and had recently been to Edgbaston on a National Express coach. A cricket fan perhaps?

Anyway, I am not sure why I even mentioned this story, I suppose recollections of this whole episode just made me want to vent the old spleen.

Right, as you were.

Wednesday September 28th 2005 – Babecast xxx

This evening I decided to cheer myself up by ordering a chicken korma, sitting in a dark room and listening to *Leonard Cohen* music. I also printed out five more letters which, over the following days, would be sent to the disparate quintet of **Guy Richie** (who I never got round to cornering at his premiere, coward that I am), **Vanessa Feltz**, **Irvine Welsh**, **Vivienne Westwood** and **Professor Stephen Hawking.**

The last 48 hours had been a rather depressing and exhausting period. Not only had I discovered that some putrid little reprobate, with connections in East London and Birmingham, had been rifling my already empty bank account, but my drive home on *this* evening saw another's behaviour plumbing equally appalling depths.

So what if I turned onto York Way in King's Cross slightly hurriedly? Just because the young lady (loosest sense of the word) had to, lord forbid, actually slow down slightly, I personally don't believe that merited driving behind me all the way up to the junction with Agar Grove (about 500 metres) with her hand pressing her car's horn and her middle finger up in the air. Perhaps she was late meeting her probation officer. The look of unbridled rage on her absurdly distorted face was truly a sight to behold. However, I did manage to make it home without turning into a pillar of salt.

If you need any further insight as to why society seems to be becoming less and less forgiving the older we get, I suggest that you do what I did when I got home. If you have Sky TV, pick up your remote control and press the blue lozenge shaped button that looks like a rubber Viagra pill (or so I've been told), and that has 'tv guide' written on it.

Note, if you will, the name of one particular programme, *Grab a Grand*. That to me sums up everything that is wrong with the world today. Grab (to snatch greedily) a Grand (money). Then note if you will the plethora of other so-called quiz shows that aim to con the poorest members of society out of their pension money.

Keep going, and what other diversions of delight did we have on offer? Some excremental smear of a programme called *Babecast XXX* one page up, and the ubiquitous pieces of detritus devoted to the game of poker on virtually every other channel.

Although I do actually quite like poker.

Anyway, sorry for whingeing on, but I've got an inner ear infection.

Thursday September 29th 2005 – Another Right Honourable Agreement

A better day, as I heard back from two more females from my list, one of whom had agreed to meet in the near future and thus would become the first individual with the double X chromosome to shake my hand.

The individual in question was MP for Maidstone and the Weald, Ann Widdecombe and obviously I was very grateful to her for being such a good sport. I still appeared to be faring pretty well with the honourable Members of Parliament and spoke to a friend about why this might be.

She argued that politicians were not known to be adverse to publicity, be they kissing babies heads, claiming to drink 27 pints per night or meowing and getting Rula Lenska to rub their whiskers.

I pointed out to her that she had clearly missed the point. There was no publicity to be gained from meeting me. In fact, as you will have noticed by the lack of any stories in *The Sun* about what I was doing, or appearances of myself with Peter Sissons on *London Tonight*, the media didn't have the slightest bit of interest in a bet undertaken between two random blokes from North West London. Besides, they had far more ground-breaking stories to concentrate on, such as the one I saw this day where a Frank Sinatra impersonator was arrested by a policeman called Dean Martin.

Hold the front page.

No, I assumed that everyone who had granted me an audience up until this point, had done so out of the goodness of their heart and because they couldn't really think of any good reason not to. I shower every day, I'm sane and I wasn't trying to claim paternity rights to any child.

Meanwhile, as someone once said, you take the crunchy with the smooth and today the crunchy that complimented Ann Widdecombe's smooth, was provided by Davina McCall.

Her agent Polly emailed me to say:

Dear Julian,

Thank you for your letter dated 24th September '05 for Davina's attention.

You'd be surprised at how many requests we get for people to meet Davina *(No, I wouldn't)* and I am afraid we're not able to fulfil them.

Only suggestion would be that you go down to one of her shows.

Good luck with it.

Best wishes...

A very prompt reply it seems, and one with the best intentions as well, but sadly the 'just popping to one of her shows' thing wasn't going to happen since my co-betee had become something of a stickler for the rules. Any meeting without the subject having prior knowledge of my arrival was strictly *verboten*.

Friday September 30th 2005 – That's A Bullseye!

◇◇

There was a story in a newspaper that I'd bought as I boarded my morning tube, about a dog that accidentally sent a fax by standing on its owner's fax machine.

Fascinating.

'I notice you've included the darts player Mervyn King,' I mentioned to Michael, soon after he handed over the list of 500 for the first time. I love the 'sport' of darts, y'see.

'I haven't. I've included the Governor of the Bank of England Mervyn King,' he clarified.

I was impressed for two reasons. First, that Michael's list had, as we had agreed, encompassed people from as wide an array of professions as possible, and second, that he knew who the Governor of the Bank of England was... In fact, that he knew *what* the Bank of England was.

I wonder if the two Mervyns frequently get mixed up? Other than name, I couldn't imagine that there's a great deal that the two have in common... Actually, come to think of it, isn't a £50 note sometimes referred to as a bullseye... and did not the preceding Governor of the Bank, Eddie George, also have a name that was similar to that of a darts player?

Perhaps once Mr King retires, we can expect Jockie Bristow to take up the mantle.

Apologies, not for the first time am I spouting poop – the point being that Mr King will, unfortunately, not be able to meet me, as stated in his letter received today.

Likewise, with my third response from Avalon Management (I like them. They are most efficient), I was informed in an anonymously written letter that '*David Baddiel will regrettably not be able to help me on this occasion*'.

Oh well, another time maybe.

CHAPTER 5 – October

Replies received: Cliff Richard, Tim Rice, Tony Robinson, Clare Balding, Lisa Rogers, Asad Ahmad, Bruce Forsyth, Chris Tarrant, Zoe Wanamaker, Lorraine Kelly, Bill Oddie, Geoff Boycott, Jonathan Edwards, Mike Leigh, Bernard Matthews, Paul Smith, Helen Fielding, Nicky Clarke.

Meetings achieved: Bill Kenwright, Lisa Rogers, Cherie Blair, Asad Ahmad, Tim Rice, Gary Lineker, Lorraine Kelly, Mike Leigh, Jonathan Edwards.

Saturday October 1st 2005 – Greeting 8 (Bill Kenwright)

I worked out that by the beginning of October I had somehow managed to attend or arrange fourteen of these meetings. Thankfully, it therefore seemed, and mercy be to him upstairs (and I don't mean Mr Rumsey in flat 4), that barring miracles, neither Michael nor myself would be forced to skinny dip in the sea off Brighton Pier during the mid-winter, and there would be no bearing of our souls, in a manner of speaking.

Jules Segal

The last day of September had seen me shake hands with the theatre impresario Bill Kenwright in the Maida Vale area of London.

While initially fearing that I would be late, it turned out that I made it to the meeting 25 minutes early, and that was including a five-minute *tour de A40* looking for the correct building. While standing by my car supping on Original Tropicana with juicy bits, and debating which house I was supposed to be going into, I spotted Bill walking up the street towards me, possibly midway through an afternoon stroll.

After brief introductions, the handshake was performed there and then in full view of the residents of this west London suburb and once complete, I was promised a couple of tickets to a West End show, not for myself sadly, for having found this rather complicated address, but to put towards the RNIB charity auction. A most generous gift indeed.

Well, that was the previous day and as for today, I was oh so tired as my sleep patterns continued to be quite badly disturbed.

I was awoken at 5.15 a.m., and despite desperately trying to drop off again, my mind was awash with all sorts of thoughts, such as whether or not all of the radioactive material from the former Soviet Union had been accounted for, what would happen if one looked at ultraviolet light through infrared goggles, and whether I was the only person who feels the need to belch when eating melon?

I received a letter from a lady called Gill, who is an assistant to Sir Cliff Richard. She seemed desperately upset that she and Sir Cliff would be unable to help me, for alas '...*he is overseas for much of the next two months.*' However, she did state that '*I will keep your letter by me and if some unexpected gap appears in Sir Cliff's schedule between now and Christmas, I'll let you know.*' And so I elected to create a new 'maybe' pile.

I also worked out that I might soon be forced to eat a hat and a cupboard, as you may recall.

As for my problem with fatigue, to be honest, I've always had a problem with peculiar sleeping patterns. Not surprising really as I used to suffer from narcolepsy but thankfully I am alright n...

Monday October 3rd 2005 – Doctor, Doctor

Something of a mixed bag for this first Monday in October. On the plus side, I was buoyed to hear in the news that Ai Ai the chimp had managed to quit smoking, since this shows great fortitude of character and acts as a lesson to us all.

Apparently, she started the dirty habit following the sad demise of her mate, and swiftly became a 20-a-day *Pan troglodytes*. The fact that she was caged in a Chinese zoo, however, does beg the question as to how was able to nip down to Londis to buy her 20 Rothmans.

Actually, this isn't a laughing matter. I must quit this evil habit too, particularly as I suffer from acute hypochondria. Yes, although I'm as fit as a butcher's dog, the dog in question is a mangy shitzu with ringworm that wolfs down trays of offal.

On the subject of health issues, closer scrutiny of the forfeits and I noted that if by some strange quirk of fate I managed to pass the '275th greeting' mark, it would be *Michael* who would have to run the Marathon (that I'd like to see). I'm not saying that he's out-of-shape, but put it this way, he irons his shirts in a wok. I decided that there was no way I could force him to run 27 miles – but I changed my mind a minute or so later.

Anyway, two more replies to tell you about, one was a 'yes' and the other a 'no', a further illustration of this curate's egg of a day.

Tony Robinson, comedy actor, archaeologist and Baldric, would sadly not be able to make it. Sir Tim Rice, on the other hand, had kindly agreed to meet me, and for that, I salute him as a gentleman, and no doubt a scholar.

I myself had another epiphany. I finally realised that many of the oblique references that I was using on my website, be they quotes from Nietzsche or expressions used by the Chuckle Brothers, were not being understood by everyone. I was of this belief because people were still emailing me to tell me so.

From this day forth I pledged to tone down my pomposity, to stop being so self-indulgent and pretentious in my choice of phrases and to knuckle down with only writing about my challenge.

Also Sprach Julian.

Jules Segal

Tuesday October 4th 2005 – One of the Greatest of Them All

◇◇

...and not just thought of as such by me. He was voted Number 16 of the Best Comedians of all time by other famous funnymen.

I, like everyone, was very upset to hear the news about Ronnie Barker. While I was certainly not qualified to make any particular statement about this news, I do know that as a child growing up in the 70s and 80s, I remember him as one of the best comedians around.

Sometimes I wish that life today could be like it was back then, when no-one listened to iPods on the tube, there weren't 17 free London newspapers to choose between and when you didn't have to swear, shout or humiliate people to be entertaining, and to raise laugh after laugh.

He was obviously a comedy genius and I just wish I could have met him. Michael mentioned to me that Ronnie Barker was one of the first names that he came up with when thinking about comedians to put on my list of 500. He really was an icon to people of our generation. At some stage in the future I would need to add a new name to the list. Basically, I would have to replace an irreplaceable name.

Thursday October 6th 2005 – It's Oh So Quiet

◇◇

Forgive me for quoting the lyrics of a strange Icelandic elf but there was very little to report. I had two meetings arranged for the following week, one with a noted barrister, a.k.a. the Prime Minister's wife and one with a famed lyricist, yet only two replies from the 60 or so letters I'd sent out little over a week earlier.

On the subject of figures, and without wishing to mention the lovely plump little Scarlett Johansson, I had now written to 207 of our nations most well known, well respected and greatly admired country-folk. Thirty-seven of these individuals (17.9 per cent), or the agents thereof, had gallantly replied to me, eight of them (3.9 per cent) had indulged me on my curious whim and I was scheduled to meet another six over the coming months.

I was obviously a long way short of my 20 per cent target, but I assumed that was largely down to my own stupidity in addressing many of the envelopes incorrectly, or indeed using addresses that were well out of date.

I felt like a poorly made soufflé, yet despite being rather deflated, I was of the opinion that as it was October, when the weather closes in and daylight recedes, some of the remaining 170 had only failed to respond because they were still away in Marbella, St Tropez, Miami Beach or Hull, getting some late autumn sunshine and that it was just a case of playing the waiting game.

My dad tracked me down on this day as well. He wanted to voice his concern about how I was neglecting both my 'real' job and my Gillette Sensor Excel and so he gave me a bit of the old father to son advice.

He basically told me to take my time and to think a lot, to think of everything I'd got and that I'd still be here tomorrow though my dreams may not. I stared at him with a vacant expression, because I'm not a fan of Cat Stevens or Boyzone.

'Take my time?' I was nearly at the halfway stage of this project and I was already starting to tread water. There were no prizes for second, or to quote the finest ever film made about time-travelling Scottish clansmen with the gift of eternal life, when it came to winners between Michael and I, 'There could be only one'.

Interest in what I was doing, which for a period had definitely been waxing, was now starting to fade. In the beginning, apart from everything being created, just two people had looked at my website, my mum and John Lucarotti (a friend – you don't know him).

Following Yahoo!'s help, an average of 1400 people a day visited to see that I hadn't updated my website for 48 hours. That number had by now slid to an average of about 800.

Perhaps I didn't write with enough pizzazz or I wasn't fashionable enough. I've never even heard of Goldfrapp, a musical group which I had been led to believe was now the benchmark of all that is trendy.

I sent an email to a prostitute the other day.

I promise you that's not as seedy as it sounds. The previous Friday's *Evening Standard* had an article about popular 'weblogs', (just for your information, mine was strangely overlooked) and one was a so-called '*amusing take on life*' by this anonymous lady of the night, or more likely some male Oxford graduate writing it from his Hampstead garret.

OK, so I'm a little jealous.

Jules Segal

I was hoping to have a link to my website placed on hers/his and so got in touch via the *Belle de Jour* website.

No response. Goodness me, what had we come to when even an information superhighway-based working-girl-cum-scribe was too important, sorry busy, to reply to me?.

Saturday October 8th 2005 – Two Great Ladies
◇◇

Brilliant, absolutely brilliant is the only way I can describe the response that the lovely Lisa Rogers sent me following my request for help. Not only had she agreed to a meeting and to bring a gift, which would obviously help me raise money for the RNIB, but she also laid into Michael, my most irritable of friends, who had set me this difficult challenge.

I hope she will not mind me including some of the text of the email here:

Dear Jules,

Your friend Michael sounds completely hilarious, and a total grumpy ar*e. If I can, therefore, help in any way that means he has to pay unpleasant forfeits, I am more than willing to do so. You can meet me… *(Details of meeting arrangements)…*

PS If you do get well over the 100 mark set by moody Mike, are we allowed to watch as you make him dance naked round Leicester Square painted blue? (or whatever else it is you get him to do).

In my reply, I pointed out that she wasn't only welcome to attend, but actively encouraged, as long as she turned up with a pointy stick with which to prod his heaving carcass as he danced over hot coals.

Further grist to the mill was provided by the witty-as-you-like TV presenter, Clare Balding. She was gracious enough to offer me a vast array of dates on which I might be able to have my photograph taken with her.

One was for the Sunday morning of the Lord Mayor's Parade where she would be commentating, although as that would have meant having to get up early on a weekend I opted for another day at the races in

November, because I was still desperately skint and therefore need to bet. With logic like that, I couldn't lose.

I would now just like to reply to an email that I received from a lady called Brandi who lives in El Paso in Texas. I am not sure if she lives in the 'Old' part where the meat sauce comes from. Anyway, I'll simply reply by saying that I have NO IDEA what Bill Murray whispered to the lovely Scarlett at the end of *Lost in Translation*, although I was told it was ad libbed.

Oh, and it was on this day that England managed to qualify in style for the World Cup Finals in Germany. Yup, the style of a slightly injured racehorse that manages to somehow stumble over the line.

Sunday October 9th 2005 – Halftime Oranges

Before creating my website I made three vows to myself: I would never discuss politics (you'll always be pissing someone or other off); I would never use profanities (I was finding that one difficult to keep to); and I would never prefix any adjective with the German word *über*, like some pretentious, recently-graduated, music journalist that has disappeared up their own point of no return (if I was going to write pretentiously, I would do it in English thank you very much.... well, maybe with a bit of French and Latin).

No, I didn't want to mention any of these things.

Some things that I would like to mention, however, are the fact that, in my opinion, the UK produces the finest milk on the planet, the fact that *Aliens – The Director's Cut* appears to be the same as *Aliens* and the fact that, as I discovered on this day while almost slicing my hand off, trying to open a tin of lychees ('oooh, la-di-da!') with a screwdriver is a fruitless exercise. Quite literally come to think of it.

I was nearly halfway through my challenge, which was to officially end on January 14th. Therefore, and in order to celebrate, other things that I did on this day included eating a scone in Louis Patisserie in Swiss Cottage, replacing a lightbulb, and compiling another 28 letters, which took me just 15 short of the halfway 250 mark.

They were sent, the following day, to **Roger Moore**, **Lisa Faulkner**, **Stella McCartney**, **Simon Rattle**, **Caroline Aherne**, **Jeffrey Palmer**,

Richard Curtis, Jermaine Defoe, Alan Ayckbourn, Nicky Clarke, Simon Pegg, Anthony Gormley, Mackenzie Crook, Pete Waterman, Norman Foster, Keith Floyd, Alan Sugar, Chris Evans, Oona King, Darcey Bussell, Barry Hearn, Nick Ross, Clive Woodward, Helen Fielding, Alan Yentob, Michael Winner, Cameron Mackintosh and **Zoe Wanamaker.**

Monday October 10th 2005 – The Main Headlines Again...

It was Monday morning and not for the first time I was absolutely exhausted. I couldn't have been more shattered if I was a Wedgewood tea-set in a Hotpoint CTD40 Polar Condenser Tumble Dryer (with fluff filter and end of cycle alarm).

After a late night, I was awoken at 7.00 a.m. by Mrs Rumsey getting busy with the Dyson in the flat upstairs, and I didn't drop off again. Not to worry, more pleasant neighbours you couldn't wish to have. Mr R has on more than one occasion invited me in for a glass of Chateaux Something and he frequently offers me winning racing tips that I never seem to bet on.

Anyway, here is the news. In other stories, BBC London newsreader Asad Ahmad had most kindly agreed to meet me. I would be greeting him in three days time, in between meeting Cherie Blair in the morning and Sir Tim Rice in the afternoon (and my mother in the evening, who wanted me to try and mend her dripping fridge).

Meanwhile Bruce Forsyth had also written to me. Good old Brucie's always been a man of the people and one that I have greatly admired as I share his passion for humour, golf and tap dancing (cue a joke about falling into the sink). I think everyone loves Bruce.

Sadly, he was about to embark on a long stint of filming for a new series of *Strictly Come Dancing*, and had no time to make my acquaintance, yet he had very kindly sent me a signed photograph which included the amusing personalised message, '*to the winner of the RNIB charity auction, what a bargain you've got!*' Well, I suppose that depends how much it goes for.

To round off an encouraging day, an email from Sue, PA to Chris Tarrant, stated that while her boss barely has time to catch his breath during the average day, he *would* afford me the time I needed (what a nice guy) if I travelled up to Elstree during the shooting of *Who Wants to be a Millionaire* and no, I didn't suppose I would get a go in the chair.

Funnily enough, a Turkish friend of mine once told me that in his home country, the currency used to be so unstable and in such a constant state of flux, that the show there is named *Who Wants 500 Billion?*

Tuesday October 11th 2005 – Greeting 9 (Lisa Rogers)

Lisa Rogers or Lisa Rogers-Phwoooar, as I used to think her name was, kindly granted me an audience. I know that this Welsh beauty/TV presenter/former girlfriend of Ralf Little/host of *Scrapheap Challenge* had glanced at my website in the past and may well do so in the future (so sorry for mentioning Ralf, Lisa) as she had sent me an email to tell me as much. In fact, her email even mocked Michael, and I was most delighted that she saw fit to enter into the spirit of things.

Before I get to the meeting, a little background info.

I'm not sure if I've mentioned my track record with the fairer sex in the past. Oh, I have? Well, I'll do so again anyway. Let's start with school, where as a six stone, 5ft 1 inch 14-year-old, I really used to struggled with the girls. Then one day I just decided to let them *take* my dinner money without a fuss. As for trying to steal a kiss off any of them, HA! You were more likely to have seen Captain Hook stealing an eel (with his bad hand I mean).

In my late teens and early twenties I fared only slightly better. Sure enough, girls were now willing to occasionally play share the mattress, it's just that within a month or two they tended to get frustrated with me and scarper.

To be honest, I was never very good at relating to female issues, such as why a woman could never have enough shoes or why she might refuse 'Death by Chocolate' in the restaurant but then go home and eat a whole tube of Jaffa Cakes in bed. In fact, it took me many, many years to realise that coming out with statements such as, 'You look tired, honey. Can you come here and give me a head massage...' was in fact a bad idea.

In my mid-twenties everything changed. I was given a book called *Men are from Earth, Women are from Earth. Deal with it.* Well, to be honest that isn't entirely true, but I did gradually get to grips with the mechanics of the female brain and started faring slightly better.

So why, in the name of all that is holy, am I mentioning this now? Well, because, and this is going to sound really stupid, I did actually think just for one iota of a second that my occasional ability to make women laugh, and I mean with me and not at me, might just give me a glimmer of a shadow of hope in convincing Lisa, that most beautiful and blondest of blonde sirens (unless it's out of a bottle, which I doubt) to go out for a drink with me at a later date. But would I have the gall to ask her? Well, wait and see...

For the time being I had other problems. I had a blazing row with Mickey Boy prior to the meeting. He had been throwing his toys out of the pram and wanted nothing more to do with *Greeting the 500* as he didn't like the way I'd been portraying him on the website.

He mentioned that he didn't like the way I had been 'speaking for him'. The thing is I hadn't been speaking for him, I'd just been speaking *about* him.

Despite wanting 'nothing more to do with the stupid bet', when I informed him that I would be shaking hands with the delightful Lisa Rodgers, he rather predictably changed his tune. 'Right, this is the last one I'll be coming to,' (until the next one no doubt).

You see Michael, who obviously had an active role in this bet, albeit a passive one, had been showing the same kind of stinky attitude that many other people that I'd told about my bet had shown. When the going was good, when it was all picnics and rainbows and chocolate éclairs, and meetings with Cherie Blair, everyone was fascinated about it. However, when I was struggling or not getting any meetings, or replies, when my sponsorship page had been inactive for weeks and I'm having panic attacks in the bath, who encouraged me then? I'll tell you who: effing nobody. It's then that my friends and family and work colleagues all thought, 'What the hell is he doing this for? Why is he wasting his time?'

So for Michael, when there was no news about any future meeting, or when I told him that I was struggling to find contact details for some of the 500, or that only 22 people had looked at my website in two weeks, he had this ridiculous aloof expression as if he'd almost forgotten about the bet and that he was wondering why I was sweating away and rushing off to the post office every other day or down to the south coast to meet Sir Patrick Moore.

I really wanted to know if I was actually busting a gut here for no reason whatsoever? Had Michael truly lost interest in this? Could I pack up now without having to bare my necessities on Brighton Beach or was this Michael's idea of a bluff? To be honest, I really couldn't be sure, but I supposed time would tell.

Well, back to *this* meeting and the two of us were directed by Lisa to meet her outside some fashionable shop on Argyll Street in the afternoon. And there she was at the pre-appointed time, coming out of the shop like a stunning Venus emerging from a large clam. I really wanted to appear unflustered and aloof but I think that for the first time in all of my meetings so far, I was rather tongue-tied.

The young lady was an absolute gem. Up close, you can see why she's ideal for TV. She was a rare beauty indeed, although a bit of an upset one when we first approached her, as apparently some utter shyster in a post office had run off with all of her stamps which she had neatly laid down on the counter next to her. The bastard! If I ever get my hands on him I'd show him what for - unless of course he's bigger than me.

I really wanted to give the poor lass a consoling hug as she looked a little forlorn, but as everything was going quite well to that point, I decided not to. However, I did mention to Lisa that I had approximately 248 stamps at home and although theoretically they'd all been earmarked for my letters, had I known her plight in advance, I'd definitely have brought one or two.

I don't think she heard me, partly because I was mumbling a bit through nerves and partly because I think she was distracted by the ominous form of Michael grinning at her, like a mountain with teeth. So we traded insults about each other's respective football teams (I'd like to think that we bonded), and had three - count them, three - photographs together, including one where Lisa suggested that we both put on a mean and moody expression.

Lisa could never look mean and moody. Well, actually, I don't know, had the stamp thief been around...

Following that, as we prepared to depart, we accepted her unbelievably generous gift which turned out to be one of her outfits from the TV show *Scrapheap Challenge*. It included a blouse (do women still call them that? I'm not sure), a grey trouser-top combo and a warm looking jacket with a fur-lined hood.

Lisa apologised that it was a bit grubby and hadn't been washed since she last wore it, and then Michael in his untactful and oafish manner said, 'Don't worry, we'll probably get more for it that way'.

The guy is a flaming liability.

'*Scrapheap Challenge*, that's a good name for the challenge that you're undertaking,' he said to me as we were walking away, 'just without the 'S''.

Oh, and by the way, did I actually get round to asking her out for a drink? Whadda *you* think...

Thursday October 13th 2005 – Greeting 10 (Cherie Blair)

I had three 'meetings' pencilled in, my most productive day so far, and a day in which three per cent of my entire challenge could be accomplished in the space of five hours.

In days of old, when knights were bold et cetera, witnessing the sight of Halley's Comet was said to be an ominous sign. Likewise, during Macbeth's lifetime, kings tended to be terrified when they were informed that their horses were eating each other, as this often heralded fateful news. Like the news that the 2.30 at Ascot would have to be cancelled.

My own ominous portent does not relate to bright lumps of rock in the sky, or equine cannibalism, it revolves around the showing of the film *Apocalypse Now* on TV.

The first time I viewed it was the night before my economics A-level, when I became so engrossed in the action that I forgot to revise the importance of price elasticity of demand to the producer of goods, and ended up getting an 'N' in the exam. I then viewed it several years later, and ended up staying awake so late to watch the climactic scenes of Marlon Brando at his wheeziest best, that I overslept and missed my flight to Alicante.

Having again watched it the previous night, I faced this important day with a certain amount of trepidation.

Before describing what happened, I would like to point out that I shall do so in as much detail as possible. I'm aware that very few people are fortunate enough ever to get to see the inside of one of the most famous buildings in the country and I would, quite rightly, like you to be able to soak up the atmosphere, the sights and sounds and smells, well, most of the smells (I was, again, a little nervous) as if you'd been there with me.

That having been said, I'm well aware that detailing the layout and the floor plan of the Prime Minister's residence could be deemed something of a risk to national security and so rather than having MI5 smash down my door with one of those miniature battering ram things, I hope you'll appreciate that I have to tread somewhat carefully with my descriptions.

OK, so it was raining heavily as I left for 10 Downing Street, not the end of the world. The fact that the Northern Line wasn't turned on, rankled me only slightly. I made my way to Marylebone to take the ever-reliable Bakerloo line instead. I then accidentally left my umbrella on the tube but, nevertheless, made my way towards Whitehall in the face of what had become monsoon-like conditions that wouldn't have looked out of place in a Bangladeshi rainforest.

As I was a little early (I thought it only polite not to rock up to No.10 15 minutes late for my appointment with the PM's wife), I decided to stare into the window of a pizza restaurant by Trafalgar Square for several minutes, even though it was shut. I was trying not to draw attention to myself, you see.

After a few minutes had elapsed, and by now resembling a sodden sheep, I decided to make tracks, or more accurately, hoof-prints.

Outside the gate at Downing Street, I encountered a thick metal railing that seemed to have no viable entry point and so, I must confess, I started to panic a little. Well, whoever said that 'There's never a policeman around when you need one' ought to hang around at the Met's training centre in Colindale, or else ought to see how far they would get trying to hold a rave at No. 3 Downing Street. Actually, they had better not as there were about 12 long arms of the law there (that's six policemen).

I explained to one staggered looking officer what I was there for – 'To shake Cherie Blair's hand' – and after looking at me for a short while as if I was soft in the head, he sent me along the railing, around the corner and through the gate at the side of the railing. Aah, I'd found it.

I then found myself in a small low-level building that had an X-ray conveyor belt contraption and a walk-through metal detector within it. It was a building akin to one that you'd find in a small airport – say, Gibraltar.

Anyway, after completing a brief name-check – phew, I *was* expected – I apologised to another officer that I was five minutes early for my meeting. 'Don't worry,' he replied, 'after going through all the security checks you'll be five minutes late'.

Right.

Then we had the walk up Downing Street itself, as trudged by so many harried cabinet members before me. As I strode along, I spotted a rather smart Jaguar driving past me away from the building. I remember thinking to myself that it was the sort of car that David Niven might have once driven in a film, if it had been set in Monte Carlo. I also noticed a small patch of grass with a large tree that I considered to be a lovely place for a summer barbecue, although again that might be a bit of a security risk.

I soon arrived at the famous door and announced myself to yet another policeman, who simply looked at me as I stood there in the rain waiting to be ushered in. We stared, squinting at each other for 15 seconds or so as if he was 'the Good' and I was 'the Ugly' and we were in some version of a Central London spaghetti Western, until he eventually said, 'Well, you have to knock'... and so I did, while at the same time pondering whether I was the first person ever to pass through this famous portal in a brown hooded tracksuit top.

Apart from Mrs Thatcher...possibly. (Happy Birthday by the way, Ma'am.)

Once inside, I gasped (silently) and took it all in, while rather rudely and inadvertently forgetting to answer the question asked of me by the police officer just inside the front door. You see, it was so beautiful in there and such was my excitement, that I felt like that evil archaeologist at the end of the Indiana Jones film, who'd been the first to witness the inside of the Lost Ark of the Covenant (although without having my head blown apart). There were so many lovely paintings on the wall and a beautiful rug and some stunning urns and a fireplace and an antique (or possibly Argos) clock. I tell you, Hugh Scully would have had a field day.

When I came round from my reverie, I informed the officer that I was there to have a photograph taken of myself next to the Prime Minister's wife and he promptly telephoned up to the delightfully efficient Sue, PA to Cherie, before inviting me to take a seat in a chair – the chair right next to the notice on the wall that read 'Under no circumstances are mobile phones or cameras to be used here'. Oh dear, I thought, fallen at the first fence.

Sue came down and was as nice as a particularly nice pie. We had a little chat where she informed me that despite having worked there for some time, she also still found it incredible to believe that she was wandering up Downing Street every morning, sometimes even bustling through the front door with supermarket carrier-bags in tow. She also told me not to worry about the 'No Cameras' notice. These were extenuating circumstances after all. I mean, I had a ridiculous bet to win. She was ever so kind to me and even took a picture of me outside the famous Number 10 door.

Cherie appeared soon afterwards with a pleasant smile and wearing a very appropriate red coat (she's a Charlton Athletic supporter... not really, she votes Labour). She looked almost regal, but then again I haven't yet met the Queen so I wouldn't really know. I would describe the rest of her outfit for any interested woman reading this (sorry, that's very sexist of me) but my head was all over the place and I can't really remember. All I do remember is that Cherie was particularly warm and welcoming and so I stopped shaking and was put at ease, and for that I was, and am, very grateful.

I thanked her very much for helping me and was introduced to her fantastic young son Leo, who made me smile very much. He was particularly sweet as he held his mum's hand and hid behind her.

I complimented him on his great trainers complete with flashing lights on the heels.

It was explained to me that he had the day off school today, as part of his classroom had flooded. Well, young Leo appeared most delighted about this. 'Maybe I'll have the week off school,' the beaming youngster suggested to me. 'Ooh yes. Maybe you'll have the year off school in fact,' I winked to him. He digested my comment and with an innocent smile, turned to his mother and said, 'Yeah, maybe I'll have the year off school!'

'Umm, no, I don't think so,' said Cherie, putting us both in our place.

Cherie was so down to earth that I was bowled over. We had our photo taken in front of a lovely oil painting, and as I shook her hand for the snap, I gave her a bit of breathing space from my rain-soaked attire. However, Sue, who took the picture, told me to move in a bit and Cherie agreed, 'Yes you can come a bit closer you know. I don't bite.' I was tempted to reply, 'Yeah, but maybe I do,' before thinking that on this occasion, discretion being the better part of valour, I ought to keep my cakehole shut.

I was then given a signed copy of her book *The Goldfish Bowl* for the auction before Cherie informed me that the RNIB was a charity that was close to her heart and that she tried to help them whenever she could (presumably even if it meant having to meet idiots like me).

And that was it. I left Downing Street to be greeted by an audience of chattering Oriental tourists behind the railings at the end of the road, who possibly mistook me for the Minister of Sloppy Dressing, and made my way back to the tube still in a state of shock.

It had all gone just swimmingly and how apt bearing in mind the drippy conditions. So it looked as though my fears had been unfounded after all. Apocalypse when?

Thursday October 13th 2005 – Greeting 11 (Asad Ahmad)

It was then, however, after leaving Downing Street to return home to pick up my car, that things started to go quite seriously wrong.

I was due to meet Asad in the *BBC News* studios on Marylebone High Street at 12.30p.m. but wasn't helped by the fact that when I got back to my car, it was blocked in by a white transit van which, from what I recall, had something to do with landscape gardening in Potters Bar.

Not for the first time in my life, I felt as though a panic attack wasn't a million miles over the horizon, so I scanned the pavement for a brown paper bag.

That wasn't necessary though, because a minimal blast on my car horn (approx. 70 seconds) saw a red-cheeked, red-headed man bound down the street towards me with an expression of embarrassment and a raised hand of apology. I muttered the first two letters of a curse before realising that he was actually quite large and so instead slammed my car door with a vigour I didn't know I possessed, and drove off.

I was destined to be late.

Lesson one: When meeting anyone on your list of 500, who has kindly agreed to give you a couple of minutes of their time, **DON'T BE LATE.**

As I drove past London Zoo, in an act of desperation I phoned my dad, who lives nearby and is retired and spends a lot of his time dozing on the couch, to ask him if he could drive me to the edge of the congestion-tax zone, drop me off, and drive my car back to his house. He agreed and I was soon at my destination.

'Hello, I'm here to shake hands with Asad Ahmad,' I blurted out to a security guard who gave me a most quizzical stare. The sort of stare you give someone you've just engaged in conversation with, only to learn that they have recently escaped from Bedlam. 'I haven't seen him today,' announced a lady named Dominique behind the reception desk, and just as my heart started to slowly sink, the man himself walked through the front entrance in full motorbike gear and introduced himself.

After a quick change, he re-emerged and thoughtfully ushered me through to the BBC London News studio as he thought I'd get a nicer picture there. You see, it's little gestures like that...

I made various inane comments, such as 'Gosh, the studio looks small in real life,' and the even more embarrassing, 'Is this a BBC News studio or a London News studio?' before looking up at the screen above me that read 'BBC LONDON NEWS STUDIO', but Asad kindly let those pass.

A young lady then came out, took our photo and left before Asad mentioned that he would be sending me something for my charity auction, for which I thanked him very much.

He even suggested, in response to my cheeky email asking whether this project might make a decent quirky story to end the *BBC News* with, that he'd see what he could do, but I wouldn't for one second hold him to that.

Anyway, that was that, I thanked the security guards, did an Elvis, left the building and strolled up towards a drizzly Harley Street.

Thursday October 13th 2005 – The Wreck and the RAC

...and so to the third 'Greeting' of the day and the inevitable curse of *Apocalypse Now.*

The plan was to pick up my reliable VW Polo from my dad's house and drive down to Barnes in South London, to shake hands with the most famous theatrical lyricist in the country, Sir Tim Rice.

From time to time I criticise my dad for his slightly erratic driving. I'm of the opinion that he confuses the rev-counter with the speedometer. I wouldn't say that he's leaden footed, but put it this way, I wouldn't want to ice skate next to him on a frozen lake.

So, by the time I got back into my car, the car that had been working when I picked him up and he had dropped me off to meet Asad, it had a very strange smell coming from it. A sort of burnt-wiry smell. To cut a long story short, I lost my mind because my dad had managed to wear out the clutch of my car in the space of a two-minute drive.

I had a breakdown in every way possible. It was just past Maida Vale, just short of Bill Kenwright's office (I decided not to pop in again) and WAY short of Barnes.

While waiting for the RAC to arrive, I telephoned Eileen, Tim's friendly assistant and apologised for not being able to make the meeting and to rearrange it for the following week.

I then phoned my bank manager, who had phoned me earlier in the day to ask why my finances were in such a state of disarray.

I then phoned the RAC to find out when they might be arriving. A very amusing and friendly mechanic named Shapour turned up shortly afterwards, and after hearing what had happened, advised me either to change my car or change my father.

On reflection I decided to do neither.

By the time I got home, I was so exhausted that I decided to the hit the sack, yet I was too tired even to do that so I just went to bed instead. I did so, though, safe in the knowledge that I wouldn't be woken by Mrs Rumsey hoovering in the flat above me at 7.00 a.m. the next day, as she had since told me that she never gets up at that time, never mind getting involved with domestic chores, and that the real culprits from the other day were the industrial cleaning company who look after our block. They don't come on a Friday, praise the Lord, but the gardeners and their petrol-driven chainsaw would no doubt be in attendance.

Sunday October 16th 2005 – Bird Flew
◇◇◇

No, I haven't spelled the above title incorrectly, since I am not about to have a topical discussion about the terrifying prospect of pigeons coughing and spluttering everywhere and making us all ill.

This is simply a potted reference, and a slightly non-politically correct one, to the depressing night I had in a pub the previous night, when instead I should have been trying to find contact details for Fatima Whitbread.

The title above refers to the young lady who I was talking to and who I was hoping to get to know better, yet she turned on her heels and fled while I was ordering a drink for the two of us at the bar, and presumably found a dark alcove in which to hide from me for the rest of the evening.

I have since decided never again to use the line '…but us men honestly like big-buttocked ladies like you…'

I had also come to the decision that should Bernard Matthews, owner of possibly the largest poultry farm in the world and one of the 24 individuals I had just written a letter to, agree to meet me in Norfolk, then I would not jokingly inform him that I had just heard one of his turkeys sneezing, as the poor man would probably become sick with worry.

Just 70 shopping days until Christmas, after all.

There was some other important news about *Greeting the 500* as I also unilaterally decided that my challenge would no longer end in mid-January but instead on January 31st.

By now, you may be aware that one of the most important rules agreed between Michael and I when setting up our bet, was that in the interest of fair play, the 500 people on the list should all be based on these shores, so as to give me a sporting chance of garnering a handshake.

I had since written to George Michael and Sheena Easton in California, and to Simon Rattle, leader of the Berlin Philharmonic Orchestra in, erm, Berlin. I am not sure if Simon Rattle spends all of his time in Germany; perhaps he only works part-time there and spends some time in England – a semi-conductor if you like – but this situation was getting seriously out of hand. I had since discovered that others I had written to lived abroad, including Roger Moore (Switzerland), Keith Floyd (South of France) and Anthony Hopkins (Los Angeles). The world renowned neuropsychologist and author Oliver Sacks, to whom I had also recently written, apparently lives and works in New York. In fact, when I discovered this, I let slip a string of short sharp expletives. Ironic, then, that on further scanning his website I learned that Professor Sacks had been investigating the 'neuroanthropology of Tourettes Syndrome'.

Anyway, the cherry on the proverbial black forest gateau became clear when I phoned Michael to ask him who on earth the 'David Jacobs' on my list was. 'He's the fashion bloke. The one who makes that perfume you wear (he meant aftershave). He's British, isn't he?'

I decided to check the profile of *Marc* Jacobs on Wikipedia, the first line of which read, 'Marc Jacobs is an American fashion designer who was raised in New York'.

We therefore agreed that I would be allowed to replace Marc/David Jacobs with someone else, seeing as how my pea-brained colleague couldn't even get his name right. My target of 100 would remain the same, but I would get an extra two and a bit weeks to work with.

Michael didn't really have a leg to stand on. Just as well then that he spends most of his life lying down and watching *Star Trek Deep Space Nine.*

Following the sad passing of Ronnie Barker recently, we could not decide whether to subsequently include the up-and-coming tennis star Andy Murray, or the up-and-coming boxing star Amir Khan. With Mr Jacobs being taken off the list, both of these bright young things were now added.

So these are the 24 protagonists to whom the next batch of letters were sent: **Bernard Matthews, Anthony Hopkins, Oliver Sacks, Willie Carson, Nick Hornby, Chris Kamara, Cilla Black, John Virgo, Lynda La Plante, Mike Leigh, Sally Gunnell, Jeremy Paxman, Sanjeev Bhaskar, John le Carré, Martin Kemp, Joan Collins, Ronnie O'Sullivan, Sue Barker, Robbie Coltrane, Billy Connolly, Lawrence Dallaglio, Liz Hurley, Simon Cowell** and **Steve Davis.**

Tuesday October 18th 2005 - Breaded Ovum

‹‹

On the way into work this morning I yet again cursed the constant problems with London Underground's Northern Line and its constant array of extraordinary faults. OK, it gets me to work via King's Cross, but then so would a skip full of urine if it had wheels and a motor.

I'd just been explaining to my South African work colleague what a Scotch egg is. I don't think I was too wide of the mark telling her that if food was people, a Scotch egg would be wearing a Burberry cap and a gold sovereign ring. She soon understood that it wasn't exactly haute cuisine and then asked if it was called a 'Scotch' egg because it was in batter, similar to the famous battered Mars bars one can buy north of Hadrian's Wall. I suggested it was more likely to be because the only time you'd fancy eating one would be after several large Scotches.

I digress.

An email I received from someone called Mr Mason – very formal there, I'll just call him M – mentioned that having forgotten about my website for a couple of months, he visited recently and was both surprised and pleased to see how well I was doing on the old handshake count. Thanks, Mr M.

I was starting to get a bit concerned myself, as I hadn't heard back from anyone on my list for almost a week; not since Chris Tarrant and Bruce Forsyth the previous Wednesday.

Well, all I can say is praise the sweet lord above for Lorraine Kelly. Just as despair was seeping into my head, or more accurately, the amygdala in the front medial part of my temporal lobe, I receive an email from a kindly lady at GMTV, who informed me that this Scottish damsel would ride to my aid and had agreed to meet me the following Tuesday. Once again, therefore, numerous gratitude and platitudes emanated forth from my humble gob.

I momentarily considered going out and celebrating by buying an egg from Lorraine's region of the country. On the flipside, I noticed that the popular show *Little Britain* was about to go on tour and that Messrs Lucas and Walliams, the latter of whom I wrote to a couple of weeks earlier, would soon be incommunicado (which I believe is just South of Rhyl).

I therefore hurriedly decided to contact the representatives of Matt

Lucas, to ask them to pass on the gist of my request (30 seconds, photo, handshake) to this young man of comedy, possibly by email or phone, and preferably before his show travelled further north than Leighton Buzzard. Would it be a case of 'agent says no...'? Well, that was up to them.

Having had quite an arduous day, by the time I returned *chez* squalid tip, I was just about ready to make some amendments to the likes and dislikes columns that you might have read somewhere else, namely:

More dislikes: trying to vacuum up feathers that are stuck in wiry carpet, Graham in Camden's Council Tax department, anything micro-waved, finding long female hairs in my fridge, being ripped off by car mechanics AGAIN, the City of Scottsdale, Arizona, USA (don't even go there), people who ring every buzzer in the block at 7.00 a.m. because they don't know where Mr Gonzalez lives, water ingress in a sock drawer, treading on my glasses in the morning, the smell of napalm at any time of the day.

More likes: tube workers who let me pass without rummaging around in my back pocket for my Oyster Card, Kwik Fit, *72 Virgins* by Boris Johnson, item 47 on the Weng Wah House menu, Mido.

Thursday October 20th 2005 – My Family and Other Sitcoms

Americans have fascinating surnames, they really do.

Within the preceding few weeks I had added a Mr Crapple, a Mr Nutbrown, a Ms Beanblossom and a Mr Cakebread to our company database. And what did we Brits have, to counter these colourful appellations with? Well, a Mr Teets was about as entertaining as it got.

Whether this was confidential information and I would be fired for divulging these names, I am not sure, but it is a risk I am prepared to take to try and garner a cheap laugh.

Meanwhile, Marli my Namibian line-manager departed for a spot of lunchtime yoga the other day and I took the opportunity to update my website with information on the three – count them, three – replies I'd received.

The agent of Zoe Wanamaker, who I last spotted playing a witch at Hogwarts (Zoe, not her agent), sent me a very pleasant letter stating that Zoe had really wanted to prove Michael wrong, (so she gets huge brownie points from me for that at the very least), but sadly she would be too busy filming the new series of *My Family* to be able to assist.

I also received an email from a lady called Carolyn which included an apology and went on to say that unfortunately Bernard Matthews, a man to whom we should all raise a glass before we tuck into Christmas lunch (apart from vegetarians and people who don't have Christmas lunches), wouldn't be able to meet me, since he was recovering from illness and was under orders 'not to take on additional diary commitments'.

I wished him well.

Finally, a young lady called Abi rang to inform me that the writer and director of one of my favourite films (*Secrets and Lies*), namely Mike Leigh, had a ten-minute window in his schedule in which I could meet him, and so the following Friday was pencilled in.

I thanked Abi and informed her that, like a porthole on a cramped yacht, a teeny window was all that was required, since I needed no more than 30 seconds for the handshake. I supposed that I could spend the other 9 minutes and 30 seconds trying to palm off a script about a schizophrenic, stand-up comedian.

I wasn't sure whether my inner ear infection had returned, but at that time I happened to be suffering from the mother, father and extended family of all headaches.

Perhaps my lifestyle and diet was contributing to this. After all, man cannot live on M&S 'Luxury Sherry Trifles' alone, but at least I knew that my diet was healthier than Michael's, (he survives on meat, wheat and anything covered in melted cheese). In fact, I had to explain to him just this very day that crisps don't actually count as 'roughage' even if they were crinkle cut.

I was, as you can see, on speaking terms with him once again, partly because he had been one of my best friends for 20 years and falling out over one poxy argument seemed ridiculous, but mainly because I needed to borrow his digital camera.

He did make me laugh today though.

Jules Segal

As I have mentioned in the past, although he is blessed with a fair amount of wit and savvy, his knowledge of literature and the great authors of our time is not what it might be. This possibly stems from the fact that he left school at the age of 14, because, in his words, 'It was either me or them'. I've never really understood what he meant by that.

I was, therefore, slightly surprised when he announced to me out of the blue that he had found a book in his flat by a notable German writer and on reading some of it had come to the decision that 'Kafka is sh*t. I can write better than him.'

Lord knows how it got there.

Friday October 21st 2005 – Greeting 12 (Tim Rice)
xxxxxxxxxxxxxxxxxxxxxxxxxxxxxxxxxxxxxxxxxxxxxxxxxxxxxxxxxxxxxxxxxxxxxxxxxxxx

This greeting was meant to take place eight days earlier, yet owing to a *force majeur*, or more accurately the force of someone's foot on the clutch pedal of the metallic grey dustbin that I drive, I was immobile until this week.

This time it was a far more relaxed affair. Woke up. Got out of a bed. Dragged a comb across my back and shoulders and then had a quick shave. However, on reflection, in other words when I looked in the mirror, I noticed that the shave with a disposable blue plastic razor had been a little too quick and I'd have been only slightly less disfigured had I used a scythe.

It's no exaggeration to say that there were so many spots of blood on my face, that it had an air of the 'King of the Mountains Jersey' from the Tour de France, about it. If you don't know what that looks like, think white with red polka dots.

Fortunately, I found a bottle of '2-in-1 Combined Cleanser and Toner – with witch hazel and AHAs(?)' lurking at the back of the bathroom cabinet, presumably left there by some absent-minded ex-girlfriend, before I too was left on the shelf by her.

I soon found myself making my way to South London, stopping only to buy a frugal lunch from my favourite Lebanese Restaurant on the Edgware Road, *Maroush*.

Just in case you happen to be interested, I plumped for *wahad chicken schwarma* (kebab) and *wahad tabbouleh* (parsley salad). I was contemplating also getting a portion of *beid ghanam*, but then I remembered that I'd already eaten lamb's testicles for breakfast, so I said my *shukrans* and left.

I arrived at my destination in good time although my drive was a slightly surreal experience having noted both a blue plaque informing me that the classical composer Gustav Holst lived in a house under Barnes Bridge (I wonder if the tube kept him awake at night?) and numerous posters informing me that the 'World Famous Moscow Circus' would soon be playing on Putney Common.

After a bit of trouble I found the office that Sir Tim was working from and indeed found the man himself.

We had a friendly chat, together with his assistant Eileen; they were keen to know how it was all going and who I had met. It turned out that a couple of others on the 'yes' list, namely Tony Hawks and Mike Leigh, are good friends of Tim's. He also suggested that from my point of view, there may be a book to be written about *Greeting the 500*. Now there's a thought...

Tim suggested that we had the photo taken out through the French doors and in his lush garden, where it was a bit brighter. Sadly, at that stage my cowardly colours truly came to the fore again once I noticed that a boxer, canine not pugilist, was lying in the middle of the lawn outside.

'Will I be alright with the dog? I'm a little uncomfortable around them to be honest,' I whimpered.

At this Sir Tim chuckled, drew in his breath and said, 'Oh yes, she's a bit of a killer'.

Tasha turned out to be a puppy of probably less than two years of age. I shame myself sometimes, I really do. Anyway, Eileen took our picture, I gratefully received a CD for the charity auction, (and a signed copy of a book for myself), and was soon once again caught up in the permanent snarl around Hammersmith roundabout.

Alright, alright, the 2-in-1 cleanser is mine.

Despite receiving Gary's letter back on August 25th, in which he stated that he would be happy to shake my hand and have a photo taken in order to 'enable me to cross one more name off the list!', that meeting wasn't scheduled to take place for almost two months, or in other words, until this day.

As I journeyed down to BBC TV centre White City for the second time in two months, with my slightly crotchety, cowboy-hat-adorned passenger, I wondered whether Gary might have agreed to this meeting in haste and subsequently forgotten all about his prearranged obligation. I didn't let it bother me too much though, as I was more preoccupied with trying to find the lit cigarette that had rolled under Michael's seat.

We made it in one piece and even in good time that day, despite the fact that Wood Lane looked like a cross between Lake Nyasa (by virtue of a burst water main) and a mobile Jackson Pollock painting – Norwich City (yellow and green-wearing supporters) were playing QPR (blue and white hooped-supporters) around the corner.

Parking was a bit of a worry, since Michael, in his usual shy and retiring way, screamed his head off when I mentioned that we might have to tip-toe through the flood water to reach our intended destination. He emitted a series of staccato outbursts along the lines of 'stupid (expletive) prat!... wearing suede shoes!... not as if we're late!...'

I therefore drove up to the gate of the BBC and asked a security man, on the off chance, whether I could park within the complex. He directed me to his colleague, who shrugged and directed me to *his* colleague who was working inside a large glass box by the gate. I popped my head round the door and explained the situation.

This helpful soul asked me to wait outside his opaque cube, and I was comforted to see through the window that he was indeed speaking animatedly down the phone, no doubt trying to track Gary down, in an industrious and workman-like fashion.

After about four minutes of looking at my watch and growing a wee bit impatient, I popped my head around the door again, fully expecting him to be fighting my corner and shouting at some BBC gofer to 'Hurry up and find Mr Lineker', but what he was actually saying was 'No! *Two* king prawns and *one* special fried rice...'

I drove through the flood.

We eventually caught up with our footballing deity in reception and, much as I had suspected, it didn't take Michael more than five seconds to embarrass me by adopting the clichéd 'bowing down' position to this former Spurs hero.

I laughed this off (and punched Michael's arm when Gary's back was turned) and the three of us briefly discussed the chances of our team securing a victory up at Manchester United that afternoon (Gary was reticent to make any prediction; Michael and I went for a loss), before we made our way outside for the photo.

While we posed by a fountain, waiting for our Annie Leibovitz impersonator to check his imaginary light meter, I asked Gary if he had been the one who was kind enough to plug my project to John Motson or David Gower, as they too had both met me, but he said no.

A bit of a coincidence then, I suggested. 'Well, we're all good eggs here at BBC Sport,' he said with a cheeky grin and I must confess, I have to agree.

Just to prove the point, no sooner had the picture been taken and Michael and I started to wander off, that I noticed Gary had been cornered by a beaming Asian guy and was merrily signing an autograph and chuntering away.

'Damn!' I said to Michael as we drove home, 'That reminds me, I forgot to ask him for something for the auction. Maybe I can get him to send me something at a later date.'

'If he does, I'm having it,' replied my charitable friend, which led me to the decision that on this occasion, I wasn't going to force the issue with my latest subject.

Final score: Manchester United 1, Tottenham 1.

Monday October 24th 2005 – Alas Smith and Fielding
◇◇

... so yes, sorry about being so sartorially challenged, and for enjoying day-time TV quiz shows, for still listening to Duran Duran, and for going clothes shopping in Matalan, for having the cheek to occasionally say positive things about America and Americans (oops, that won't go down well with my 'right-on' comrades of Belsize Park), and for driving a dented VW Polo (girl's car according to Michael) with fluffy dice and for wearing an Elizabeth Duke gold chain.

You see, the thing is, the inescapable and inalienable thing about me is that, sadly, I don't have the slightest crumb of fashion sense about me.

Not that my outré style of dress is in any way an affectation, or that I revel in it, it is just how I am – always six months behind everyone else. In fact, when asked to comment about fashion, all I can say is that it's never been one of my favourite David Bowie songs.

One person who could certainly teach me a hell of a lot about how to dress is Paul Smith, as this son of Nottingham has risen to become one of the most famous fashion designers in the world today.

Sadly, I wouldn't get the chance to ask him for any hints or tips about how I might be able to make myself look slightly less slovenly, since his secretary Carla sent me a very nice letter which read:

Dear Julian

It is a very interesting concept and thank you for thinking of Paul Smith. However, as Paul's schedule is particularly hectic over the next few months, unfortunately it is impossible for us to find a time for you to meet with him – sorry!

Good luck with the challenge and thank you for thinking of Paul...

These thanks were passed on to Michael, who came up with the list, although I'd like to say that apologies really are not necessary.

To be honest, despite my bold assertion that I would easily shake hands with 20 per cent of the 500, no problem, when the day of sending out my first few letters actually dawned, my tune was changed and I was seriously thinking to myself that it would be amazing if *anyone* were to respond to my daft letter, let alone agree to meet me.

Therefore, at this stage in the day, while receiving a 'Yes' to a meeting was cause for massive cheer for me, simply getting a reply of *any* sort made my day. So two in one day and it really was party time down my way.

However, I did once again hurl abuse at Michael when I next saw him, because his promise that all 500 of the people that I was expected to write to would be based here in Britain was starting to look as flimsy as a polystyrene tow-rope.

This is what Leah, the agent of Helen Fielding (author of *Bridget Jones's Diary*), stated in her email today:

Thank you for your letter of 8th October asking to meet Helen Fielding as part of your challenge in aid of the RNIB.

I am afraid that it will not be possible for Helen to meet you, the primary reason being that she in fact lives in LA and will not be in the UK before the end of the year.

With best wishes for your challenge and your fundraising efforts...

Michael's slapdash approach was really starting to get my ruddy goat.

How I wish I were in the shoes of Helen Fielding or indeed Samuel Pepys or Sue Townsend.

Oh to be writing an *interesting* diary.

Tuesday October 25th 2005 – Greeting 14 (Lorraine Kelly)

Waking up at 7.00 a.m. should not have been too alien a concept to me as I am normally up with the larks. In this instance, though, I am talking about Mr and Mrs Lark on Adelaide Road, (he's a night watchman and she's a hooker), who are rarely out of bed before noon.

I woke at the uncivilised hour of 7.00 a.m. because I was meeting Lorraine Kelly, fresh from her stint on GMTV, at 9.15 a.m. at the South Bank headquarters of ITV.

The 8.30 a.m. journey in the cattle truck otherwise known as a rush-hour tube train was a pretty miserable affair. No one wanted to be there and it wasn't long before the migraine inducing lights and a**e-crushing confinement of my carriage started making me feel really unwell. More than just a headache, an entire body ache of sorts.

By the time I arrived at my destination, and to incorrectly paraphrase a certain Swedish pop group, my my, at Waterloo my bones were feeling tender.

Fortunately, a glass of water in the foyer of television centre acted as a cure-all, and by the time Lorraine's assistant Gaye came to fetch me from the foyer, I felt right as rain. She really was an absolute darling and we chatted away merrily as she escorted me past open-plan offices where news crews appeared to be looking at me as if they were wondering why the photocopier maintenance man was being given a guided tour.

While we strolled along the corridors chatting, one very interesting topic of conversation did crop up though. It just so happened that Gaye also looked after another individual from my list, one that I wrote to several weeks back.

'By the way,' she said to me, 'I had a glance at the 500 names to see if I could help you out with anyone else and noted from your list that you've also written to Fiona Phillips. The thing is, I never received that letter and I'd hate you to think that she was rude or ignoring you.'

So there we had it, my worst fears were realised. In any project where you are attempting to greet 500 famous people, you're only as strong as your weakest link. For a while, I assumed that my weakest link might be incorrectly addressed envelopes or agents who binned my letter without opening them.

Following this revelation, a new, more sinister thought crossed my mind – that some employee of Her Majesty's Postal Service might have been too intrigued by an envelope marked 'T. Blair, 10 Downing Street' to pass it on, or even that someone who lived in the same block as me might have been intercepting the replies.

I'm not paranoid – I know you all think I am (that 'joke' © Jerry Sadowitz), but this non-arrival of my letter seemed rather suspicious.

I soon met Lorraine and bless her, what a little sweetheart she was. Maybe it was the reassuring squeeze of my shoulder or the fact that she complimented me on the originality of the idea (dare I say it, that's also a compliment to Michael), but I was truly entranced.

She even asked Gaye who else from my list might be around for them to rustle up for me, but unfortunately no-one was.

The picture was taken by Gaye and a fantastic gift was offered for the auction, one of Lorraine's dresses, together with a signed photo. In fact, both ladies were so nice to me and I was in such a fragile state of mind courtesy of the tube journey and my paranoia about my letters, that I just wanted to have a big group hug. However, that probably wouldn't have been a good idea because I do recall the security guard at the entrance being of a particularly stocky frame.

As I made my way back to the tube, I contemplated how on earth Lorraine managed to looked glamorous having presumably woken up unbelievably early, while I, who'd got far more sleep, had a face like the proverbial 'blind cobbler's thumb'.

Back at Waterloo, I encountered the 9.30 a.m. brigade leaving the station. They had an altogether jauntier look about them than their 8.30 a.m. counterparts. As for me, I just thanked the Lord that getting up at this hour was the exception and not the rule. For that matter, I thanked my boss, Marli, too.

Wednesday October 26th 2005 – Vertigo

...a great film by Mr Hitchcock, I am sure you'll agree, but in this case it refers to an affliction that I've suffered from since the age of about seven, when I fell off one of my grandmother's particularly high stools (no jokes please). Sadly, it seems to have got a lot worse the older I've become, and I now cannot get on any plane without at least two of the -*pam* pills rattling around inside me, be they *Diaze* or *Nitraze*.

Forfeit number five, in other words, one of those that I'd have to undertake should I fail to register more than 30 handshakes, was to ride Britain's largest roller-coaster.

I did a little research into this situation, only to discover that the future heralded the possible darkening of my underwear and passing out on a ride known as the Pepsi Max Big One at Blackpool Pleasure Beach

Wikipedia cruelly informed me that this ride is 213 ft high, 5 497 ft long, has a drop of 205 ft, a maximum speed of 87 m.p.h. and a ride on it lasts for 2 minutes 30 seconds.

It happens to be not only the tallest, fastest rollercoaster in England but also in Europe (forgetting the German one). On the plus side, there is a minimum height requirement of 4 ft 4 inches to ride it, so if all else fails I suppose I could hack my legs off as we approach Stoke on Trent.

Jules Segal

As desperate times call for desperate measures, another 12 letters were sent out today to **Terry Venables, Anna Friel (if only), Trevor Horn, Jasper Carrott, Willie Carson, Steve Cram, Simon Groom, Neil Kinnock, Kelly Osbourne, Ronnie Corbett, Naomi McLean-Daley** (a.k.a. Ms Dynami-Tee-Ee) and **Julian Clary.**

One letter each, I mean.

Thursday October 27th 2005 – Jumpers and Twitchers

Having informed the readers of my website of the above facts, I promptly received no less than four emails all informing me that if I were forced to go through with it, I would *love* my ride on the aforementioned 213-ft high reinforced tubular-steel fairground attraction. I assured them that they were all completely wrong. A man by the name of Barney T told me not to be 'such a pussy', so I reminded him that at least a cat lands on its feet.

I might actually do a B.A. Baracus, in the finest traditions of the *A-Team*, and get someone to knock me out before I ride the contraption (form an orderly queue) because I don't think that being flung around a carriage at 87 m.p.h., while in a state of unconsciousness, would be all that unbearable. In fact, that happens to me most mornings on the Edgware to Morden via Bank.

I needed to achieve more than 30 meetings to escape that particular forfeit, and considering I was already almost there, I wasn't actually losing a great amount of sleep about a potential date with my worst phobia.

My cause to avoid it was aided by Jonathan Edwards, without a shadow of a doubt the finest leaper into sand that this country has ever produced, as he had kindly become the latest from my list to agree to spare me some of his time.

I wasn't lying when I included in my 'Likes' list, 'Watching England, GB or the UK winning things', because I love my sport I do, and I suppose even the *Eurovision Song Contest* and *Miss World* and the Oscars are OK, so I distinctly remember getting very excited when watching Jonathan break the world triple jump record (18 m 29 cm, Gothenburg). After all, that's further than I can walk without getting a stitch.

As for myself, I was useless at athletics at school. I actually once threw the discus negative five metres. I also remember running the high-hurdles once and actually jumping *onto* one of them instead of *over* it, and almost cleaving myself in two at a particularly sensitive crease of the body.

Sadly, Bill Oddie will not be able to meet me.

In a rather long-winded way to contact Bill, I had sent a letter to his agent in Hampshire. I say long-winded because I had been led to believe that Bill himself actually lives just up the road from my residence and from time to time frequents Bacchus Greek Taverna for his souvlaki.

Such were the difficulties, you see, in trying to find *home* addresses for anyone on my list. Nigh on impossible, in fact, and rightly so: we are all entitled to our privacy.

Friday October 28th 2005 – Hair Today Gone Tomorrow

I had 95 days of my challenge left – I already had 55 per cent of my allotted time and was only now creeping up towards the 20-meeting mark. Barring a minor miracle, Michael had this bet in the bag, and it was simply a damage limitation exercise for me as I tried to stem the bleeding and plug up the dyke.

Brilliant, five clichés in of one sentence – a new personal best.

I would say that Nicky Clarke is the most famous hairdresser in the country. I can't think of any others myself (is Vidal Sassoon British?), apart from Charlie and Antonio, my Lebanese and Palestinian barber friends in Paddington, who shave my head once a month.

I don't think that 'Antonio' is the latter's real name, but more a nickname because he looks like Mr Banderas and he is just as smooth. From our discussions, it sounded as though he'd dated most of North London: women of every nationality, religion, colour and creed. He's done his bit for race relations.

So where was I? Oh yes, Nicky Clarke, who surely must be among the busiest of the 500, also turned out to be a real trooper. I was informed by his assistant that if turned up to his salon the following week, I would get the obligatory snapshot handshake.

Jules Segal

I have a lovely head of hair, but unfortunately it is on my back. I actually had a very pertinent question to ask Nicky: Why on earth is men's hair-dye so much more expensive than women's? For that matter, why is there gender specific hair dye at all? Hair is just hair, no?

I say this because I have to come clean, I *have* been known to dye my grey hairs from time to time, much to the mirth of everyone I know, although it's never been a secret.

Yes I know, I'm male, so string me up for even considering it. Not that I have to justify my actions, or Antonio's, but the reason I 'colour' *my* barnet is because naturally my hair is rather funny. I don't mean that it does some comedy stand-up routine (although often that's the case), but basically because it resembles the torso of a skunk.

'Salt and pepper' all over would be OK, but mine is generally salt on the side and pepper on top, like a fussy man ordering a fried egg.

Imagine if you will, someone with black hair standing in the middle of a room. Now imagine someone standing next to him with a thick paintbrush covered in white emulsion, putting the paintbrush to the man's temple and walking, say, 270 degrees around and behind the man until reaching the other temple (the top of the hair being unsullied). That is the direction that genetically my hair decided to take. I look like a negative image of a pint of Guinness. I was simply sick of being stared at on the tube, so...

Friday October 28th 2005 – Greeting 15 (Mike Leigh)

I was strutting my way down Hades Boulevard the other day (second turning on the left off Purgatory Lane), when I saw a plaque on the floor which read, 'Here lie the good intentions of Jules's so-called friends'.

I can honestly say that the preceding few weeks had been one of the most educating phases of my life. A real eye-opener. So much had been promised, by so many, with so few delivering.

I know that many people reading this will be thinking, 'Welcome to the real world', but in the past my default setting had been stuck on 'naivety'. It has now been switched to 'cynicism'.

I am not even talking about *Greeting the 500* here, or about friends and family members who claimed that they could 'help' me with my challenge, I'm talking about so many aspects of my life:

○ The lady in the movie business who might have offered me some work. A few weeks earlier I had sent her an example of my writing (the schizophrenic comedian thing), as she had requested, and stupidly thought that maybe one day she would send a reply, as one does, even if it was just to say, 'Sorry but your script is abysmal'. Nothing.

○ The former flatmate who frequently gushed, 'Oh you *must* come and visit me up in Edinburgh.' Now I actually needed somewhere to stay when I went to 'Greet' Iain Banks and left her FOUR messages. Nothing.

○ Potential tenants that viewed my spare room and said, 'Yes, very nice. I am seeing others, but I'll let you know.' Nothing.

○ A former school friend and his sidekick (a 22-year-old agent?) who claimed, 'Oh, I can *definitely* get you to meet another 36, no problem.' Nothing.

To quote the former England Manager Graham Taylor in one of his less articulate moments, 'What sort of thing is happening here?' Most mobile phone rates are still only 8p a minute, for heaven's sake.

Sorry to harp on, It is just that all of these examples happened in a very short space of time this October and my view of man and womankind had suddenly been adjusted accordingly.

I had, however, worked one thing out. It related to a number of people I had recently encountered who, on learning what my project involved, had said things such as, 'Oh, I can definitely get you a meeting with Dennis Waterman!' What they were actually doing was no more than running me through a list of any famous people they had ever encountered, as if having once spotted a celebrity at a party in Clapham would enable them to act as some sort of go-between. It actually turned out to be no more than basic showing-off.

This brings me back to one of the earliest points that I made in this book, namely how, and more importantly WHY, are we slowly developing into a nation of people, a collective consciousness, that heaps so much importance on the concept of fame?

Maybe it's because our top footballers regard a £100000 fine as pin money, or because our soap-stars are so readily invited to bring out pop songs, or because a majority of the well-known faces that we see on TV are able to behave so disgracefully in public, and get away with it, that we all want a piece of this action.

We are, as a nation, a living, breathing, 55 million-headed starry-eyed leech, desperate to suckle at the sour-milked bosom of Mother Celebrity. Well, lots of us are anyway. One thing's for sure, you'll never catch *me* name-dropping famous people.

By the way, I met Mike Leigh on this day.

What a top man he was. I was down at his offices in Greek Street and despite being rushed off his feet (having an interview with *The Guardian* lined up directly after me) I received the requisite handshake together with a signed photo for the auction.

So why did he agree to meet me for absolutely no personal gain to himself? He didn't have to. Maybe altruism does still exist. Hmm, let me just consider that one for a second.

Blood pressure dropping. Bile and spleen calming down. Cynicism levels decreasing. Yes, that's better.

Sunday October 30th 2005 – The Mercy of IA

The London Borough of Camden seemed to be getting more and more terrifying with each passing week.

Having talked about 'the road to hell' (the expression, not the Chris Rea song) in a recent offering, I was, coincidentally enough, actually *in* Chalk Farm on this lunchtime. It's just down the road from my home and bears all the customary scars and pockmarks of your average inner city suburb, dried bloodstains on the pavement outside the pub, public telephone box used as a lavatory... that sort of thing.

I'd gone there with my friend Emma, because we'd decided that after the excesses of our respective Saturday nights, we ought to try and eat healthily for Sunday lunch.

On leaving *Marathon Kebab*, I witnessed something that I'd never seen before as two young lads sitting by the door, were trying to light an 'outdoor' firework, 'indoors'. Possibly they were not well-versed on the Health and Safety at Work Act 1974, or indeed the firework code.

Remarkable? Well, I just remarked, didn't I?

As the title suggests, today I threw myself upon the mercy of the International Artistes talent agency. They had the capacity to hugely help me in my quest, merely by passing on the gist of my letters to the 10 respective individuals from my list whom they represented. If that were to happen, I was hoping to get at least one or two meetings out of the fruits of their labour. Alternatively, I was aware that they might simply throw all of my letters in the bin.

I prayed that they take the former course of action.

So, 23 DL plain white 100g/m² A4 Fast-seal envelopes, were duly sent out to **Julie Walters**, **Paul McKenna**, **Ellen MacArthur**, **Damon Gough** (*Badly Drawn Boy*), **Michael Mansfield QC**, **Colin Jackson**, **Jim Davidson**, **David Puttnam**, **Steve Redgrave**, **Jamie Oliver**, **Jason Queally**, **Jimmy Tarbuck**, **Paul Merton**, **Barry Davies**, **Lisa Riley**, **Paul Daniels**, **Eddie Large**, **Derren Brown**, **Nigel Havers**, **Martin Offiah**, **Leslie Ash**, **Les Dennis** and **Joe Pasquale**.

I needed help. Fast.

Monday October 31st 2005 – That's Bad Technique is That

According to health and safety rules*, anyone who works in front of a computer screen in an office is allowed at least ten minutes off in every hour, in order to give their corneas a breather. So if your boss asks you why you're reading a book at your work station, just tell him/her that I said you could. I'll take the rap. I don't mind.

A recent ten minutes off of mine involved closing my eyes, reclining in my seat and listening to *Heroes* by David Bowie and then *No More Heroes* by The Stranglers in quick succession on Youtube (www.youtube.com). I am not sure if Marli, my boss, had a problem with what I was doing because I had my eyes shut and headphones on, but if you see me down the DSS office next week you'll know why.

---

*This information might not be correct.

Anyway, my concentration was finally broken by a strong vibrating sensation in my genitalia, so I removed my mobile phone from my trouser pocket and left my open-plan workspace for a closed-plan toilet cubicle, where I could speak in private.

Rachel Boycott was a delightful lady. We had a good old chinwag where she apologised that Geoff, her husband (who if you do not know, happens to be one of the most accomplished cricketers that this country has produced) had not yet got back to me, but that he had been in South Africa.

He was then scheduled to jet off to Singapore, then South Africa again, then Pakistan, and sadly would not be around in this country until long after my project was over. I told Rachel that unfortunately no, I wasn't planning to be in Islamabad the following spring (Autumn maybe), but not to worry and that it was good to talk to her and that I'd plug Geoff's website on my website.

That I did, so I'd like to think that Geoffrey now owed me one.

Monday October 31st 2005 – Greeting 16
(Jonathan Edwards)

After a short drive across North London, and an act of violence threatened against me by an agitated driver on the number 23 bus that I cut up, I arrived at the Paddington Hilton, where I met Jonathan.

I do like ambling around in marble-foyered hotels, particularly in London because it makes me feel as though I'm on holiday, which reminded me, I had to go to work later that day.

I've managed to stay in the Hilton for free before. It was in Bangkok. I found my room slightly cramped and was puzzled by the bars on my window and the fact that I was expected to wallow in my own filth... Actually, I'd better stop there, before this particular hotel chain decides to seek compensation for slander. The Bangkok Hilton is of course the nickname given to the notorious Bangkwang Prison in the Thai capital and no, I was never incarcerated there.

I fled the country.

Back to this morning then, and on arrival I tiptoed through the tourists looking for our world-class triple jumper, but I'm not very fit and Jonathan is, so I found a chair near the revolving door in the hope that *he* would find *me*.

Thirty-five minutes later, and as hope was starting to ebb, we eventually caught up with one another by the huge weeping fig, which was just behind the nattering Spaniards. Jonathan apologised that his prior meeting had overrun and for the fact that he was in a bit of a hurry, but I reassured him that the whole process would take no longer than the duration of an Olympic 400-metre race.

A kindly concierge, whose name I didn't catch although he looked like a 'Leonard', took the fine photo you might find somewhere in this book (if Jonathan allows me to use it) – a photo spoiled only by the fact that I was in it. Then with a hop and a skip (but no jump) I was away again.

Back at work and I took the opportunity to quickly update my website so that I could personally wish anyone reading it a happy Hallowe'en/ All Hallow's Eve/Samhain or whatever they might call it in their house, although I'm not sure if this pagan celebration of the dark months is meant to be a particularly 'happy' one.

It would be happy for me though, as I was off to a party that night, where I looked forward to supping wine and wearing a superbly designed costume that would make me look like one of the 'undead'.

In other words, one of the 'living', so just a T-shirt and jeans then.

CHAPTER 6 – November

Friday November 4th 2005 – Greeting 17 (Nicky Clarke)

The only problem with having a bright idea is that someone else has probably already had it first.

It was my intention to write to Channel 5 back in 2004 with a concept for a game show that I first saw on Australian TV while living in Sydney and which I became hooked on. I was going to sell that idea for £2.25 million (despite not having the rights to it) and retire to the Hotel du Cap Eden Roc in the South of France, to live the rest of my life smeared in Hawaiian Tropic, basking in the sun and wolfing down plates of *foie de veau* and *crevettes*. Then I noticed that Channel 4 had recently discovered *Deal or No Deal* for themselves and my plan was scuppered.

I'm sure that the concept of asking a glut of celebrities to rally around a total unknown in order to raise money for charity had been done many times before.

For example, after talking to a friend of mine at about this time, I was informed about the work of Andy Gotts, a photographer, who had spent eight years taking snapshots of A-listers in America, each subject being asked to refer Mr Gotts on to another of their A-list friends in a real life game of '6 degrees of separation'.

Eight years he spent! Poor guy. You get less than that for ABH. I couldn't bear the thought of trawling round the country for eight more *weeks*.

The news that I was merely the latest in a long line of those to have 'challenged' the famous did help my general mood and melancholy air. The recent mildly depressive mindset had come about through a number of factors:

○ my failure to yet break through the '20 Meeting' barrier;

○ my failure to garner a solitary response in the preceding week;

○ my failure to interview a potential new flatmate who wasn't either (a) insane, (b) Austrian or (c) an accountant;

○ my failure to secure 'extra borrowing' (due to peanuts income);

○ the fact that my most serious relationship in the last few months had been with Lara Croft;

○ the fact that my left lung hurt when I inhaled.

On this day I greeted Nicky Clarke. In my opinion, the world needs more Nicky Clarkes. Not only is he a gifted craftsman, teasing the hair of his customers into a state of sheer perfection and thus providing a valuable service to improve the lives of countless well-to-do women, but he is also prepared to offer some of his precious time to aid some daft bloke complete his daft celebrity meeting project.

I left work early to attend Nicky's salon in Mayfair and emerged blinking into the crisp November air at Bond Street tube station at 5.15 p.m. where, fortunately, there was no cold November rain.

It was here that the pungent Oxford Street aroma hit me, a smell that is no doubt familiar to so many frantic shoppers. That sickly sweet smell of nuts being swilled around a wok-full of sugar and being roasted by a man who, to be unfair, wasn't the most hygienic of looking vendors I had ever seen. The sign read 'caramel roasted nuts', but judging by the proximity of this cooking apparatus to one of the busiest thoroughfares in the world, a more accurate description would have been 'part peanut, part caramel, part sulphur dioxide and a trace of polycyclic aromatic hydrocarbons'.

The other familiar smell was the cloying stench that was oozing out of every scented-candle shop this side of Christendom, which instantly reminded me that there are only 51 shopping days until Christmas, and that I now knew what to buy for everyone I hated.

So it was, in this queasy state, that I made my way down South Molton Street, around Grosvenor Square, past fortress US Embassy and onto Mayfair.

I was still 35 minutes early, so I decided to do a quick circuit of Berkeley Square in the hope of finding a discreet watering hole that was devoid of any chirping nightingales. As I plodded round, I stopped briefly outside the exclusive *Annabel's* club, to consider whether or not I should pop in to enquire about membership prices for this prestigious establishment, but then remembered that I was wearing the wrong shoes, wrong clothes, wrong face.

Eventually, I found a crowded little pub, the sort of pub that I like, i.e. instead of being full of polished wood and chrome, one that had migraine-inducing patterned carpet, thick fabric curtains and could double up as your average living room in Penge.

I had a wee dram of the rare mountain dew, completed the Sudoku puzzle on the back of a beermat (fantastic idea) and retraced my way back to Nicky's salon.

I didn't have to wait by reception too long before I was whisked upstairs, where my generous host was midway through applying curlers to the hair of a very glamorous young lady. This young filly happened to be Nicky's daughter and so interrupting him made me feel a little guilty, but he was fine about it and within 30 seconds of having the photos taken, I was out of everyone's hair for good – because they swept it up.

So, what we were left with, not for the first time, was a picture showing the smiling face of one of the 500 individuals from my list, next to my ridiculous gurning and unphotogenic expression. Unbelievably, I once again looked like a cross between a startled camel and the class idiot in some backwater Mississippi school. Amazing.

Sunday November 6th 2005 – Kate Moss…

(I thought that would get your attention) …had returned to Europe from America and was at this time engaged in a number of photoshoots around the continent, none of which, regrettably enough, included mine. She had her own problems to deal with.

Ben Fogle was rowing across the Atlantic, Jim Davidson was on his way to the Dubai Comedy Festival, Salman Rushdie, I believe, was still incommunicado and I had been told that Michael Barrymore had emigrated to New Zealand. And here I was, wondering why I hadn't received any replies from the recipients of my letters for a few days. I had clearly gone about this in a stupidly haphazard way. If I had even the tiniest shred of nous or wits about myself, I'd have found out the contact details for the entire 500 before the six-month bet had started and sent all of the letters off on day one; but I didn't.

I deserved everything that might befall me. All I could do was just plough on regardless, like an ox in a trance and so I therefore compiled another 17 letters that would hopefully soon be opened by: **Paula Radcliffe, Kirsty Young, Alexander McQueen, Todd Carty, David Dimbleby, David Beckham, Sacha Baron Cohen, Richard Stilgoe, Miranda Richardson, Hugh Laurie, Sting, Sue Townsend, Phil Tufnell, Alan Titchmarsh, Kate Moss, Keith Flint** and **Jane Torvill**, or the agents thereof.

Monday November 7th 2005 – Greeting 18 (Chris Tarrant)

I am not one to argue with songwriters of the ilk of Burt Bacharach, but I have to disagree with his findings to the rhetorical question, 'What do you get when you fall in love?' Forget all of that nonsense about girls bursting bubbles with a prick, the answer, at least to me, is a hefty overdraft.

I only mention it because that was one of the songs that I listened to as I drove up the A1 to Elstree to meet Chris Tarrant on this rain-spattered evening and yes, a journey which, amazingly enough, my decrepit car did just about make.

While I'm on the subject of song lyrics, I read the news today, oh boy, about a fight somewhere near Leicester Square. And while the news was rather sad, well I did actually have to laugh (although there was no photograph). A friend of mine from University who had somehow become something of a movie mogul in recent years, was spotted trading blows in a gutter with George Clooney. The story was on the front cover of the Currant Bun (*Sun*).

Perhaps this ex-friend of mine was currently engaged in his own project, I thought: 'Duffing up the 500'.

Today I was expecting to greet two of *my* 500. I turned up at Ann Widdecombe's office very early doors although I still do not know what that expression means.

After the rigmarole of going through security at her Westminster office, where the receptionist worryingly told me that Ann wasn't expected in for a while, I waited in the foyer until her assistant Annalinda arrived shortly afterwards, walking towards me with a piece of paper in hand.

That paper turned out to be a print-out of the email that I had sent to her several weeks earlier, confirming that I would be arriving at 9.00 a.m. on *Thursday 10 November.*

So, not just egg on face but a complete full English, even including one of those small bits of black pudding that everyone leaves. My head had been so vacant recently that if someone had offered me a penny for my thoughts I'd have been forced to give them change.

The evening's 'Greeting' went much more according to plan. I was welcomed to Elstree by a delightful, and dare I say it, stunning Antipodean lady. Oh, I do like Australians and their habit of starting sentences with the word 'Look...' when they are mildly annoyed.

Shona wasn't annoyed, she was lovely and after a walk and a chat, she ushered me into the *WWTBAMillionaire* studio where I was taken under the soft, downy wing of the floor manager and was allowed to watch that evening's contestants being put through their paces by Chris.

They all looked rather nervous in their plain monochrome shirts, shirts of many pastel colours, which, combined, would have made a lovely coat for Joseph. I guess by the time that you read this, one of them will be considerably better off, while I will still be involved in constant financial wrangles with the bank that doesn't listen.

Chris was extremely amiable, and suggested that we have the photo taken by the *Millionaire* 'Hot Seat' which was actually quite thrilling for me. It was a lot taller than it looks on TV, and I was left to imagine what it would be like to sit on it for real.

My general knowledge is actually quite strong. For example, I know that honey is the only food that never spoils, there are more psychotherapists per capita in Buenos Aires than anywhere else in the world and a bluebottle's average speed is 4.5 m.p.h.

However, I baulk at asking how you like 'those apples', as I already did so on September 19, but not bad, eh?

Tuesday November 8th 2005 — I am Buzzing

I'd hate to ruin the Charles Dickens masterpiece, *A Tale of Two Cities*, for anyone who hasn't read it, for example by announcing that the wizard dies after being thrown off the tower at the end of the book, but I can reveal that for those living in eighteenth-century Europe, it was the best of times and strangely enough it was the worst of times.

As paradoxes (or is that paradoxen?) go, that one's a bit of a head-scratcher, but here's one I made earlier: I hate wasps, I love Wasps.

In my opinion, the stinging insects serve no discernible purpose other than to procreate, eat and attempt to induce anaphylactic shock in yours truly.

The rugby club on the other hand, sometimes known as the London Wasps, shall from this time forth and forever more be close to my heart.

I confess I know little about rugby, but the sporting icon Lawrence Dallaglio, who has won just about everything there is to win in the game and who currently plays as flanker for Wasps, had agreed to meet me at a later date.

I was severely put off rugby at school because of my 'Twiglet' physique and my balsa-wood endoskeleton, for although I grew to an average size for a 14-year-old, that wasn't until I was about 20.

Wednesday November 9th 2005 – Big Ben Strikes Again

On the subject of my search for oxygen, with which to fan the flames of publicity for my project, several days prior to this date I had written to Typepad (as in www.typepad.com) who host my website. I had learned that they promoted a handful of 'blogs' from their pages every few weeks and hoped that they might show just a glimmer of interest in mine.

I must say, I was a tad insulted, therefore, to note that this week in question they had instead decided to bang a drum for such mundane fare as: *Forest Project* (forest 'scapes from an aspiring forest photographer), *Ben Roethlisberger* (Big Ben's personal entries and photos) and one called *Healthwise Agewise*, that seemed so tedious that I dropped off while thinking about how to describe it.

Who the hell was 'Big' Ben Roethlisberger anyway and why the hell should he get special treatment? I decided that he was probably having an affair with someone in the Typepad offices.

Elsewhere, and this is entirely true, I was hovering around some run-down looking church on this evening when I was shot at and almost killed by a lunatic wielding an MP5 SMG semi-automatic rifle. That honestly *is* a true story.

Therefore, if anyone has any hints about getting past level 3 of 'Medal of Honour: European Assault' on the Playstation 2, I'd be most interested to learn how as I've still not completed it. Not that I had a misspent adulthood, it was just far more entertaining than trying to track down contact details for Christine Hamilton.

Meanwhile, I also had some extremely positive news, as I was informed that two fine and upstanding members of the 500 had agreed to a meeting with me, both in the same place and at the same time, so not only would my tally increase by two, but the whole shooting match would be a very simple procedure (unlike the one on 'Medal of Honour' it seems).

Crimewatch's Nick Ross and Fiona Bruce are obviously both very good sports and I would soon get to know the reception area of the BBC like the back of my hand.

Happy in this knowledge, I decided to round off the evening by reading 'Big' Ben Roethlisberger's diary to see what he'd been up to over the last few days. Chewing several large hamburgers no doubt.

Thursday November 10th 2005 – Greeting 19
(Ann Widdecombe)

I believe that it was the famous philosopher Ludwig Wittgenstein, in his great work *Tractatus*, who asked '...Why so many aspiring writers feel the need to quote from famous philosophers in order to pretend that they are intelligent'.

I'm not intelligent.

Earlier this week I turned up for my meeting with Ann Widdecombe two days early, having copied down the date of our meeting incorrectly. When I met her this time, I was ten minutes late, although on this occasion my own stupidity wasn't to blame, rather the stupidity of the bloody Jubilee Line train that decided to park itself in a tunnel just south of Green Park station for 15 minutes.

At least I had my iPod to keep me company, listening to *Hits of the Eighties* on loop. I never realised how good the music of A Flock of Seagulls was, including their seminal hit *I Ran So Far Away* (possibly only known by individuals born between the years 1960 and 1978, or owners of 'GTA San Andreas' on the Playstation), although I cannot agree with what Rose, an American friend of mine at work, says.

She tried to convince me that the song is basically about the failure of democratised Western nations to foresee the danger that is presently emanating out of a certain Persian state, purely because it is on the other side of the world.

I, however, noticed the space between the 'I' and the 'Ran' and also that the song was written in 1985 and concluded that it was actually about someone who was running a great distance.

Bearing in mind my errant journey earlier in the week, this entire morning was a case of *déjà-vu*. I felt as though I now knew the ticket collectors at Westminster, as well as the security guards and receptionists in Ann's building personally.

Ann herself, and indeed her PA Annalinda, were most welcoming. My tardiness wasn't in the least bit held against me, and I was invited to have the photo taken with the fantastic backdrop of the Houses of Parliament behind my noggin, as you may see.

Following a brief chat, where I tried to garner Ann's opinion of the death penalty (I think she pretended not to hear my question), the Right Honourable MP for Maidstone and the Weald asked who the other MPs from my list were. On being informed, she immediately picked up her phone and dialled the office of Boris Johnson, to see if he was around, which I thought was extremely kind of her.

I confess to feeling slightly embarrassed that Boris might actually answer the call only to be ordered against his wishes to shake the hand of a random stranger, so I think I said something like, 'Ann, don't worry this really isn't a three-line whip. I don't want to trouble him', to which she replied, 'Nonsense! Boris would be happy to do something like this, it's just that getting hold of him can be a bit difficult as he's sometimes a little disorganised.'

I replied that I'd noticed.

Although I didn't further reply that he'd looked positively all over the place the time I nearly knocked him off his bike on Shaftesbury Avenue.

He wasn't about, anyway.

As I left, I was given a generous gift for the RNIB auction, a signed copy of Ann's book, *The Clematis Tree*.

Here's a thing. I once had a number of clematis plants growing on my balcony. That was before my flat was let out to a couple of idiot Scandinavian vegetables (or Swedes as they preferred to be called). They clearly had brown fingers, not in a rude sense, but it's just that when they vacated my apartment and I moved back in, I noticed that

Jules Segal

all of my plantlife was dead including said clematii.

I was heartbroken.

Saturday November 12th 2005 – Tour de Forces

I was beginning to get tired, so very tired of this little game that I had started playing on July 1st. If I could go back in time, aside from stealing some of the Brinks Matt gold, and asking out the lovely Nathalie who used to sit in front of me at White Hart Lane all those years ago, I would have reconsidered shaking hands with one person in particular – Michael's when I made the bet.

Anyway, at least I had discovered the root cause of my trivial health problems and vivid nightmares over the recent months. You see, rather than spending the preceding four months doing what any normal young man in his early 30s would be doing, that is to say, getting plenty of exercise, eating well, earning money, spending that money on alcohol and searching for his life-partner, I had been spending all of *my* spare time licking envelopes and updating a pointless diary. In fact, this was the reason that I had been forced to come into work on this particular Saturday.

When I arrived in Farringdon at 9.00 a.m. this morning (Saturday, I would like to reiterate), I wondered why I hadn't yet heard the news that Britain had been invaded during the night.

Apart from the special forces operatives standing outside my office building holding their Hechler & Kochs, there were literally billions of police swarming all over the City of London – no exaggeration.

There was also a Challenger CR2 Tank blocking my way on Aldersgate Road, and a Band of Her Majesty's Royal Marine Commandos strolling down Long Lane and piping out *Who Do You Think You Are Kidding Mr. Hitler.*

It was only then that I remembered that this was the day of the Lord Mayor's Show, the day when the 'City' part of the city of London comes to a standstill and that somewhere down there Clare Balding was freezing her bits off while narrating this procession of the nation's armed forces to a much warmer TV audience.

154

TONY HAWKS

JIMMY CARR

JOHN MOTSON

'Pleased to be in the book,
even without my sheepskin coat!'

JEFFREY ARCHER

PATRICK MOORE

DAVID
GOWER

'Meeting Julian was all too easy.
It is probably only because he was far too polite
that he failed to meet all 500.'

LISA
RODGERS

'I thought he would have been
taller in real life
– Lisa Rodgers (5ft nothing).'

CHERIE BLAIR

ASAD AHMED

'I think Jules squeezed me in between Tim Rice and Cherie Blair. It's not often I find myself in that position!'

TIM
RICE

'Those who refused to meet this great 21st
Century hero, clearly have a distorted view of
their own self importance.'

GARY
LINEKER

LORRAINE KELLY

MIKE LEIGH

'Frankly I thought he was stark raving mad.'

JONATHAN EDWARDS

CHRIS TARRANT

ANN WIDDECOMBE

'It must have been one of the most inventive bets ever thought up! I wish I had been half as inventive in the cause of charity.'

CLARE BALDING

'Well done.'

NICHOLAS PARSONS

'It is always nice to meet someone who is a little different and has an eccentric idea.'

JASON QUEALLY

'Good man.'

JOHN
FRANCOMBE

JOHN
McCRIRRICK

'I met Jules Segal and survived!'

LAWRENCE
DALLAGLIO

IAIN BANKS

'Dearie me. What a pillock I look.'

NICK ROSS

'He didn't look too happy to appear
on *Crimewatch*.'

FIONA BRUCE

'I've always wanted to meet David Beckham. Perhaps I should try your tactic.'

ALAN TITCHMARSH

RICHARD WILSON

'Meeting Jules was one of those life enhancing moments. It simply changes you evermore.'

DAVID SUCHET

BRUCE OLDFIELD

DERREN BROWN

'I thought Jules was extremely charming and had impeccable taste, as exemplified in his blog statement that I was much nicer than any of the other 'celebrities' that he met. I just hope he mentions this in his excellent book.'

NEIL KINNOCK

'Very British: bit crazy, quite harmless and a nice fellow. Raises cash for good causes.'

ANDREW MARR

'Funny way of not earning a living but fair play.'

BOB HOLNESS

'What a nice chap. Asked me for a 'P'. Luckily I know where the gents is at the National Theatre so I pointed him in the right direction!'

CARL
FOGARTY

'I was happy to help with Jules' quest to
take over the world.'

JOE
PASQUALE

EDITH
BOWMAN

SIR
RANULPH
FIENNES

'Good luck with all
you do Jules.'

LESLIE
GARRETT

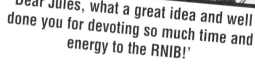

'Dear Jules, what a great idea and well
done you for devoting so much time and
energy to the RNIB!'

AINSLIE
HARRIOT

GARY BUSHELL

'A pleasure wasting time with you. Next time bring beer and borrow Britney's clippers. Well done for raising cash for the RNIB, now name and shame the bums who snubbed you.'

TOBY ANSTIS

'Julian you're a top man with an infectious sense of adventure! We and the RNIB are dead proud of you!'

It could be argued, then, that this morning wasn't the best day for me to turn up to work to find contact details for the senior vice president of Walmart Stores Inc. and to enter it into our company database. You see my concentration was slightly broken by the 45 or so brass bands that thundered past the window.

Before long, the sights and sounds, impressive though they were, started to wear a little thin, thanks largely to the nature of my hangover. That was, however, until I sojourned to the roof for a sneaky cigarette, while watching (despite my vertigo) and listening to a band made of young RAF cadets, as they passed by five stories below me.

Smiling away in the mid-morning sunshine were 40 or so young men and women of every race, creed and colour, marching in unison under the flag of our nation, sworn to defend it as friends and as comrades.

I've got to say, that really did give my usually bitter and twisted heart a massive fillip and I was soon aware of a non-phlegm-based lump that had appeared in my throat. God bless this great nation of ours, I thought, before driving home in my German car.

I want to, nay need to, inform you of a couple of replies that I received on this day, both in the affirmative to a handshake.

Jason Queally was the only cyclist on my list of 500. Having won an Olympic gold medal for GB and having laid claim to being the fastest man on the face of the earth without use of a motor, I think Michael did very well to include him. I hoped to make his acquaintance outside the Oval Cricket Ground in the not too distant future.

Meanwhile, the Right Honourable Neil Kinnock or, to use his correct title, Baron Kinnock, former leader of the Labour Party and former VP of the EC, had also kindly agreed to accept my request. He therefore became the first of the Welsh participants to agree to a meeting, although I could find just three others on Michael's list: **Charlotte Church**, **Colin Jackson**... and **Anne Robinson**(?).

As I took to the wheel of my car that afternoon and drove past what looked like a camel and *was* in fact a camel, being led past Barbican tube station, I heard the roar of nine fighter jets as they soared overhead. I am not sure what sort of craft they were, but if I were to hazard a guess, I'd say airplanes.

Jules Segal

◇◇

Well, there you go, just a couple of days after talking about my dead clematis, not to mention the yucca and the ficus, I got an email from the personal assistant of Alan Titchmarsh. She wasn't writing to suggest that I move my plants nearer to the window, or I give them less water, or even to inform me that the renowned gardener would be arriving in person to resurrect my balcony on a shoestring budget, but just to let me know that Alan *would* be available for a photograph the following month. Much obliged.

I had awoken early this day, partly through fretting that it was taking me far too long to send out the 500 letters and partly because of another peculiar nightmare that I had suffered. I don't want to bore you with the details of it.

But I will. My history teacher of 16 years ago, Mr Winterbottom (real name), had set us an exam on the historical significance of the film *Casablanca*. He started shouting at me because I had written about an exploding sheep, '...In all the bars in all the world ewe had to walk into mine.' I got 17 per cent and was expelled.

So, despite once again being cream-crackered, I was still able to summon up enough energy to reel off another 70 letters in just 25 minutes.

For my next trick I will sit for 92 days in a hollowed out block of ice suspended over the Statue of Liberty, eating only tinned corned beef and Aquafresh.

The next recipients of my requests coincidentally included three former sets of sweethearts, a mother and daughter, the female cast of *The Good Life*, the male cast of *Men Behaving Badly*, three-fifths of the cast of *The Young Ones* and almost the entire cast of *Jonathan Creek*, so there's a little quiz for you.

In alphabetical order they were: **Donna Air, Nicole Appleton, Tom Baker, Helen Baxendale, Sean Bean, Kate Beckinsale, Ian Botham, Kathy Burke, John Cleese, Martin Clunes, Steve Coogan, Hugh Cornwell, Alan Davies, Bobby Davro, Darren Day, Angus Deayton, David Dickinson, Adrian Edmondson, Ben Elton, Colin Firth, Dexter Fletcher, Andrew Flintoff, Emma Forbes, Martin Freeman, Emma Freud, David Frost, Richard E Grant, Lesley Grantham, Ainsley Harriot, Amanda Holden, Bob Holness, David Jason, Natasha Kaplinsky, Peter Kay, Penelope Keith, Ross Kemp, Felicity Kendal,**

Jude Law, Robert Lindsay, Maureen Lipman, Nicholas Lyndhurst, Rick Mayall, Neil Morrissey, Tara Palmer-Tomkinson, Nicholas Parsons, Billie Piper, Eve Pollard, Su Pollard, Caroline Quentin, Esther Rantzen, Alan Rickman, William Roache, Linda Robson, Patricia Routledge, Julia Sawalha, Alexei Sayall, Suzanne Shaw, Michaela Strachan, David Suchet, Liza Tarbuck, Emma Thompson, John Thomson, Johnny Vegas, Dennis Waterman, Rachel Weisz, Paul Whitehouse, June Whitfield, Richard Wilson, Claudia Winkleman and Ray Winstone.

I headed off to the post office, to spend a fortune on stamps.

Tuesday November 15th 2005 – Bits and Bobs

Sadly, the runner Paula Radcliffe would not be able to take part in my challenge as she was currently involved in warm-weather training on the other side of the world and would remain there for much of the winter.

Although I was informed that she may be in the country over the immediate Christmas period, perhaps on the day itself, I guessed that the last thing she would want to see over the sprouts and brandy butter was someone grinning inanely with an outstretched arm and a camera.

My friend Michael, who as you well know by now set me this bet, was by mid-November happier than the proverbial 'fat kid with cake'. He was by now almost certain to win the wager, as I was still 82 handshakes short of my target and had only 77 days left. He had therefore started to strut about like a particularly proud cock(erel).

Not only that but he had also just started his new job, shifting vases around the stage of the Garrick Theatre and had been talking about Edward Fox, the lead actor, as though they were best mates.

'Yeah, he's a really nice guy. We've got loads in common...'

'What do you mean?'

'Well, we both work in theatre and we've both worked the Palladium.'

To cap it all, would you believe it, he'd only got someone of the female persuasion to accompany him home the previous week and apparently she wasn't, as I had suggested to him, a cycloptic lady wearing an eye-patch.

For my part, having recently been moaning about a lack of physical contact with those of the cellulite-afflicted gender, I would like to inform you that I had spent much of the previous evening with a delightful wench called Melanie. I met her in the Hill Tavern and she had agreed, amazing as though it felt at the time, to actually see me again.

I think I hit rock bottom, sex-wise, on Saturday morning while watching the Lord Mayor's show from work; it was then that I decided that I would try to spring into action with a bit more vigour. After all, three and a half months without female company through the night is a long stretch in anyone's books and I'd like to think that my new-found desperation had paid dividends.

If there is one thing I know about women, it's that they are REALLY attracted to desperate men.

My website also seemed to be ticking over nicely, I was getting about 3200 'hits' per day at this stage, not as many as the BBC's site, I suppose, but probably more than the official Liechtenstein Office of Tourism page.

Things were slowly but surely starting to look up.

Apart from the bet of course.

Saturday November 19th 2005 – If it is Broken – FIX IT!

Amazing really, in an age where we can put men (and theoretically women) on the moon, and where we can make a healthy and nutritious snack out of dried noodles, a plastic pot and boiling water, it is still sometimes impossible to connect to a website for over three days.

Now, I've never been one to apportion blame, but in my opinion it was all Typepad's fault. The bad news was that because of their inability to function as a reliable organisation over those few days, they had major problems in hosting websites. The good news was that I would be receiving a little bit of financial compensation.

So actually that's bad news and irrelevant news to you... an expression I've heard once before in fact.

In the 'real' world, a lot had happened since I illegally posted a copyrighted picture of Paula Radcliffe on my website four days earlier. The daily stories of horror and carnage continued to flood in from around the world, 50 deceased starlings had been found in quarantine and an angry Irishman had left a famous football club. Oh, and I had received two replies and had one 'Greeting'.

First of all, I certainly owed a quick thank-you to David Gower and Chris Tarrant, who had in the intervening days both sent me rather smashing items through the post for the charity auction. I do baulk at using the word 'Smashing' as it's usually only heard in American films starring Hugh Grant, but there's no other way to describe the great gifts. The highest bidder would be very happy with them indeed: signed clothing and VIP tickets to *WWTBAMillionaire*.

I also had to thank Fiona Phillips who'd agreed to meet me a couple of weeks further down the line. She'd been collared by the extremely industrious and helpful Gaye, who you may remember I first met on the day of my meeting with Lorraine Kelly.

David Dickinson was away in Australia at this time, a country I have a huge amount of time for. I'd have dearly loved to swapped places with him, but I don't think that he'd have been up for working in data entry for a legal publishing company in Central London.

He'd soon face the possibility of having to scoff scarabs, blowflies and the reproductive sections of a wallaby, not because there was a sudden shortage of food in Queensland, but because he was about to appear on the engrossing *I'm A Celebrity, Have You Got Any Indigestion Tablets?* or a title to that effect. You know the show.

His agent, Natalie, gave me a call and said that a meeting would obviously not be possible while he was in a tropical rainforest, as the Number 83 from Dalston takes rather a long time to get there. However, she told me to get in touch once again in January to see whether something might be sorted out at that stage.

Another for the 'maybe' pile then.

Jules Segal

Yesterday was chilly, wasn't it (although you probably don't remember it now)? Despite the cloudless sky, and even though I was cosseted in the warm interior of a VW Polo driver's seat, I could tell that at street level it was a day for mufflers and thermal long-johns. This message was hammered home as I drove through Royal Oak on my way to Windsor racecourse to meet Clare Balding, as it was there that I spotted a smattering of chubby American tourists who were dressed as though London was in the Svalbard archipelago in the Arctic Circle.

The drive itself didn't take long and I even managed to wangle myself a space in the 'Staff' car-park, meaning that my walk to the entrance of the racecourse was shorter than one that any lazy git could hope for.

On my little amble, I almost trod in a puddle which, despite having being bathed in morning sunshine, still had a covering of ice on it. I therefore concluded that the 'going' at the racetrack that afternoon would probably be described as 'Good to Concrete'.

A friendly lady from the BBC production team handed me a 'Members Enclosure' badge and ushered me through the turnstile to where Clare was pre-recording a bit of the show.

Once finished, she turned to me and announced, 'Ah, Julian I presume,' whereupon I made a crass joke about Dr Livingstone and an expedition to the Zambezi, which she kindly glossed over.

I know that I continue to mention this fact, but everyone that I had greeted so far had just been so down to earth and friendly. My cynical Cypriot friend should be ashamed of himself with his 'famous people tend to elevate themselves above the masses' nonsense. In any case, he was probably getting them confused with helicopter pilots.

Clare was most obliging. We had the photo taken and I was given an autographed race-card for the auction. I then asked her a question that she was, more likely than not, asked every day of her life. A question that she was no doubt sick of hearing...

'So, do you have any tips?' I enquired, half expecting her to reply with the old 'yes, never eat yellow snow' line.

'Not really, I'm afraid. No. Let's go and ask Richard (Pitman),' who happens to be another member of the BBC Racing team. This was good news, I thought to myself, as we approached him. Here was a former champion jockey with almost 500 wins to his name, a notable racing journalist, an owner and trainer of a number of horses and father to another notable jockey. If *he* didn't have any juicy tips, I didn't know who would. The pound signs flashed before my eyes.

'Richard, this is Julian. He wants to know if we have any tips for today,' Clare said as I stood forlornly next to her. At that precise moment, I had a flashback to my youth, where fear would get the better of me and someone else was usually roped in to asking a pretty girl if 'she'd dance with that boy over there in the corner'.

A simple 'No,' was his reply and he turned round and carried on with his work. Fair enough.

Well, seeing as I'd been given a racecard, I thought that it would be rude not to wander off and waste some money.

The 1.30 had seven horses in it, so I checked the form of the jockeys and the form of the trainers. I assessed the conditions, looked at the 'Stopwatch Ratings', checked past results, found out who the runners were sired by and finally, did what I normally do – picked one whose name was funny.

In this case I was hoping there might be one with a name that was linked to my project, such as 'The Greet Gatsby' or '500 Not Out' or 'Weirdo Handshaking Freak', but there wasn't. Instead, I went for one called Julie's Boy, for no other reason than my name is Julian.

I discovered that my pick happened to be the favourite, which translates as 'not much money back, but may still fall at a fence'. I walked along a line of gesticulating men who were taking everyone's money while looking like a group of Saint Vitus' Dance sufferers, and then I sat eating my prawn cocktail-in-a-cup, trying to work out if 10/11 was better odds than 5/6.

Whatever, the bet was struck and wouldn't you know it, my horse only went and bloody won! A £10 bet and £19.09 returned. This is so easy, thought the fool, who was soon parted with all his winnings plus more when Border Tale came in nowhere in the next.

I only stayed for the two races but revelled in the thought that I could do it all over again when I went to meet John Francome at Newbury in a few weeks' time.

Jules Segal

Progress from Windsor, where I met Clare, back to North West London was an extremely long, drawn-out affair. Fair enough, it was a Friday afternoon just short of rush hour, but I always assumed that people were rushing to *leave* the Capital for the weekend, heading for their two-up two-downs in Bracknell, not vice-versa.

As I sat motionless behind an Ocado lorry that was presumably bursting with fresh fruit and wafer-thin ham, I noticed an incoming call on my mobile phone. I believe I was just approaching the A312 junction with the M4, for anyone following my progress on Google Maps.

Well, anyway, the number was one that seemed very similar to my own home phone number so I assumed that it was either Mr Rumsey calling to tell me that plumes of smoke were spiralling out of my kitchen window, or perhaps the Haverstock Arms wanting their beer garden table returned (just a joke – I couldn't saw through its chains).

It turned out to be Nicholas Parsons.

Indeed, I'd suspected that he might live in my neighbourhood, having seen him a few weeks earlier eating in the tapas restaurant on Haverstock Hill, I'm not sure what it was, possibly *gambas al ajillo*. Anyway, he did indeed live near me and agreed to meet me the following week in what would surely be the most convenient of my 20 or so meetings to this point. We were to convene in a hotel, not the Dorchester (which is an oblique reference to a film that I once saw starring the aforementioned actor), but one that was very close to both of our respective apartments. It was no more than a two minute walk from my flat.

It certainly beat the 400-odd miles I'd be travelling to meet Iain Banks in Edinburgh.

That girl from The Hill. I'm meeting her again next Saturday.

Monday November 21st 2005 – Drug Store Psychology

Here is a précis of the work of Jill Neimark, a lady that I know little about and who you know even less about. That's assuming that you're not Mr Neimark.

I found her piece entitled *The Culture of Celebrity* on the internet on this day, and wanted to share its summary with you, not because I deemed it relevant to what I was doing, or indeed that I even understood it, but primarily because I wanted to pad out my diary entry and this fitted the bill quite nicely:

Summary: argues that the nature of fame has changed in modern times, and that celebrities, and their fans, are diminished by the process. Assertion that modern celebrities are crafted from 'images marketed, sold, and disseminated' rapidly; how technology has changed fame so that it is far more immediate, instantaneous and easily disposed; celebrity in the information age; why we know too much about celebrities; the increase in the number of celebrities; media images

Whatever.

I lost my voice again and it remained AWOL for quite some time. Every time I swallowed it felt as though I'd eaten a pin. I blamed the crazy weather we were having. Apparently, this summer had been the hottest for 50 years and we were soon to shiver in what was expected to be the coldest winter ever... not to mention all the hurricanes and earthquakes and such like.

Perhaps Doomsday *is* approaching after all. I hope not. I want to find out what happens in the last Harry Potter book and if England can ever win the World Cup.

Well, without much time to spare before Gabriel's trumpet was blown and the four seas collapsed in on each other, I decided that it would be wise to hurry up with my letter sending and so **Andy Murray**, **Moira Stuart**, **Mark Lewis-Francis**, **Jensen Button**, **Jo Brand**, **Amir Khan**, **John Simpson** and **Kelly Holmes** were my latest targets.

Jules Segal

Unbelievably, yet ANOTHER sleep-interrupted night. I was woken by what sounded like an angle grinder or some heavy artillery being used in another flat in my building. Meanwhile, the Group A beta haemolytic streptococcus had spent a busy few hours propagating in my throat, and my breakfast plate fell face down onto the living room carpet – '*oeuf à la terre*' as the French might call this dish.

No, it had not been the greatest morning. I received an email to tell me that on further reflection, BBC London News would NOT be able to do a short piece about my challenge after all (a complete 180-degree turn) and Hugh Laurie, actor, comedian, voice-over artist and general wit and raconteur, sadly would not be able to meet me.

A letter from his agent, a very reliable soul obviously, since my letter to Hugh had only recently been sent, informed me that the subject in question would be out of the country for the next few months, which was starting to become something of a common theme.

I suppose what I didn't realise when I made this bet, was that because of the very nature of the successful lives of these 500 individuals, duty would call them abroad at the drop of a hat. Perhaps I should have been given more than six months?

Or my own twin-engined Bombadier Learjet 45?

Friday November 25th 2005 - Greeting 21
(Nicholas Parsons)

Although the following sounds like a joke, it's not, and I'd wager you wouldn't have heard an exchange like this 20 years ago.

Two burly looking builders working on scaffolding on my street, one says '... it was delicious. It was a ciabatta covered in a creamy basil and pesto sauce.' The other replies, 'I've got to say, I prefer ricotta.'

Britain truly is becoming a feeding ground of multicultural gourmands. Or maybe just perhaps someone, somewhere, in some marketing company should be getting a massive bonus.

I heard the tail-end of these culinary deliberations as I made my way up the road to meet Nicholas Parsons in the foyer of the Belsize Park Holiday Inn, and while thinking about, if I'm totally honest, what Melanie's breasts would look like if released from the constraints of their bra cups.

As everyone and their parrot had been telling me that this was going to be the coldest winter since dinosaurs roamed the earth, I was well wrapped up against the elements, colour coordinated too, in brown-hooded tracksuit top, beige coat and my honey-coloured cords.

I've always thought that 'Honey-Coloured Cords' would be a great name for a pop group. Then again I've thought the same about 'Visiting Patel', ever since I placed a notice to that effect in my car windscreen when illegally parked by a large block of flats in Belsize Village (I'd simply copied someone else's note).

I digress.

I arrived slightly early at this peculiar little hotel that abuts the local BP petrol station and which can't contain more than about 12 rooms. I've no idea how it could be considered economically viable, but I suppose that's a question for David Webster (Chairman of the Intercontinental Hotels Group).

Within a few minutes Nicholas came in from the cold, like a spy, and I introduced myself before cursing the weather, without actually cursing. Unfortunately, there was no receptionist, doorman, concierge, chambermaid, porter, bell-boy, chef or, indeed, any staff member to take the photo for us, so I was forced to bother an American guest who was busy reading his *Herald Tribune*.

He made a brief joke about the idiot-proof nature of Michael's camera, 'Oh, it's a PHD camera.'

'*Is* it? *Is* it really?'

'Yes, it stands for press here, dummy.'

'Oh right, yes, very good,' I conceded (I don't think Nicholas was particularly amused, either), before the obligatory hand-clasped snap-shot was taken.

That was it, really. I had a brief conversation with Mr P about how I wasn't required to greet all 500 people on the list to win the bet (a common misconception), my target being only 20 per cent, and how much we both enjoyed the local *tapas* restaurant, and then it was once more unto the breach dear friends, or unto Kennington to be precise...

After I left Belsize Park's smallest hotel, I had a little time to spare before meeting the Olympic gold medal winning and world-record breaking cyclist Jason Queally, so I decided to spend that time catching up on sundry chores that had been nagging at me like a frustrated wife... or husband.

These included buying a birthday present for a seven-year-old girl (fluffy pink diary and chocolate coins – Toys-R-Us, Brent Cross), eating (an Anthony Worral Thompson egg and bacon sandwich – BP petrol station, Park Lane) and fretting over my finances (with bank manager Rob – South Kensington Branch), so as you can see, all the while I was gradually making my way down to South London.

On arrival, I decided to drive twice around the egg-shaped Oval Cricket Ground looking for a suitable parking space before electing to illegally dump my car just outside the gates of the OCS Stand, where the meeting was planned.

It was then that a thought crossed my mind (nothing to do with Melanie and edible chocolate underwear) for I realised that although I'd watched Jason magnificently secure his country a gold medal at the Olympics some time ago, I'd forgotten exactly what he looked like.

The next 15 minutes were therefore spent staring hopefully into the eyes of each well-dressed dignitary that passed me by to enter the ground. I suppose I must have looked like the forlorn dog in Battersea, longingly staring at potential new owners. It didn't work and I can only assume that those who strolled past me thought that I was some sort of oddball with a squint.

However, before too long a tall, well-dressed man in a heavy overcoat approached me, smiling and rather than asking to be taken back to his home to be fed Pedigree Chum, I enquired if he was Jason.

'Indeed, I am,' he replied in what sounded like a Liverpudlian accent, whereupon I decided to refrain from telling him the joke about the

Spaniard who used to park outside Liverpool's Anfield Stadium on match days (Carlos) and instead thanked him for helping me out. Just as well, really, as he turned out to be from Lancashire.

'No problem, mate,' he beamed, 'but it won't take long though, will it? I've got to go to a talk in there in a minute'.

'Don't worry, it'll take no longer than the press of a camera button.'

As it turned out, it would have been quicker to reinvent the wheel.

Unfortunately, owing to the fact that there was once again no-one around to take the photo, I decided to ask a young man in the security 'cube' by the gate whether he would do the honours for us. To say that his grasp of English was poor would be doing a disservice to a deaf Nepalese goat-herder.

I believe that I had to repeat the line 'Wiiiiill yooooou taaaayyyke a photograph of us,' three or four times before he eventually smiled, nodded and said, 'Ah yes. I understand. No, I am not allowed to take photos.'

What the ... ?

Jason and I were therefore forced to walk up to the stand to find an alternative option and while doing so, I uttered something about not understanding the link between sprint cycling and cricket (we were at The Oval).

The basic answer was that there is none. It turned out that the Oval was hosting an event geared toward helping children to succeed in sport. It transpired that many sports personalities would be turning up and, as if to prove a point, as we entered the stand, rugby player Rory Underwood brushed past us and as I recall, gave me a most quizzical and suspicious look. One that you might give to a hyena that had wandered into a crèche.

Anyway, once inside, we asked this lovely, salt-of-the-earth, northern lass named Angela if she could take the picture. She was more than happy to help, and having been told of the problem that we encountered with the man at the gate, she simply responded, 'He's obviously a moron.'

Well said, young lady.

Jason then plucked a signed cycling jersey from his pocket and handed it to me for the charity auction – what an absolute star – before bidding me farewell and skipping up the stairs.

So that was it. Done AND done. Two meetings achieved this day, no hypothermia caught, two more the following day and a date that evening.

I believe that as I retired to my cluttered bedroom to mull over all that had gone before me and that lay ahead, I couldn't but help sing that song by ABC to myself... 'Everything's good in the world, tonight!'

Makes a change.

Saturday November 26th 2005 – Greeting 23
(John Francome)

If Noel Coward was accurate when saying that only mad dogs and Englishmen go out in the midday sun, can we also assume that only jet-lagged Australians and postmen go out at 7.30 a.m. on a freezing Saturday morning in North London?

The answer is probably no, because my postman doesn't arrive until 11.00-ish; however, I was milling around at this ungodly hour on this morning, since I was preparing to enjoy a day at the races for the second time in little over a week.

Don't get me wrong, I am not an addicted gambler, the nearest I get to a fruit machine is when I walk past the electric juicer in my kitchen, it's just that my rescheduled meeting with former Champion Jockey and current Channel 4 Racing pundit John Francome, was taking place at Newbury. It was Hennessy Gold Cup day, which doesn't mean that everyone would be drinking cognac out of expensive goblets, it just meant that there was an important race on.

On my way to the racetrack, I stopped to pick up my photographer for the day, a Greek friend of mine by the name of Demitris who happens to be a waiter in Michael's mother's restaurant in Hampstead (Bacchus Greek Taverna – for a fun night out, etc., etc.), and who happened to love a flutter on the old geegees.

The two of us trundled up the A41, around the M25 down the M4 and along the A4, in the process my passenger educating me about all sorts of important titbits about the Sport of Kings, such as the difference between a Super Yankee and a Canadian (which are not simply terms for our North American friends but are actually complicated bets that one can waste money on), the difference between a Class 1 race and a Group A race (I can't remember) and why Scarlett Johansson is so undeniably beautiful.

OK, so the last one wasn't about racing, although I'd put my shirt on her any day of the week.

Once at the racetrack, we made our way to the TV trucks and once again I met the delightful Dinah, whom I first encountered several months ago at Newmarket. On that occasion I had failed to meet John, since he'd been called away at the last minute to watch his nephew play for Wales against England in a World Cup qualifier.

Dinah was again an absolute angel of delight, inviting us into the TV trailer to thaw out, tracking down our host and giving us Premier Enclosure vouchers which enabled us to access all areas of the ground. Meanwhile, her colleague gave me a satsuma, possibly because my complexion and shivering body made me look like a rickets sufferer.

Following this, and as directed, we made our way to a suite that was above the 'weighing-in room' and up a metal flight of steps. It was there that we met John and his entourage who gave us a very warm reception. Demitris took some excellent photos, John signed a copy of the Jockey Club rulebook for the auction while repeating the mantra of 'No problem, no problem, easy as pie...' to my grovelling platitudes and even his Channel 4 co-commentator Jim McGrath gave me a memento which would also be auctioned off.

I felt a bit sorry for Jim, actually, who was presumably wondering what on earth was going on, why all this fuss was being made of John by some starry-eyed autograph hunter, and why he himself hadn't been asked for a single snapshot despite his kind gift; a shame he wasn't on Michael's list.

As if all of this wasn't the cat's pyjamas, the bee's knees, and dare I say it, the canine's scrotum, I was then invited to indulge in a second and unexpected greeting, since John McCririck who also happened to be one of my 500 targets, was upstairs in the press box.

Following a brief phone conversation between the two Johns, where

Francome didn't as much ask as *tell* McCririck that he should have his photo taken with me, we were directed to the top floor of the Berkshire Stand where the second greeting would take place.

Saturday November 26th 2005 – Greeting 24 (John McCririck)

OK, it is, as they say, a fair cop. You have got me bang to rights, whatever that means.

A number of people continued to scrutinise my website every day – amazingly enough, the figure at that time possibly exceeding the average attendance for Torquay United home games – and I was sure that among all of them there were one or two who were sticklers for the rule book and who were, by then, well-versed with the regulations laid down by myself and grumbling-boy when the bet was struck.

Notably, regulation (1) – The Anti-Stalking Clause – I wasn't to approach any of the 500 listees until they have actively acquiesced to a 'greeting' in advance. Well, in the case of the betting pundit John McCririck, I had not even sent my letter out to him yet.

Seeing as how I was making pretty slow progress (76 or so meetings still needed) and how I only had a couple of months left and, most importantly, seeing as how Michael wasn't around to whinge at me and quote rules, I decided to do a Rhett Butler. I didn't give a damn.

In addition, the 'Big Mac' *had* agreed to meet me, telling John Francome as much on the phone. That was good enough for me, in as much as a third-party had passed on the news that the handshake could take place. It wasn't as though I had approached someone cold, even though I myself was.

So there you had it. Demitris, who was itching to rush off and place some bets, and I, who was just itching, took what was labelled 'The Steward's Lift' up to the top floor of the Berkshire Stand and entered a door that was marked Press Room. We were suddenly confronted with the sight of numerous newspaper hacks, all of whom had a fantastic view of the entire track and who were busy sharpening their pencils and wits.

'Hmmm, I don't think he'd be in here,' I mentioned to Demitris, who looked agitated, possibly because the 1.00 from Lingfield was moments from the off and he hadn't lost any money yet. We entered the next door along the corridor, this one was marked Press 'Box' instead of Press 'Office' and found ourselves in the same room, just ten yards further down it.

It was then that, as luck would have it, a kindly journalist, which isn't a contradiction in terms, pointed out that John was in fact in the room, sitting in the back row, so I approached him and gave a short garbled speech that included the words 'handshake', 'charity', '500' and 'celebrities'. John looked momentarily taken aback, remembered his conversation with John Francome, and then boomed, 'Happy to do it, though I'm no blooming celebrity.'

I refrained from replying, 'Well, you *were* on *Celebrity Big Brother* once,' remembering that no-one likes a smart ar*e and after all, he was doing me a favour. It appeared that the kindly journalist had differing views about smart ar**s, since he chuckled 'Another modelling assignment, John?' as we headed for the corridor.

The Big Mac was friendly and amusing in equal measures and after the photos were taken, I asked him whether he'd been pulling faces behind my back (I could see him doing it). 'Not at all,' he replied and winked at Demitris. I therefore assume that he had a passing bout of lockjaw in the picture you might be able to find somewhere in these pages.

Well, the less said about the rest of the day the better, I'll simply provide a few facts and figures: races watched, 5; bets on winning horses, 0; hairs pulled out, 370; ambient temperature, $-3°C$; swine in a baguette eaten (with crackling), 1; tailbacks caught up in on way home, 3.

Sunday November 27th 2005 – Singleton Once More

Me: 'So how's it going with that lass you met recently?'

Michael: 'Who, Julie?'

Me: 'If you say so.'

Michael: 'Not very well. I'm probably not going to see her any more.'

Me: 'Why not? I thought you said she was quite good-looking.'

Michael: 'Well, she was but she's only 21.'

Me: 'Michael, that's a *good* thing.'

Michael: 'No mate, she played silly little girl's games, probably because she's a silly little girl. Kept phoning up to meet and then cancelling at the last minute. I'd be better served cutting off my own todger.'

Me: 'What, like Geoff Huish?'

Michael: 'Who?'

Me: 'Never mind.'

Michael: 'Anyway, what about *your* date last night?'

Me: 'What, Melanie? Yeah, she stayed over. She's only just left in fact.'

Michael: 'Really? Well, I can't see it lasting more than your typical six-week relationship.'

Me: 'You're wrong, Michael.'

Michael: 'I bet I'm not.'

Me: 'You are, Michael.'

Michael: 'Yeah, right. How can you be so sure? What, are you in *love* with her already?'

Me: 'No, I've split up with her already... not that we'd even been attached yet.'

Michael: 'Eh?'

Me: 'Yeah, strangest thing. After a lovely meal, drinks, return home, slap, a bit of tickle and kip, she announced this morning that she probably couldn't see me again. Something about her ex being back on the scene.'

Michael: 'Unbelievable. I suppose it doesn't say much for your ability in the sack, heh heh.'

Me: 'Oh, piss off... I didn't hear any complaints at the time.'

Michael: 'I can't believe her mouth was *totally* full? Ha! Well, anyway, if it's any consolation, I've heard that excuse millions of times before.'

Me: 'Really? Me, just four.'

Michael: 'You know what this means, don't you?'

Me: 'Yeah.'

Both of us in unison: 'They're all nuts.'

Incidentally, on the subject of scrotums, and I promise not to dwell on such an unappetising subject, I do hate to say 'I told you so,' but if you scan my words earlier this month, where I mentioned the reply I received from David Dickinson, I also mentioned that this year's particular entrants on 'I am a Celebrity Get Me Out of This Rat-infested Rain Forest', could well end up having to eat the naughty bits of a kangaroo – from this evening's television viewing I was right.

Tuesday November 29th 2005 – Greeting 25
(Fiona Phillips)

I went to my barber's in Paddington, for a short back and sides. The sides turned out fine, but the hair on my back still wasn't short enough. Anyway, while I was there a thought crossed my mind.

My barbers are Lebanese and Palestinian, my dentist is Indian, my local cabbies are Portuguese, my grocer is Turkish, my golf buddies are Irish, my plumber is Polish, my boss is Namibian and my neighbour is Columbian. After work, I drink in a Japanese bar with Brazilian barmaids. My last three girlfriends were Scottish, Italian and South African and my best friend was a Greek-Cypriot Englishman. My point is this – I love this melting pot that is London.

I met Fiona Phillips today, TV presenter and one who has just finished dancing in a ballroom in a strict manner. I have to say, what an utterly, utterly lovely woman. Now, I've been accused by one friend, who would from to time to time skim through my diary, of brown-nosing the people I'd met so far. This is possibly true, but to be honest I was just giving the facts. I was reacting to first-hand evidence.

Jules Segal

At the ITV offices I was met by Gaye, who'd looked after me in my previous greeting of Lorraine Kelly. Unfortunately, I looked a bit dishevelled and bleary-eyed because the builders upstairs from my flat were by now banging one pipe *each* at a stupidly early hour and they weren't even in rhythm with one another. If I had a hammer, I certainly wouldn't hammer in the morning – it's just plain selfish.

Anyway, after waiting for a short while in '*la chambre verte*' as we pretentious types like to call it, and having nabbed a cinnamon Danish that had my name on it (that edible ink is a fantastic invention), Fiona turned up.

This greeting turned out to be the longest I'd spent with any of the 25 individuals I had so far met. Gaye took the photo, and I couldn't resist a hug with Fiona although I would like to point out that it was she who offered, as I myself am a stickler for protocol.

After that we chewed the fat about subjects such as *Strictly Come Dancing*, Fiona's tip as to who might win it (Zoe Ball), reality TV shows in general, having to eat the tail of a rat in an Antipodean rainforest, my project and how it was going, the possibility of having a short feature about it on GMTV (out of Fiona's control unfortunately), the correct way of addressing Patrick Moore (Sir, we both concluded) and the fact that I wasn't some geeky autograph hunter as Fiona thought I might be.

Geek or no geek, I'll let you decide. I'll simply highlight the fact that very first sentence that I used on my very first website posting back on July 1st – 'And so it begins...'. It was a direct quote from *Lord of the Rings* Part I. Enough said.

Wednesday November 30th 2005 – Better Read Than Dead

Good news. According to the front cover of this day's *Evening Standard*, doctors could now perform face transplants.

I let Michael know. I don't suppose I can talk, really – not exactly the face that launched 1000 ships, more like the face that buffered 1000 trains.

I read another interesting article on Ceefax. Apparently children with

174

lower levels of growth hormones swilling around inside them, along with the turkey twizzlers and sunny delight, tend to have lower IQs.

May I respond with the following: I am both short (5 ft 9 ins) and a member of MENSA (141).

The other week, I learned that actress Zoe Wanamaker, who appeared in such roles as Susan Harper in the sitcom *My Family* and Madame Hooch (a name that conjures up images of a dominatrix alcopops drinker) in the Harry Potter films, would sadly not be able to meet me due to work commitments.

On this final day of November I learned that Robert Lindsay who plays Ben Harper alongside Zoe in *My Family*, would also be unable to meet because of a heavy workload, so perhaps I have the full house?

I first remembered seeing Robert in the show *Citizen Smith* in the 1970s. It was a comedy about a character called Wolfie, a Marxist-Leninist urban guerrilla who was a member of the Tooting Popular Front.

That made me think of Michael and I. Michael was an urban gorilla and I was a Marxist–Leninist. I'm a big fan of Marx and I often quote him. Just the other day I said to someone, 'I never forget a face, but in your case I'll make an exception.'

Actually, I'm a dyslexic Marxist. I live by the motto, 'Workers of the world, untie!'

OK, I'll stop now.

CHAPTER 7 – December

Replies received: Bob Holness, Joe Pasquale, Derren Brown, Robbie Coltrane, Richard Wilson, Jamie Oliver, David Suchet, Freddie Flintoff, Richard Branson, Kelly Holmes and Ian McKellen.

Meetings achieved: Lawrence Dallaglio, Iain Banks, Nick Ross, Fiona Bruce, Alan Titchmarsh and Richard Wilson.

Thursday December 1st 2005 – Wholly Cow

◇◇

...and so we entered December, the cruellest month. Or is that April, I'm not sure? I had just six weeks left of this little project, one that I had found, on occasions, enjoyable, but more often than not time-consuming and expensive.

As far as the bet went, I was slowly starting to pick up. I no longer had to undertake several naked swims off Brighton beach the following February, for which I was eternally grateful. Apparently, the Gilthead Bream of the English Channel are very partial to maggots so I'd been spared a bit of pain if nothing else.

Jules Segal

I no longer had to run the following year's London Marathon which was fortunate since, as several people had pointed out to me, it was unlikely that Flora or whoever organised the whole shebang would have permitted my brittle frame from entering it. I'm a heart-attack waiting to happen.

With several more meetings pencilled in, I no longer had to conquer my fear of vertigo by riding the UK's biggest roller coaster. No, at that moment I was stuck on Forfeit 4 and unless I received a couple more agreements to meetings in the following two months, I would soon be having to put my hand up a cow's rectum.

Please do not lambast me if you happen to be an animal lover (I am too – you should see some of my exes), this wasn't an act of cruelty, it was just that Forfeit 4 read: 'To help a rural vet in checking on a cow's pregnancy situation (by sticking arm up rectum of said cow) *although* I wasn't too sure how we'd find a vet willing to help us, or a willing cow for that matter.

Bob Holness had become the latest from my list to agree to a meeting. His PA Ros, whose phone call I accidentally returned while she was in the 'cereal aisle' of her local supermarket, sent me an email two days prior to this. It brought massive cheer to my heart after reading just the first sentence:

Dear Julian,

Bob was intrigued by your letter and is happy to help you to try and achieve your goal...

What a fantastic man. I would be meeting him outside a theatre in Drury Lane the following week and then could celebrate by ceremoniously burning a pair of rubber gloves, as the bovine surprise might have to be put on hold after all.

Friday December 2nd 2005 – Greeting 26
(Lawrence Dallaglio)

Before I detail my meeting with this legend of Rugby Union today, I would like to briefly mention another sport that uses the oval ball.

This other sport sees its heavily padded and helmet wearing players, whose names are invariably Antwan, Terrell, Le Dwayne or Andre, grouping themselves in a huddle and shouting out a series of random, unconnected numbers, like an overeaters convention in a Chinese restaurant.

So why do I briefly want to mention American Football? Well, only because it appears that I had done a large man by the name of Ben Roethlisberger a huge disservice.

You may recall that I was whingeing about Typepad.com, who rather than showing interest in promoting *my* website, were highlighting other tedious looking efforts such as *Forest Photography* by A. Dullard, or Ben Roethlisberger – *Big Ben's Personal Entries and Photos.*

Well, it transpires that Typepad.com were not in fact simply promoting the observations of some random fat bloke, but were in fact puckering up and kissing buttock of the rich and famous themselves, since 'Big Ben' happened to be the quarterback for an important team called Pittsburgh Steelers, so little wonder then, that he had his site splashed all over the Typepad home page.

Therefore, I hereby formally apologise to Ben... because he looks massive.

I made my way to Wasps Rugby Club in Ealing on the preceding Friday at the invitation of team manager Nolan Miller and Lawrence Dallaglio (The one on the right in the photo).

I was a little apprehensive to be honest, as in my paranoid way I'd envisioned the team of boisterous young sportsmen stripping me and leaving me tied to the goalpost, or worse, pointing at my scrawny body and laughing hysterically.

I need not have worried; everyone I encountered was most genial. I had a chat with Nolan about my project and then Lawrence was waved across to the touchline even though he was in the middle of a training session. This was despite my protestation of 'Oh please don't disturb him if he's busy', to which some wag who was warming up behind me jokingly replied, 'Don't worry he'll just batter you to the ground.'

He didn't.

Lawrence was an absolute gent, we took the photos, he mentioned that the club charity rep would send a couple of mementos on to me for the RNIB charity auction and he gave me a couple of autographs.

Jules Segal

He therefore not only made my day, but also the day of Ify, a work colleague of mine. She'd spent a good portion of our office Christmas Party the night before, eulogising about rugby players and Lawrence in particular. She would apparently be placing the autographed sticker I gave her under her pillow (although I believe she may have been joking).

So, a huge thank you to Lawrence then, and to Nolan and indeed to everyone else connected with Wasps (obviously apart from Rentokil or the like).

Sunday December 4th 2005 – Greeting 27 (Iain Banks)

The undeniable fact is that yes, I must have been completely barmy. I don't mean totally Crackersville, Tennessee, I just mean in a single-digit IQ sort of way.

I was cavorting around the country spending money that I didn't have, trying to shake famous people's hands and all because some crabby man believed that well-known people were self-serving.

If you don't believe me when I say that, at this stage, I was seriously considering selling my poky flat since I could barely afford to keep it, please feel free to phone Mr Bradford, Mr Bingley, Mr Egg-Creditcard or Mr Norton who financed my Personal Loan and ask them how much they were owed.

On the Saturday of this weekend I took a day-trip to Edinburgh to meet my favourite author Iain Banks, or Iain M. Banks if you prefer. I wasn't too sure how to go about getting there; should I take the high road or should I take the low road? In the end I opted for the very high road – I flew. (BAA London Heathrow to Edinburgh – £110.50 incl. airport tax.)

Honorary photographer for the day was one of my oldest and dearest friends Eddy B, who like me was a big fan of Iain's work. His surname hasn't been foreshortened to preserve his anonymity, he's always been know as Eddy B.

This good mate of mine has a fair few 'Roberts'. What I mean to say is that he is not short of a bob or two, although far be it from me

180

to discuss anyone else's finances (which I appear to have just done, oops); he also happens to be ridiculously generous.

Having already written out a healthy cheque to the RNIB at my behest, for which both they and I shall remain eternally grateful, he also offered to drive me up to Edinburgh in his new sports car, although when he mentioned 'I've only just bought it and I'm a bit worried that I might kill us both,' I suggested taking the plane.

The flight itself wasn't too terrifying although midway through it, so round about Leamington Spa I suppose, I got a little concerned when I stared out the window and thought that I saw a shape in the clouds that resembled Christ's head. I feared that this might be a bad omen. On reflection though, it looked more like David Seaman, which I feared to be an even worse omen, bearing in mind I am a Spurs supporter.

I soon calmed down though when I reassured myself that seeing this Turin Cloud was probably a good thing and that I wasn't likely to plunge to a fiery death because Jesus actually 'Saves' (as did David Seaman come to think of it... occasionally).

We arrived in 'Auld Reekie' in good time, yet despite being 90 minutes early, we took a cab ride to our meeting point with Iain (The Café Royal Bar), because we heard that it had a very fine restaurant and because we were hungry, and because Eddy B was paying.

I had the venison paté followed by the salmon and my dining partner opted for the langoustine, a bold choice as it so happened.

I must confess I was a little edgy during lunch, as on returning from the toilet I thought that I noticed Iain dining on a table near ours. The man in question was sat behind me and I asked Eddy B to scope him out in the mirror beside us. Ed confirmed that he did indeed have glasses and a beard.

How embarrassing, I thought. 'We must look like a right couple of stalkers,' I said to Ed, who replied, 'Oh, so what. Just shut up and eat your deer offal.'

Thankfully, it turned out not to be the famous author after all, since, having scoffed our posh tucker, we popped next door to the bar section of the building at the allotted hour and were just in time to see our host enter through the external door in a smashing autumnal light-brown ensemble.

Once again a 'greetee' who turned out to be extremely hospitable and friendly. We exchanged pleasantries while I waited for my photographer to emerge from the crapper and then we all went outside for the official picture and handshake ceremony, where we were hindered only by some idiot tourists waving behind us while Eddy B was waiting to take the snap. Presumably, they were French.

So that was it then, a 4-hour round trip for the purposes of a 2-minute conversation, a photograph and a brief hand-warming. Iain signed some autographs for me, signed Ed's copy of *The Wasp Factory* and mentioned that he would post me a signed copy of his new book for the auction, before going on his way.

As for us, we wended our way up a steep hill towards Edinburgh Castle where we briefly took in a stunning vista of this historical part of the world before deciding that we'd rather spend the hour that we had left in the city, drinking whisky in a smoky beer cellar. After all, you can't do *that* in London.

Monday December 5th 2005 – Santa's Grotto

Now 'tis the winter of our seasonal affective disorder, yet in this gathering hibernal gloom I had accumulated quite a little collection of gifts for the charity auction that was to be held come the end of the whole debacle.

I was rooting around in my cupboard where all the gifts were kept, the other day, much as a fat pig would root for a truffle, when I accidentally fell through a secret door at the back of the cupboard that I never knew existed.

It was weird. I was suddenly transported to a mysterious, freezing, wind-swept wasteland where a frightening yet regal lady all dressed in white offered me some Turkish delight and a large feline pranced away in the background.

So now if I ever need to go back to that pet shop in Wood Green, there's no need to take the tube. By the way, if you're wondering, yes that was a reference to *The Lion, The Witch and The Turnpike Lane Shopping Precinct*.

The story above was, of course, made up apart from the rooting in the cupboard (hmm, reminds me of an office Christmas party). Here is one that wasn't.

I was standing in line in a Hampstead post-office the day before this (100 from my list still to write to), listening to a Danish couple arguing behind me, and watching a dear old pensioner slow everyone's progress by scooping vast quantities of 1p and 2p pieces from her purse as if she was some sort of fairground game, when I noticed a rack next to me containing dirtily cheap CDs.

A mere £1.99 for 'A Complete James Bond CD'. 'Cor blimey guv'nor that's cheap,' I thought to myself in an affected cockney manner, while checking that the album did indeed contain all 22 theme songs. I am not a huge Bond fan (just 5 ft 9... sorry, I've used that one before), it's just that I do love Carly Simon's honey-on-toast voice and particularly the theme song from *The Spy Who Loved Me* and even more particularly the end bit with the manic violinist.

Imagine my disappointment, therefore, when I got home having bought it and discovered that the theme tunes were not in fact originals, but were performed by some miserable charlatans.

The young lady who mangled Carly's song into a bloody pulp, truly had the voice of an angel. Yes, an angel with numerous polyps on her vocal chords and a crushed windpipe. It was like amateur karaoke night at the OK Coral.

So that was my day. The only real thing of note (unlike the lady above) was that I now had a new flatmate, Lois, a charming young lady who happened to work in a profession where, from time to time, she would come into contact with people who really can sing.

I would, therefore, briefly like to thank her for passing on details of my challenge to the agent of a certain Aled Jones.

Wednesday December 7th 2005 – It's Just an Illusion

Two replies received, both from generous souls agreeing to help me on my way.

An email from a fine young lady by the name of Nicola, mentioned that a former king of the celebrity jungle, Joe Pasquale, would be happy to meet me. I would, therefore, be making my way to Birmingham in

January whence the funnyman would be appearing on stage in a J. M. Barrie classic.

Another email was from 'Coops' who looked after the affairs of Derren Brown, illusionist of huge talent and a man who doesn't need to sit in a glass box sucking glucose off a blanket in order to wow *his* audiences. I was very excited about this one. Perhaps he might be able to look into the future and tell me whether I was going to lose this bet. Then again, that one wasn't exactly the most puzzling of conundrums.

I spoke to the Cypriot Leviathan, just five minutes after receiving this second email and told him of this latest progress.

'Dan Brown? I don't remember putting the author of *The Da Vinci Code* on your list of 500.'

It was good to know that Michael was aurally dyslexic as well.

Thursday December 8th 2005 – Another Bumper Crop

A few drinks after work (well 'tis the season to be merry) saw me stagger home late last night to a heaving postbox, which coincidentally enough wasn't the only thing that turned out to be heaving, although that's another, rather unpleasant, story.

I drunkenly opened said letters while listening to Handel's *Zadok the Priest* on the TV. It's not that I'm a particular fan of classical music, it's just that this happened to be the theme music for the UEFA Champions League and I was tuning in to watch Manchester United's decline and fall against Benfica.

So what quirks of fate had befallen me? I'd received one jiffy bag sent by Orange in order to return the Nokia N70 that I didn't wish to upgrade to but *would* like to smash to pieces for being confusing to use. I had one letter from Camden Council demanding £100 for the cardinal sin of straying into a bus lane on Kilburn High Road on my way back from meeting John Francome (maybe he'd pay?). I had one letter from Egg letting me know exactly how much money I didn't have and one note from Royal Mail informing me that they couldn't quite cram a large fragile packet through my letterbox. I'd also received three replies.

The assistant of Jamie Oliver went to great pains to explain all of the charity work that the young celebrity chef was currently involved in, including his 'Fifteen' restaurant project. I didn't doubt any of it for a second. In fact, on this very day I read an article in *The Evening Standard* entitled 'Jamies's Jammin' Session' with a picture of him playing the drums in the company of Joss Stone and Cat Deeley at a Great Ormond Street fundraiser. That's a shame, I could have had a triple greeting.

Suffice it to say, unfortunately, he had no time to meet me.

Richard Wilson, on the other hand, was able to agree to a meeting. He wrote me a lovely personal letter to say that he'd soon be appearing in panto in Wimbledon, and if I was to turn up one day and mention *Greeting the 500* at the stage door, he'd give me 30 seconds of his time (and the stage manager would no doubt give me an odd look).

So far then, panto-wise, I had *Peter Pan* in Birmingham and *Cinderella* in South London.

I therefore decided to take a cursory look at www.its-behind-you.com, the definitive guide to this quintessentially British phenomenon and blow me, if there weren't at least 30 names on my list appearing up and down the country in make-up and frocks. Amongst others we had one of my personal heroes, Richard O'Brien, appearing in *Snow White* in Milton Keynes. Darren Day was in *Cinderella* in Derby, Sir Ian McKellen was in *Aladdin* at the Old Vic and Scarlett Johansson was in *Mother Goose* at the Worksop Civic Centre. (OK, I made the last one up.)

The final letter received was from the agent of Robbie Coltrane, a.k.a. Cracker a.k.a. Hagrid, who mentioned that as Robbie lived out of town and was something of a private person, he sadly wouldn't be able to meet with me.

Sunday December 11th 2005 – Extension II

There was something of a black cloud hanging over me on this day.

Actually there were two, one courtesy of the massive explosion at the Buncefield oil depot, which was sweeping down from Hertfordshire as I slept, and another that was brought on by my consistent failure to

185

find a well-paid job, a sane female companion and contact details for Salman Rushdie.

I had a row with Michael over the weekend, and I don't mean that we went sculling in a small boat on the Serpentine, I mean we had an argument.

'It's ridiculous, how am I meant to get anyone to agree to meet me between Christmas Day and New Year. They'll be too busy trying to get refunds on unpleasant cardigans or watching *The Sound of Music*,' I moaned.

'Shut up and get me some chips,' he replied (we were in the Coral Bay Fish Shop on Cricklewood Lane). To cut a short story shorter, I was magnanimously granted one final two-week extension to my challenge, which would now end with all the finality of Mongolia's chances of winning the World Cup, on February 14 2006 – Valentine's Day, or the day that my postman might as well sit at home and put his feet up (although that would require vast quantities of KY Jelly).

I also finally got round to sending out some more of my letters, as I still had 108 of them to churn out. And so, it would come to pass that the following 18 people would get more than just Christmas Greetings from their local curry house through their letterboxes over the coming few days: **Richard Branson**, **Tim Brooke-Taylor**, **Sir Ian McKellen**, **Greg Dyke**, **Boy George**, **Naomi Campbell**, **Richard O'Brien**, **Nigel Benn**, **Jimmy Greaves**, **Wayne Rooney**, **Colleen McLaughlin**, **Aled Jones**, **Andrew Marr**, **David Bailey**, **Bernie Taupin**, **Michael Barrymore** and **Sir Alex Ferguson.**

I could name at least one or two in this group who, to put it mildly, probably wouldn't have replied to me in a month of Sundays. I was thinking about the ones who don't get out of bed for less than £300 000 (and might be seen on a catwalk/in court charged with assault) and others who are Scottish, chew gum and berate referees, But we would see, would we not.

Monday December 12th 2005 – An Inspector Calls
(or His Agent Does)

Emails continued to flood in offering pearls of wisdom such as '*...have you tried contacting Alan Shearer via Newcastle United?*' (yes, strangely enough I had) or '*I saw Ronan Keating just off Dean Street in Soho recently, if you hang around there he might come back*' (the less said about that the better).

As David Byrne, the talented if somewhat peculiar lead singer of Talking Heads once sang, 'You may find yourself in a beautiful house, you may find yourself with a beautiful wife and a beautiful car and you may ask yourself, how did I get here?'. And I will answer him – through a fallopian tube. The only reason I extraneously mention this oblique reference is because its title happens to be *Once in a Lifetime*.

Bear with me here.

I received a phone call from a very helpful lady named Angela, who happened to be the assistant to David Suchet. David is perhaps best known for his portrayals of Agatha Christie's world-famous moustachioed Belgian detective inspector. No, not Mrs Marple after she'd let herself go a little bit but Hercule Poirot, of course; he of the little grey cells, or am I getting confused with Parkhurst Prison?

Anyway, David was currently appearing in the play *Once in a Lifetime*, which happened to have nothing to do with finding yourself 'behind the wheel of a large automobile', but was in fact a comedy set in the time of the silent movie scene in Hollywood.

So David told Angela to tell me that he would be happy to help me out and that I should proceed directly to the National Theatre in early January (picking up £200 and a congestion charge fine as I pass 'Bow'). For that, I was abundantly grateful, even if it did mean traipsing around Waterloo again.

With another affirmative reply safely tucked under my belt, the evening was spent panic-buying some petrol.

Tuesday December 13th 2005 – Greetings 28
and 29 (Nick Ross, Fiona Bruce)

10½ stone; alcohol consumed: half an M&S sherry trifle; cigarettes smoked: 14 (was with Michael for much of the day).

Bumped into Mark Darcy. He reminded me about a former girlfriend of mine who tried to constantly gnaw away at my ego by telling me how Colin Firth was far superior to me in every conceivable way. Remembered that a different girlfriend did the same using Thierry Henry as an example. Thinking to myself that it's not long before some future girlfriend compares me unfavourably with Pol Pot.

Today was BBC TV studio visiting day again, as both Nick Ross and Fiona Bruce were recording an episode of *Crimewatch UK*. Ironic then that Michael should agree to accompany me on this one, as much about him was criminal, although not illegal.

'I'm covered in Skips crumbs,' he said to me as we got out of the car to walk to the studios, since he'd just devoured a large pack of the prawn-flavoured snacks on the journey while resting the packet on his gut.

'Lovely, Michael, do you think that'll create a nice impression?'

'You know, Jules, it's amazing you've never been punched to the floor before, you sarky git,' and with that we strolled into Bush Centre or whatever it's called.

With the help of our chaperone-cum-aide-cum-fixer Laura, we wound our way through the maze of corridors and ended up in a large blue and black themed studio; most appropriate I thought in view of the police themed nature of the show.

So there we stood, taking in our surroundings and it wasn't long before Michael pointed to the ceiling and spoke with pseudo authority about the studio's complex lighting system, or 'Grid' as I was corrected, which was hanging above our heads.

'Oh yes,' he said to Laura, who pretended to be interested, 'If there's one thing I know about, it's lighting gantries and grids. I work in West End theatre you see,' before regurgitating his familiar patter of 'I'm fed up of people rushing up to me when I leave the stage door. They obviously think I'm famous...,' and it was with that sentence that I finally grasped the major difference between myself and my good friend.

You see, whereas I generally downplayed and disregarded my rather humdrum existence, career, lovelife and in fact everything about myself, Michael always seemed to have done the opposite. He tended to loudly crow about every aspect of his life, even though like myself, he didn't really have one.

I couldn't help but think that the way the two of us viewed our own respective lives may have had something to do with the arguments that we had put forward in the Crown back in June. Michael wasn't so much trying to educate me as to how the well-off and the well known view the general public, but was in fact indirectly informing me as to how *he* viewed them.

He'd always had minor delusions of grandeur, and perhaps regarded himself as famous by default, primarily because he once promoted nightclubs, had appeared for three seconds in a pop video by Shed 7 and regularly walked out of 'Stage Doors'.

Fair enough, he was known to quite a few people who live around the Hampstead Village area, but I didn't then and still don't feel that this qualified him to make sweeping statements about 500 people he'd never even met. In a nutshell, just because he was crabby and got fed up with people who waited outside stage doors, it didn't mean that everyone else hated being hassled in the street.

...back to reality and we didn't have to wait too long for Nick and Fiona to make an appearance. Nick came over first, yet before I was barely able to thank him for agreeing to the handshake, you-know-who next to me butted in with, 'I've actually met you before, Nick, at a garden party.' They had a bit of a chin wag – Michael in ar*e-licking heaven – before I wrenched Nick away and we got the photo taken.

Fiona then approached, and as in one of my earlier meetings, I was a little tongue-tied by the elegance of the person before me. Perhaps one day I might be able to wed someone like Fiona, a true English Rose, although I guess it would have to be a version of her with poor eyesight.

Michael faffed with the focus for a minute or two and I got to hold Fiona's hand for a pleasingly elongated moment of time. The second photo was taken, following which we thanked both of them heartily and bade them *sayonara* in English.

As we drove away from White City, Michael did the inevitable, 'I'm not sure if you know this about me but *I've got a police record*' joke (*Walking on the Moon*), at which point I told him not to stand so close to me... even though we were sitting.

Friday December 16th 2005 – Greeting 30
(Alan Titchmarsh)

◇◇

There's nothing like having a day off work on a crisp and sunny December morning.

Actually, there is. Someone, somewhere was presently lying on a sun-kissed beach sipping on a pina colada. I was simply lying in my furnace of a bedroom planning that day's two meetings in South London.

As I got ready to leave home I noticed that the sub-Saharan temperature in my flat (still trying to get rid of an infernal cough) had seen the weeping fig in my living room shed most of its leaves and rather than weeping, it now looked positively inconsolable. That's one to ask Alan Titchmarsh about later today, I thought to myself.

Our meeting was scheduled for the temperate house at Kew Gardens – so from one temperate house to another. I feared I'd be late as the traffic, when I approached my destination, was totally static. Basically, there was a massive queue in Kew.

I did, however, make it on time and a huge thanks to Vince on the gate, who, on learning of my charity-based intentions, let me off with the £10 entrance fee (I'm sure it used to be a nominal 2p to get in) and gave me a complimentary pass.

The gardens themselves were a delight to behold. I love plants and trees and the like – they are the lungs of our planet, aren't they? (perhaps slightly less wheezy and tar-lined than mine) – so I must say that I was a bit upset to see so many people ignoring the beauty of mother nature as they rushed off to slide around on a rink of frozen water.

The Temperate House was just lush, yet I'd arrived slightly too early and Alan was still posing for a famous sculptress who was building a clay replica of his head.

Once that was all done and dusted, Alan had a brief photoshoot with several people and then I took my opportunity to approach.

I've got to say I felt slightly sorry for him. Sat stock still for the best part of two hours as a clay squeezer's model, then being bossed around by a gaggle of camera clickers, yet still having enough time to sign a few autographs and exchange pleasantries with a group of swooning elderly Yorkshire ladies and all the while the genial smile never left his face.

Fearing that he'd forgotten about his most important duty of the day, I was soon put at ease as it transpired that he *had* been expecting me and my fretting was unfounded. In fact, Alan had even ensured that his PA had bought a signed picture for the charity auction. So it was a very swift affair: the handshake, the giving of thanks on my part, the 'Good luck with it all' from Alan, the 'I've got copyright over that picture' from the unforgiving Irish press photographer who took the snap with MY camera, and then back outside.

Back past the buffoon ice-skaters (what is this recent national obsession with ice skating?) past the sweet group of young kids who were making an imaginary wildlife documentary among a row of Douglas Fir trees, past Irish Vince on the gate, and off to Wimbledon for more of the same.

Friday December 16th 2005 – Greeting 31 (Richard Wilson)

After greeting Alan Titchmarsh in Kew Gardens, it was back to my car, which I'd hurriedly parked in an extremely narrow little conduit called Branstone Road, where ironically enough I got into a bit of a pickle, having to perform what can only be described as a thirty-two point turn.

Despite living just down the road from Richard Wilson in NW3, I was scheduled to meet him at the Wimbledon New Theatre where he was appearing in that enchanting tale that we all associate with this time of the year. That one with catchy songs and ugly sisters and a nasty villain – *The Sound of Music.*

No, just a joke (I'll shut my von Trapp) I mean *Cinderella* of course.

As it was such a beautiful day, with the sun shining, the flowers blooming and the birds getting frisky with the bees (as is my understanding), I decided to take the scenic route to SW19 through Richmond Park. Sadly, there was no wildlife to be seen, not a stag, buck or doe in sight. Where they all were I couldn't tell you – no eye-deer. I assumed that they were hibernating and that some friendly park ranger had put them in a massive cardboard box full of straw.

Before long I was there. Back in Wimbledon. Back to where it had all started several months ago where a rather confused looking Tony Hawks had shaken my hand and stared nervously at Michael.

So, at 4.45 p.m. on this nippy December eve, I found myself outside the Wimbledon Theatre stage door.

By that, I don't mean that I evaluated my life, my psyche and my motivational triggers and finally gained a true understanding of who I really was, I simply mean that is where I was situated geographically. With a clutch or troop or whatever you might call them, of autograph hunters.

After a brief conversation inside, I was informed by an apologetic young lady at a desk that Richard was still having a bit of physio for his bad back (these panto-watching kids can be ruthless you know) and I was forced to venture back out into the icy breeze where I noticed that only two of the hardiest 'hunters' remained (one with snot coming out of a nostril).

Although, in a way, I viewed these two middle-aged men as kindred spirits, after all I was simply undertaking a glorified version of what they were doing, I must say that I had little in common with them, although they had much in common with each other.

Both toured the country going to numerous pantomimes every year, trying to fill out their autograph scrap-books, both had strange voices (the sort you might hear if you asked someone to mimic a train-spotter), both laughed inanely at the drop of a hat (well my hands were cold) and both were possibly unmarried.

I shall call them Colin and Colin.

Colin had travelled up all the way from Eastbourne, while Colin had laboured in from darkest Kent... Actually, I'm going to stop all this. Who the hell am I to judge them; anyway, they both seemed friendly enough. Colin even excitedly showed me his autographs of Danny La Rue and someone from *Crossroads* who'd been appearing at the Croydon Coronet.

Back inside the building I eventually caught up with Richard who was extremely obliging, especially considering he had just been performing to several hundred screaming children and was about to subject himself to several hundred more 'it's behind yous' and 'oh no it isn'ts' in an hour's time.

After very nearly calling him Victor, much to my absolute horror (fortunately only the V came out), I informed Richard that I didn't want to keep him too long as he probably wanted his tea (I think his reply had something to do with Kentucky Fried Chicken), so we had the picture taken in the corridors of the theatre before he returned to his dressing room to fetch me a signed photo for my auction. I then thanked him and made my way to the exit.

It wasn't until I'd left that I noticed that Richard had followed me out, possibly to get his food, poor chap, and had unwittingly stumbled right into the clutches of the two autograph-hunters.

'.. and who shall I make this out to?' I heard him say politely to one of them as I ambled off to my car.

'Oh, it's for me – huh, huh – sign it 'to Steven' – huh, huh,' said Colin.

Monday December 19th 2005 – Right Said Fred

Just four and a half days until we broke up for Christmas, so in other words just six days until we breakdown *at* Christmas. I was really looking forward to the big day, where for the nth year in succession I could look forward to no less than three generations of my family asking me why I didn't have a 'proper job' or 'How's that lovely young girl from Bradford you're seeing?' – 'Erm, I broke up with her eight years ago.'

I don't suppose there was ever going to be any doubt as to who would be winning the 2005 Sports Personality of the Year award, such was his impact in our round thrashing of the Aussies. Indeed, it was good news on my part, as it appeared that Andy Flintoff and I might have an appointment to meet in the New Year.

It wasn't really a case of 'Right said Fred', because he was still playing cricket in Pakistan, and I didn't recall my letter being addressed to anywhere near Karachi. However, a lady by the name of Kate did get back to me with the following:

Dear Jules,

Thanks for getting in touch.

We think that at some stage in the New Year this could happen. However, we can't put something down as a fixed date as we just don't know when we can fit this in. It will have to be a very

193

Jules Segal

last minute thing if it is going to happen as Fred's diary is
crammed. But if we give you short notice in the future you are
more than welcome to come to our offices when Fred drops in and
take a photo.

When that is, though - we will have to let you know…

What a totally fantastic lady Kate was. I sincerely hoped that she would
be getting everything that she wanted under the Christmas tree that
year - present-wise, I mean.

Wednesday December 21st 2005 - It is Better to Receive than to Give

Oh joy and celebration and sounds of seraphim blowing brass
instruments! Only three more 'panicking in John Lewis' days until
Christmas.

As of the Tuesday of this week, I promised never to inflict upon myself
the misery that was doing the Christmas shopping in Brent Cross
Shopping Centre. To sum it up, Brent wasn't the only thing that was
cross.

Admittedly, there was no shortage of stores to choose from in this
hypermarket, ('hyper' being the operative word), in fact there are
millions (says Geoffrey) all under one roof, but being buffeted around
by young girls with big hooped earrings who were pushing prams
containing even younger girls with dummies in their mouths (and
painted fingernails), didn't float my particularly large cruiseliner.

For the salvation of my ear-drums from high-pitched infants I also
gave the Grotto a very wide birth, although seeing it did remind me
about the funny story of the dyslexic devil-worshipper who sold his
soul to Santa, but then you've probably heard it before.

The only things that were sold to me were one aromatic candle, whose
scent I currently forget (although I think it might have been lavender,
peach, tetrachloride 1.2.1, stabiliser and E36), one shrink-wrapped pack
of soaps that were ingeniously shaped like sea-shells, presumably to
stop people using them and one of Mozart's harp and flute concerto
CDs. Funny that, I thought he was a pianist.

Well, I was sure that, as usual, my family would be completely

194

underwhelmed with what the bearded fatman had left under the tree for them, but why break with tradition, that's what I say.

Enough of this irrelevant tittle-tattle.

I had none of my 'Sleb' meetings lined up until the New Year and I expected the week ahead of me to be rather quiet on that front; it was the mass of Christ after all, which was partly why Michael, in an unusual act of generosity, gave me this final two-week extension in the first place.

I'd be spending much of the next ten days, when I wasn't either (a) drunk on eggnog, (b) watching Humphrey Bogart or (c) suffering clinical depression because of the one hour of sunlight I was getting per day, in trying to find contact details for the remaining 80 or so of the 500 on my list that I'd not yet written to.

On that subject, I forgot to mention that a few days prior to this I had sent out another 12 of my letters, to a ventriloquist, a comedian, a TV vet and doctor, another comedian, a motorcyclist, a football chairman, an artist, an opera singer, an adviser to the Mayor of London, a royal correspondent, a world famous musician and someone that I don't know how to describe. In other words: **Peter Davison**, **Lesley Garrett**, **Tracey Emin**, **Rory McGrath**, **David Sullivan**, **Carl Fogarty**, **Nick Hancock**, **Lee Jasper**, **Keith Harris**, **Jennie Bond**, **Chris Martin** and **Darren Day**.

You work it out.

Thursday December 22nd 2005 – The Virgin Mirth

The seventh richest man in the country (Source: *Sunday Times* Rich List 2005), keen balloonist and investor in other more orthodox modes of transport, Richard Branson, wasn't available to meet me... and to think I was going to buy him a tie for Christmas.

My thanks went to a lady by the name of Jacqueline, who incidentally had a beautiful and exotic surname, and who worked for Virgin Management in their Campden Hill Road headquarters.

I had sent my letter off to Richard only a week earlier and had already received a response, albeit in the negative, so gratitude was certainly owed for their efficiency. I quote what was written:

```
Dear Julian,

Many thanks for your letter addressed to Richard Branson.
Because Richard is currently travelling for so much of his
time, I am afraid he is unable to do justice to your request.

I am so sorry…
```

The fact that Jacqueline's signature was printed on and not signed, didn't dampen my spirits one iota. It just hammered home the fact that there must have been simply thousands of grovellers penning begging letters to Richard every day. I'm sure that somewhere, someone at Virgin actually read what I had to say before deciding not to pass it on, and for this I prostrate myself before their, no doubt, sweet-smelling Gucci leather loafers.

In fact, seeing as it was nearly good old Crimble, I also wanted to heartily thank anyone who had been in the least bit interested in following my progress or lack thereof over the preceding six months, or indeed anyone who had followed with bated breath the incessant tripe flowing forth from my fingers, like gizzards flowing from so many disembowelled turkeys.

Friday December 23rd 2005 – Holmes Sweet Holmes

'So you're doing this project, right?' a friend of mine asked me, having read the latest offerings from my website, 'where you're writing to 500 celebrities asking to shake their hands...'

'Yup.'

'... don't interrupt me. Yet on your website you mention things such as disembowelled livestock. D'you think that this will incline them to meet you should they glance at it before replying?'

To be honest, I think he made a valid point. So there would be no more discussions of incomplete farmyard animals, and that was a promise that I stuck to.

I received an email from the assistant to Dame Kelly Holmes a day or two before Christmas, which brightened up my day no end. I was a big fan of hers (Dame Kelly's, not her assistant, although Mary seemed very nice too) and she had certainly done our country proud.

I distinctly recall that before the Athens Olympics in 2004, I was banging on about her and talking up her chances of success to my friend Joanne. Back then, Joanne hadn't heard of our heroic runner as she was from Australia where apparently everyone is heroic.

You may recall, at the time that the papers were all making a song and dance about the guaranteed gold that Paula Radcliffe would bring home and were paying scant regard to Kelly's chances, dedicating very few column inches to her. Little did they know that they were backing the wrong horse.

Sadly, Paula subsequently wilted in the Greek heat while Kelly went on to win two golds, earned herself a title from the queen, and helped to ensure that the 2012 Olympics would be hosted in my favourite City.

Joanne has certainly heard of her now.

Anyway, this is what Mary said:

Thank you for your letter to Dame Kelly. Unfortunately, she is inundated with mail and her schedule is absolutely hectic, so she has not had an opportunity to see your request. She leaves the UK immediately after Christmas until mid January. I will bring your letter to her attention when possible and get back to you if she is able to help.

Well, I couldn't say fairer than that, and as with Sir Cliff Richard, Freddie Flintoff and David Dickinson, Dame Kelly would go in the 'maybe' pile.

I did like that name, Mary, and not just because it was Christmas. It reminded me of a poem.

Mary had a little lamb

I opted for the duck

We left The Ivy

Went to bed

Then Mary said 'Let's

Just go to sleep because I've got another one of my headaches again, I'm afraid.

Jules Segal

◇◇

I had suddenly become fascinated by the darts. Not the obscure 1970s a capella pop group, but the large-gutted men who were, at this time, throwing tungsten projectiles at the cross-section of a cork tree on a wall in Essex.

The big question was... would the 'Pieman' beat 'Hawaii 501'?

While watching the drunken antics in Purfleet (which conjured up images of cats on boats), I remembered that I still hadn't even tried to contact Eric Bristow or Phil Taylor, or if you prefer, the 'Crafty Cockney' and the 'Power', both of whom appeared on my list of 500.

I actually once had a friend from Canning Town who somewhat narcissistically, took to calling himself the Crafty Cockney (despite the fact that he was thicker than the proverbial bacon milkshake and hailed from Weymouth). As for myself, I decided that if I was ever to become a darts player of world renown, my nickname would be 'The Sore Throat', basically because I was a hypochondriac.

Despite still not being able to track down contact details for Phil and Eric, I had managed to prepare another 33 letters in the lull that followed Christmas. I think that I now had only 45 or so of the 500 to send out. Then again, I only had six weeks left of the challenge.

As for *my* Christmas day, well, a pleasant enough family affair I suppose. No massive arguments. From what I remember, the main topics of conversation that we oscillated between as we chowed down to Bernard Matthew's finest (get well soon, by the way), were hiatus hernias, Ugg boots, a play of Harold Pinter (although I can't remember which one), conspiracy theories about the Bilderberg Group to take over the world, emigration to Australia, acts of violence against Christmas cracker joke writers and my sister's (wise) decision to go to Cornwall instead of attending.

The only other point of note was that sadly, despite being quite hungry, I found a hair in my stuffing early doors and couldn't really eat much more as a result.

As for that evening, I suppose I did what many people up and down the country did, in other words, cooked some boiled eggs, sipped alcohol and watched the Colin Firth and Hugh Grant-orama on TV.

Goodness, what was on offer? *Bridget Jones, Love Actually, Bridget Jones II* and *The Importance of Being Earnest.* I suppose it was little wonder that your average American thinks we in Britain all live in stately homes and wander up and down the corridors shouting out 'Bugger!'

As for the 33 fresh letters, they were to be sent to the following just as soon as I could be arsed to buy some envelopes: **Vinnie Jones, Norman Cook, John Leslie, Noddy Holder, Gary Oldman, Dr Fox, Ridley Scott, Jimmy Hill, Hugh Grant** (Oh bugger!), **Simon Fuller, Barry Cryer, Sadie Frost, Alan Bleasdale, Damian Hirst, Murray Walker, Sean Connery, Darren Gough, Rustie Lee, Tom Jones, Bruce Oldfield, Ringo Starr, Audley Harrison, Kerry Katona, Sam Mendes, Bob Mills, Ronnie Wood, Keith Richards, Louis Theroux, Alistair McGowan, Robert Kilroy-Silk, Anthony Minghella, Matthew Pinsent, Thom Yorke** and a partridge in a pear tree... although possibly not the last one.

By the way, sorry about the Purfleet joke... and for that matter sorry about writing the word 'arsed', but the season of goodwill was basically over and we had drifted into the season of short tempers and general loutishness.

Thursday December 29th 2005 – Gandalf the Great

... Well, that was a first. I'd received an email from Kenya: a man named Joe praised my website and wished me luck in my quest.

So the details of this odd little bet had now reached the shores of Africa, as well as America, France, New Zealand, Germany, Italy, Australia, Brazil, Spain, South Africa and oddly enough the Czech Republic where it weirdly appeared to have something of a cult following(?). Perhaps a story on it featured in *Blesk*.

Another email that arrived on Wednesday was from the delightfully named Bellescheisse who lived in Sheffield, despite having a Franco-Teutonic name. She asked a number of questions about Michael and sounded as though she had a soft spot for him, maybe even somewhere near her bosom – presumably because she hadn't met him.

She asked if I had bought him anything for Christmas, and I did, a packet of Cadbury's Revels.

199

Jules Segal

It's what he wanted.

In three days time it would be a new year and we would all have a clean slate. My own resolutions were to decrease the number of fags I chuffed my way through and to decrease the amount of sarcasm I used (as if).

It also appeared as though my faith in the film *Lord of the Rings* had been repaid, as one of Britain's finest actors had agreed to meet me and had even given me a choice of dates. I simply had to turn up to the stage door of the Old Vic, where Sir Ian McKellen, was appearing in *Aladdin*, before January 22nd in order to achieve another successful 'Greeting'.

I therefore raised a metaphorical glass to the kind Sir Ian for humouring this scrawny Orc-faced young man of Middle Earth.

CHAPTER 8 – January

Monday January 2nd 2006 – Happy New Year?

Mine wasn't and it wasn't a case of 'bah humbug', but surely this is the most overrated night one could spend in the company of drunken idiots. Who enjoys getting crushed to death in a pub and spending the final three hours of a year queuing up for a white wine spritzer? Then, come midnight, we are forced to stand in a circle, hold a stranger's sweaty hand and sing ancient Scottish songs as if we were attending a Glaswegian Alcoholics Anonymous meeting.

I was in some dump in Notting Hill.

At one stage I thought my luck was in. An attractive female member of our little groupette, whom I'd met for the first time that evening, was standing at the bar holding her slippery nipples and smiling at me.

Why she needed two of these Bailey's and Sambuca-based cocktails I couldn't say – maybe to help her get through the evening in the company of dullards such as yours cynically – so I walked over and tried to engage the piss-head in conversation. To be honest, my opening gambit could have been better. In fact it couldn't really have been much worse.

'Would you like to try some Slippery Nipple?' she asked.

'Maybe later, but could I have some of your drink first?' – I swear she walked straight off without once looking back. Not even in anger.

So it appears that what I mistook for a smile was probably just Rachel trying to expel some wind and that this wasn't set to be a match made in heaven, more like some shabby patchwork quilt darned in hell by Beelzebub's own fiery hand.

How ironic then, that after all of this breast talk it was me who was left standing at the bar feeling a t*t.

Enough of such nonsense, I want to discuss the finest footballer in this country. And I don't even support Man U.

Wayne Rooney, Roonaldo, The Wayne-ster, or as my mum calls him, Thingamajig who plays for England, I'm sure had a more enjoyable New Year's Eve than the one I had: he had probably been in the company of Coleen (I'd love to be with Coleen at any time of the year). I felt obliged to thank an unidentifiable individual at Proactive Sports Management Ltd whose signature I couldn't decipher.

The young prodigy who plays for Manchester United must constantly be in huge popular demand. I was therefore very impressed that one of his agents was able to get back to me so promptly. Alas, a meeting with young Wayne wasn't going to be possible because, as squiggle wrote:

Due to the massive amount of requests Wayne receives, it has been decided that he should dedicate his time visiting chosen charities in Manchester... and it has not been possible to facilitate your request on this occasion.

I completely understood and was once again simply happy to have received a response. After all, how could I possibly be upset with the man who is one day going to lift the World Cup for us? No pressure, then.

Thursday January 5th 2006 – Boxing Day Again
◇◇

Alexander, Paul, Stella, Vivienne, Jasper and Jeff all appear on my list, yet so far I'd rather limited success with our Great British fashionistas.

So what do I say? I say all hail Bruce Oldfield who had kindly sent me the most delightful email that morning, the first line of which read:

'...Seems perfectly easy to accommodate your request. Please ring xxx next monday to set up a time next week...

A gentleman a scholar and a damned fine fashion designer I'd suggest. Although I might be biased as he *had* just agreed to meet me.

Goodness knows what he would make of my honey-coloured cords and Matalan shoes when I met him. In fact, I thought it might be a good idea to let his PA know what I'd be wearing that day, in case he walked past me and tried to drop 50p into my cap.

Meanwhile, Michael had once again excelled himself. I'd already lost count of the amount of 'no' replies that I'd received as a result of the individual in question living abroad. The latest to be added to that pile was the British heavyweight boxer Audley Harrison.

I'd been on the phone to a man in the Harrison camp by the name of Ben, who informed me that said talented pugilist now lived somewhere in the USA and had no plans to come to these drizzly shores before my challenge ended in mid-February.

I considered giving Michael a left jab to the right cheek (upper) when I saw him that night.

Incidentally, a friend of mine made the snooker equipment for Mr Harrison's new billiards room... yes, he formed an Audley cue.

(Don't worry, it might not be too late to get a refund for this book.)

Friday January 6th 2005 – Would You Adam and Eve It

It appeared that a glut of poor jokes, bad grammar and an overuse of metaphors still hadn't been enough to put some people off enjoying my website.

I'd been informed by email that, quite ridiculously, it had been nominated as a contender for the 'Yahoo! Website Find of the Year 2005'. I sent them a reply enquiring as to whether the prize might be a two-week holiday in the Bahamas, but I never got a response.

I therefore put a message on my website asking anyone who read it to vote their little hearts out for mine. To vote like they'd never voted before, unless they *had* never voted before in which case not to vote like that.

Ironically, the website was actually nominated in the 'Celebrity' category by Yahoo!. I since learned that they didn't have an 'Individuals of Note in their Profession' category, so I would have to make do with the 'Sleb' one.

The only things I had won in my 35 years to date had been 'The Most Promising Student of the Year Award' when I was nine, handed out to the swot of the class, which left mater in tears (of pride I hope), and £1000 from the side of a Tropicana Orange Juice Carton. They evidently liked my poem about 'delicious juice and crisp mountain air, you'll glide along like Fred Astaire', which all seems rather vomit-worthy now, reading it back.

Friday January 6th 2006 – Greeting 32 (Ian McKellen)

I recently informed you that news of this stupid little bet that arose at a table in the annexe of the Crown Pub in Cricklewood, had reached as far afield as Bondi Junction, New Mexico and Bloemfontein.

You could now add India to the list.

Someone called Susheel sent me a lovely email in which he/she mentioned that '*I and all of India wish you a whole ton of luck in your bet against Michael*'. Thanks Susheel, it's somewhat comforting to learn that I had 1065070607 people rooting for me. Perhaps it would have been fairer if Brazil and Nigeria had rooted for Michael, just to even things up a bit.

Sadly, with the large amount of emails I had been receiving, I hadn't been able to answer them all since, regrettably, my bionic arm still hadn't returned from the dry cleaners (they mentioned something about a stubborn vinaigrette stain that they were having trouble shifting). This left me feeling rather guilty. But it soon passed.

The preceding day to this one had seen me meet Sir Ian McKellen, a personal hero of mine, as part of this bet. He was currently treading the boards at the Old Vic in South London.

As Michael was otherwise occupied, in his role of Chief Bottlewasher at the Garrick Theatre, photographer for the evening was Gids, another friend that I'd roped into coming along to press the button of a camera.

This turned out to be unfortunate, since the journey to Waterloo (yet again) turned out to be one annoying whinge-orama.

'I'm tired, the seatbelt is hurting me, I'm missing *Celebrity Big Brother*, this car's too hot, you've just knocked down that old woman, etc., etc.'

Anyway, we arrived in good time and briefly stood around the stage door, watching crew members emerge as one of them stared at us before mumbling something, possibly derogatory, about autograph hunters and we were soon ushered inside and up to Sir Ian's dressing room.

I'm not sure if I was entirely prepared to witness Sir Ian, a man who in my mind will always be associated with that most venerable of old sages, Gandalf, in Widow Twankey costume, but nevertheless he was an absolute star and was incredibly helpful.

Not for the first time at one of these meetings, my subject asked me how many handshakes I had managed so far and there seemed genuine concern about my lack of progress.

This was allayed slightly when I once again mentioned that my project had something of a misnomer and that winning the bet entailed only having to meet 100 individuals and not the entire list.

Sir Ian even helpfully offered to assist me, by suggesting that he might round up some other suspects from the show but I mentioned that alas, no one else involved in *this* particular production of Aladdin appeared on my list.

So that was it, really. What a top man.

I met Michael later in the evening to upload the photo and I also happened to mention that, surprisingly enough, my website had been shortlisted for an award.

'OUR website, I think you mean,' he replied.

I suppose that's true. Michael had indeed put as much work into it as I had. Whereas I had paid for it, managed it, written it and badly designed it, Michael had indeed appeared in a photograph somewhere on it and so I suppose he deserved equal credit. He also asked me to mention that he wasn't actually a bottlewasher at the Garrick Theatre, but rather, a very important member of the crew and a close personal friend of Edward Fox.

Saturday January 7th 2006 – Old School

◇◇

The PAs of John Cleese, Damian Hirst and Ridley Scott had all kindly sent me replies that were received around this time. Bet-wise, I am afraid it was pretty negative news as it was three more replies of '*so sorry but he won't be in the country for a while*'.

The first response was from the agent of John Cleese, a man who had attended the same school as me in Bristol. I was personally always in trouble at school, like the time I asked my Latin teacher whether the Romans had all died off because of a mass outbreak of five-five hundred.

'What on earth are you talking about, Segal?'

'You know, sir, VD.'

Melanie was good enough to inform me that as John Cleese '... *lives in California, it's not possible to help your campaign*', but that he thanked me for thinking of him and wished me every success. I wouldn't mind living in California myself, come to think of it. The miles of beaches, the raisins, the blondes...

On the plus side, I consoled myself with the thought that John, who'd spent his early years in the same inauspicious classrooms as myself, went on to star opposite the lovely Jamie Lee Curtis in several movies, so perhaps this augured well for a possible collaboration between myself and Scarlett Johansson in the future?

Sylvia kindly sent me an email which mentioned that Damien Hirst was also currently abroad and would not be returning to England until Spring and Natascha, the assistant of Ridley Scott, was replying to me at the personal behest of the eminent director himself. He was working in post production on his latest film in Los Angeles and wasn't expected on this side of the pond until after this has all finished, yet he wished me well with my '*extraordinary and very captivating project*'. Well, that's nice.

Sunday January 8th 2006 – A Message From Your Leader

Well, only 'your leader' in the sense that he was ahead in this bet.

Michael today informed me that at this juncture, I *had* to include both a photograph of himself and a message for his 'fans' on my website, and who was I to argue?

As for his message, I quote him verbatim. Bear with it if you can't make head or tail of it, he's ever so slightly dsylixec:

'Ladies and Gentlemen: here speaks the voice of a soon to be winner (no offence to my scrawny friend) but it's always nice to win. I know this might sound just a tad arrogant but I see it more as confidence, I am aware Jules has another couple of week to complete his task (more than he deserve with his palled excuses of Christmas, terrorism and British deserters) but judging by the stats (for statistics please refer to Jules), I think I did good.

But to be nice for a second about the effort he has to put in to this has been quite amazing and feel the RNIB and all his piers should be proud. It is a selfless task, I say selfless his wrist is not as limp any more from all the hand shaking and I am sure that someone might benefit form the amount of licking he has had to do! That's envelopes not the ar*s. I wish him the best of luck in the smuggest way possible but 'You never can tell sir, you never can tell'

So I hope that you enjoyed that, and if not, I hope that you at least understood it.

Monday January 9th 2006 - The *Metro*
<><><><><><><><><><><><><><><><><><><><><><><><><><><><><><><><><><><><><><><><><><><><><><><><><><>

An email from Terry in Burbankca, wherever that was, led me to believe that having displayed Michael's photo on my website, his fan base had increased to two, although I regretted to inform Terry that Michael wasn't that way inclined.

Meanwhile, I owed another debt of gratitude, this time to a journalist from the *Metro* by the name of Bel who considered my story more newsworthy than 'Dog Treads on Fax Machine and Sends Fax' and who was sufficiently interested to feature it in a piece. I also had to thank '3AM girl' Caroline at *The Daily Mirror* for bringing it to Bel's attention. '3AM girl'? You must be constantly tired like me, no?

I also wanted to thank in advance the surreal combination of **Jim Bowen, Zadie Smith, Jeff Banks, Sir Ranulph Fiennes, Mystic Meg, Fatima Whitbread, Paul O'Grady, Andy McNab** and **Jordan** for their future acquiescence to my request.

It was unlikely but it was worth a try.

Tuesday January 10th 2006 - One More For the 'Ayes'
<><><><><><><><><><><><><><><><><><><><><><><><><><><><><><><><><><><><><><><><><><><><><><><><><><>

Having thanked 'Terry' a day earlier on my website, I was forced to apologise for suggesting that he was in fact a male lover of men. 'Terri' had written back to inform me that *he* was actually a *she* and that her domicile wasn't actually situated in the peculiar sounding Burbankca, but actually in Burbank, CA (California). Perhaps if you'd used the SPACE BAR, Theresa... (but thanks for setting the record *straight*).

To someone of my age Jimmy Hill is an absolute legend, no question. His name was frequently bandied about, for one reason or another, while I was running around the school playground. I only mention this as his utterly delightful wife telephoned me to inform me that this icon of football punditry would be happy to shake my hand after he finished recording his TV show that coming Sunday, at which time I would be able to chalk another name of the list.

Wednesday January 11th 2005 – Well, Blow Me!

I'd taken today '*off of*' work, as teenagers and inarticulate professional footballers might say. I had a very busy few hours what with three meetings, but on the plus side, I would not be forced to suffer the slings and arrows of the outrageous Northern Line. No, I was going to be darting around London *en* Polo, paying £8 for the privilege of course.

Christina, an assistant to Andrew Lloyd Webber, had penned me a letter mentioning that through sheer weight of numbers of his commitments, sadly a meeting would not be possible with this world-famous composer.

Some better news, though, as it turned out that I would now be etching the name of one of the world's finest, most popular and most successful musicians onto my 'Yes' list!

Yes, Timmy Mallet had agreed to meet me.

Just a joke. Chris Martin of Coldplay fame, he of the very catchy tunes and stunning Hollywood actress wife, had instantaneously become my favourite musician as he had become the first of this particular profession to respond to my bleating semi-begging letter. To be honest, he was up there in my opinion anyway.

For this response, I really did have to thank my new flatmate Lois and her work colleague Paul, who himself does a bit of work for Chris Martin and who brought my request to Chris's attention. When Lois told me that the meeting may well take place, I gave a faux-nonchalant 'Oh that's nice' before almost collapsing in my kitchen.

What with this joyful news, it seemed quite ironic, that my favourite Coldplay song had always been *God Put a Smile Upon Your Face.*

Then again, Chris had never met Michael.

Jules Segal

Phew, what a day! I'd been tearing around London like a cat in an aviary. I felt like Ray Liotta in that scene in *Goodfellas* where he had to deliver the silencers to Tommy, then go home and stir the stew and then go and fetch his babysitter's lucky hat for the flight to Philadelphia.

However, my tasks were slightly different. I had no baby that I was aware of, let alone a babysitter, I wouldn't even know how to begin making any meat-based broths and the nearest I'd got to a gun was at Hampstead Funfair.

It only shot corks by the way.

My first 'Greeting' of the day was of the actor David Suchet. This was to take place outside the stage door of the National Theatre where he had been performing in a play, so off I went to Waterloo for my fourth meeting in that particular corner of London. Perhaps I should rent a flat there?

I entered the stage door in good time at 1.00 p.m. and asked a lady behind the counter if this was the exit that David Suchet would be emerging from.

'Yes,' she replied with a scowl, 'He'll be emerging at about 5.00 p.m. this evening.'

'Hmm, yes, actually he's *expecting* me. I've got a *meeting* with him!'

'Well, in *that* case, he's there outside the glass door you just came in through. You walked right past him.' She let out a laugh and gave a sympathetic smile and I realised that we were in fact on friendly terms.

Anyway, she was correct. In my defence, I would definitely have recognised David, being a regular watcher of Poirot, but he had his back to the direction that I'd approached from and was deep in conversation with a friend (I believe his conversation may have been about bananas if my ears weren't mistaken). I promptly introduced myself without being rude enough to interrupt the two of them.

David was most affable. We had a brief word about London pollution (I blamed our Mayor), his friend kindly took the photograph and then we parted, with my newest acquaintance wishing me the best of luck and hoping that others engaged in his line of work were not letting the side down. I replied that they were not, it was just those from different professions that I was struggling with – sports pundits and politicians aside.

Wednesday January 11th 2006 – Greeting 34 (Bruce Oldfield)

◇◇

...and so off to the plush environs of Knightsbridge, or if you prefer, 4×4 country (although it shouldn't be).

My next meeting was scheduled for 2.00 p.m. in the shop/studio of top fashion designer Bruce Oldfield which is in Beauchamp Place (or Beautiful-Field Place for non-French speakers).

Having checked the photo from my previous meeting on the way, I concluded that there was no way I could meet one of the country's most eminent creators of haute couture in my scruffy state and that it was my hair in particular that was of serious cause for concern.

Seeing as I was early and in need of severe barnet rectification, I decided to pop into Harrods to try and buy a hat, but I'm no Pete Doherty and I don't think a £300 trilby would have suited me so I chose to look elsewhere. After much searching, I eventually went into Gap to buy a cap (and fetch a pail of water) and then made my way to Bruce's shop.

Once there, and having nearly pulled his shop door off its hinges, I noticed the 'Ring for Service' plaque next to a doorbell. The word 'service' conjured up all sorts of saucy images, I take my lead from Led Zeppelin who once surmised '...there's a sign by the door and you want to be sure, as you know sometimes words have two meanings.'

Anyway, I rang the bell and no sooner had I done so than a lovely young lady named Julia beckoned me in.

'You must be Jules,' she said, though whatever gave me away as not being a *bona fide* customer and proponent of high fashion I cannot think. Perhaps it was my Matalan trainers?

While waiting for Bruce to appear, I had a good chat with Julia who I found most endearing. I learned that she had a notable background in marketing and PR and she in fact offered to do my PR for a price, to which I replied that I could afford to pay her somewhere in the region of nothing.

Bruce soon appeared, in the company of two dogs, one large and one small and once again, as was the case when I greeted Sir Tim Rice in the company of *his* large-ish canine, I showed my true colours – various shades of yellow.

So, I'm slightly scared of dogs, sue me.

Anyway, my subject turned out to be an extremely genial man and refreshingly down-to-earth.

'So Bruce, what do you think of *my* fashion sense?' I asked him, just as Julia was taking the snap.

He looked me up and down and replied with a one-word answer and a smile, 'Shite!'

Well, you can't say fairer than that.

So that was it. I left with a chuckle and holding a signed copy of Bruce's book under my arm that he had kindly donated for the charity auction and it was on to number three.

Wednesday January 11th 2006 – Greeting 35 (Derren Brown)

I'm not really a religious man, but as far as I am concerned Derren Brown is some sort of supreme being. Not only am I frequently amazed and astounded by his illusions, acts of magic and mind readings, but I don't know anyone who has seen his act and not been amazed.

My friend James, for example, who on learning of this meeting simply said, 'Oh, game over!' which is something he often says when he is hugely impressed by someone or something. He suggested that I take Derren to a casino afterwards, where his powers might come in handy.

Well, that's just morally wrong I thought, before deciding that Derren would never agree to it anyway.

The meeting itself was planned for 6.00 p.m. at the Sherlock Holmes Hotel in Baker Street and wouldn't you just know it, I was due to meet one of my favourites from the entire list of 500 and for the first time I was destined to be late. For that I blame some half-baked cabbie who pointed me in completely the wrong direction, so a curse (albeit a minor one) on him and his Hackney Carriage.

I bowled into the hotel bar seven minutes after the prearranged time, sweaty, out of breath and possibly with an unpleasant aroma clinging to me. I even made some naff joke about the Sherlock Holmes Hotel not being elementary to find, yet Derren was extremely gracious and accepted my apology without the slightest fuss.

Not only that, but this was also to become the first of the numerous meetings that I'd had over the last six months where I was actually offered a drink and invited to stay for a chat. Top class.

I agreed, but voiced my concern that I was badly parked because of my rush to find the place.

'Actually, do you think you could communicate using the power of thought with the local traffic wardens and ask them not to give me a ticket?' I enquired.

'Consider it done,' he replied.

Derren ordered me an orange juice and he opted for a hot chocolate. When the waiter brought our drinks over, I noticed that he also passed Derren what appeared to be the crust from a slice of bread, a green serviette and a saucer. Wow, I thought to myself. My host has probably asked for these props in advance and is preparing to amaze me with an astonishing trick.

As it happens I was wrong. The crust was simply a very thin slice of cake that he dipped in his hot chocolate and ate.

We chatted for a good ten minutes or so about my challenge, Derren seeming to be very intrigued about it all. Conversation turned to the City of Bristol, where both of us had spent some of our formative years and then we discussed others from the list of 500. Derren was even good enough to mention that he'd put in a good word about me to Simon Pegg who he knew (and who happens to be another of my heroes), so I was potentially looking at another great meeting.

As we parted, I was handed an incredible gift that I initially considered keeping for myself rather than putting up for bid at the charity auction. It was a limited edition print of an original Derren Brown painting of Sir Anthony Hopkins. I have got to say, it really was pretty effing phenomenal.

So that was it, we both left and as I turned to walk up the street, I glanced behind me to see someone approach my host and saying, 'Hey, are you Derren Brown?' to which Derren smiled and exchanged words with the lad. I can safely say, therefore, that once again Michael's somewhat cynical view of the successful individual was well and truly proved wrong beyond all doubt.

Oh, and I had no parking ticket.

Friday January 13th 2006 – Typical Friday 13th

Two more from my list would not be able to help me.

I believe that it was William Shakespeare who almost said, 'If music be the food of love, Debbie Harry is a peach...' Well, he would have done if he had been alive now.

I have already stated that *my* knowledge of music was pretty limited. I confess, I once thought that Andre 3000 was Zanussi's new fridge (although come to think of it he *is* quite cool).

No, I was always more into sport. Watching, you understand, not playing – not with my physique (more meat on a butcher's apron, etc.).

What I am trying to say is that although I had only a limited knowledge of music, I was certainly familiar with the great Tom Jones, considering he had been a massive presence in British music for over four decades. I was therefore rather excited to get a response from his camp, even though it was a negative one.

The prettily-named Rosie at Valley Music wrote:

Dear Julian. Thanks for your letter explaining what sounds like an interesting endeavour! Unfortunately Tom Jones isn't in the country at the moment, and has no plans to be until the end of March...

So it seemed as though I had sent out yet another of my letters too damned late in the day. Oh well, what's new, Pussycat?

Likewise, I would not be meeting the notable impressionist, or even impersonator, Alistair McGowan who was otherwise occupied for five weeks. Carla, a representative of his, phoned me while I was mid-lavatory break to inform me that Alistair was filming in Leamington Spa (I *thought* I spotted him from the plane's window) for the Beeb. Despite my offer of driving up the M1 and M6 to meet him, Carla suggested that it wasn't quite as simple as that since he wasn't sure where the filming would be taking place on a day-to-day basis.

Not all was doom and gloom, however, as some very good news had just come my way. It concerned a famous singer.

Ooooh, how exciting...

Sunday January 15th 2006 – Hill's 'Greet' Blues

I usually like to have a lie in on a Sunday until, say, 4.00-ish in the afternoon, but this Sunday was different as I had a lunchtime appointment outside the Sky Sports studios with Jimmy Hill.

It was quite a drive to Isleworth in West London, yet once again I had arrived stupidly early and so, having parked by the security cube and barrier, I leafed through my copy of the *News of the World*. The breaking story was that of our beloved Swedish national football coach had been caught speaking out of turn to a fake sheik. That's a good topic to break the ice with Jimmy, I remember thinking to myself.

Anyway, following a lengthy wait, I approached the people in the security shed and was told not to worry and that Jimmy was probably still around as his car was still there, but that sometimes he was obliged to hang around at the studios to look after his guests, which might take some time.

I was, nevertheless, handed the charity gift (one signed photo) which had been left with them to pass on to me, and in return I left a note for Jimmy thanking him for the gift and requesting a rearranged meeting time. I then decided to take a photo of myself next to a massive sign on a building that said SKY SPORTS in two-ft high letters, just to prove to Michael that I'd been there.

I still wasn't convinced, however, by all these photos that had been splashed over my website since, as mentioned, I wasn't one who was overly happy with the face that was handed to them via the genepool.

In fact, studying the photos of all of the meetings was becoming quite upsetting for one as vain as me.

In fact, I'm SO vain, I think that song that Carly Simon wrote is about me... And not *that* song either, but the one that goes 'Baby, you're the best'.

Sunday wasn't a total washout as I was able to enjoy the visual delights of the North Circular dual carriageway not once but twice (i.e. to Isleworth and back). These included the Liu Clinic (some sort of Chinese Medical Centre that abuts the A406 and had a sign in the shape of a pagoda), the Ramada Jarvis hotel on Ealing Common and of course the perennially incomplete Wembley Stadium, which I even took a snap of. I'd taken to calling the new home of British sport the Flatfoot Stadium what with its fallen arch.

On getting home I took some lunch.

I took it from the kitchen to the living room. I wasn't sure what to have but then I remembered that it was nearly both Chinese New Year and Australia Day, so I dined on dim sum and a can of Fosters.

In the evening I attended a pub quiz which our team won. It wasn't particularly memorable, although I was introduced to a delightful young lady named Lucy, the friend of a friend and this reminded me of that old TV show, *I Love Lucy*, because... well, I loved Lucy.

Lucy had a boyfriend.

I hated my luck.

In fact, to quote that fantastic line once uttered by Rodney in *Only Fools and Horses*, 'I'm so unlucky that if there was such a thing as reincarnation, I'd probably come back as me.'

Monday January 16th 2006 – Foggy Oggy Oggy

I now had just under one month left until this bet with Michael would presumably be lost. I was really going to have to crack on with sending out the final 40 or so of my 500 letters.

In the meantime, I'd received a reply from Sue who works for Carl Fogarty at Fogarty Petronas Racing. For those who are not into sport as much as others, shame on you. Carl is the Blackburn-born man made good, extremely good in fact, in the world of motorcycle racing.

On-line encyclopaedia Wikipedia even states that Foggy is considered to be 'the most successful Superbike racer of all time...'. He had ridden his Ducati to become the World Superbike Champion on no less than four occasions. We can rejoice in the fact, as we do with Andy Murray, Amir Khan, Phil Taylor, Ronnie O'Sullivan and various others, that this man of prodigious talent is one of ours; another Great British sportsman.

Sue mentioned that Carl would be happy to make my acquaintance at the Silverstone Race weekend on the 26-8th May. I soon thereafter spoke to Sue and mentioned that, money permitting, I hoped to be travelling somewhere near Koh Phangan or Fraser Island by then, as *Greeting the 500* ended in mid-February. She kindly agreed to get back to Carl to see if something might be sorted out a little sooner.

Meanwhile, I was continuing to sleep in snatches, for want of a less crude double entendre, maybe just five hours of broken sleep each night. This was now starting to ravage my Adonis-like body and my Einsteinian mind.

I could now say for the very first time, that I would be absolutely ecstatic and elated when this was all over and I'd no longer have to send out my letters to the likes of **Jilly Cooper**, **Jimmy Saville**, **Phil** 'the power' **Taylor**, **Eric Bristow**, **Barry Norman** and **Dennis Norden**, as I did this day.

Yes, by now I was desperately longing for it all to end, after which time I couldn't care less if I never came across an eminent ballerina or member of the British Bobsleigh team again.

Tuesday January 17th 2006 – Self-Abuse

As brutally honest replies go, this was certainly way out in a league of its own. I must admit I smiled when I read it, primarily because despite its slightly negative tone, I've always been a fan of people who speak their minds. Just ask the countless people that I've offended during my time, generally because I always thought it better to say it as I saw it rather than to beat around the bush like some mealy-mouthed backstabber.

Added to that was the fact that Will Self was a man that I'd often found rather entertaining and, to be fair, in his letter he did make some interesting points.

Jules Segal

Dear Mr Segal,

I did not reply to your utterly specious request for a long
time because I could not conceive how either you or your friend
believed that 'meeting' 'celebrities' would prove anything
about the human race one way or the other.

I do hope you did not pursue this senseless enterprise for too
long and that in 2006 you will spend your time more profitably.

Yours sincerely…

So there you have it. I took that as a 'No' to a meeting.

I've also since looked up the word 'specious' (it wasn't good), have
digested the rest of the contents and have concluded that, basically,
he was right.

So, Michael, both Will and I think your idea stinks.

Joking aside, this letter highlighted a number of points that, despite
the fact that they've been delved into on more than one occasion by my
good self already, probably need further clarification.

Let us once again analyse the use of the word 'Celebrities'. As I have
pointed out, this is a word that tends to prefix a large swathe of the
current crop of rather vapid programmes on TV. So much so, in fact,
that within 20 years or so, just after the last of the ice-caps have floated
up the Corinth Canal, this Sceptered Isle will be awash with glamour
models and we will be having to import our doctors and lawyers from
El Salvador.

I had always stopped short of using the words 'celebrity meeting' or
'celebrities on my list' because – I repeat once again – this project
wasn't meant to be about 'Celebrity' as in *heat* magazine or ITV light
entertainment programmes, or perhaps I still hadn't made that clear.

This bet was started because someone levelled the hypothesis that
once a person had achieved success in his or her field, ego would
dictate that they would tend to elevate themselves above the general
masses. I disagreed.

If I had ever used the term 'celebrity' on my website, and this is totally
true, it was purely because I'm lazy and it was seven words shorter
than typing out 'individuals who have achieved success in their field.'

Now, *prima facie*, my challenge appeared to be nothing more than a jolly outing, an opportunity for Julian to meet and fawn in front of famous people, but as I have tried to explain, it was simply a stupid bet, something that once started, and committed to with the RNIB, I felt obliged to see through.

I've also mentioned that as one of life's quitters, I rarely complete what I start, be it a film script or a Big Mac. I can assure you that I had wanted to knock this whole project on the head many times over the previous six months, but first, I really didn't want to let the charity down, and second, I really couldn't bear to face the knowing glances and cutting comments from my family members, having again witnessed me give something up midway through.

For the first time in my life I actually wanted to cross some sort of finishing line (other than the one in the high hurdles race that I've already mentioned, where I nearly castrated myself).

As for spending my time more profitably the following year, I couldn't have agreed with Will more wholeheartedly. The amount of money I'd spent on letters, stamps, paper, petrol and parking tickets coupled with my underpaid day-job, had seen me living off Branston pickle, cupcakes and Petit Filou, but no need to get out your violins, I am not after any sympathy. Believe it or not, and I don't care if you don't, I was actually rather thankful that Will had bothered to reply to me (he was one of the few who had), thankful that he enabled me to clarify my position, and thankful for his blunt honesty. (And that's not just me kissing buttock.)

Wednesday January 18th 2006 – Marr, He's Making 'Ayes' At Me

Day 200. I couldn't actually believe that I'd been rushing around the country for almost eleven-twentieths of a year engaged in this peculiar 'star' trek. At least I'd only got seven-hundredths of a year left to go.

Although I tried to stick to my guns about not including the unholy trinity of politics, profanities and the appendage '*über*' on my website, I fear that at this point, I was forced to go back on my word.

The former political editor of the BBC, Andrew Marr, had become the latest person to agree to a meeting. This man, who would often be seen on the *BBC Evening News*, standing outside Number 10 (possibly wondering why a scruffy young man in a brown hooded track suit top had just been granted an audience with the Prime Minister's wife) would be available for handshaking duties the following week.

My tally was still gradually being pushed towards the 40 meeting level, so it was looking unlikely that I'd have to insert my arm inside a piece of beef that was still mooing.

On that subject, I give you an exchange that occurred between myself and my friend Polly at about this time:

'So one of your forfeits is to help a rural vet as he checks on a cow's pregnancy situation?'

'Yup.'

'Well, what makes you think that you'll have to delve your hand into the cow's waste pipe as opposed to the more obvious cavity?'

'Oh yeah, that's a point. Then again, I never *was* very good at biology.'

'Well, let's hope you never want kids.'

And although that's how we left it, I subsequently discovered that my hazy recollections of a certain scene from *Vets in the Wild* HAD actually been correct all along. Here is an excerpt from the *Southern Regional Beef Cow/Calf Handbook* as revised by A.M. Sorensen Jr and J.R. Beverly:

'*The following discussion describes a way of improving the calf crop percentage through pregnancy determination and elimination of non-pregnant cows. This determination, called palpation, is made by inserting the arm into the rectum and feeling the reproductive tract for pregnancy indications.*'

So shove it (quite literally).

I also owed a certain talk-show host named Jonathan Ross a huge debt of gratitude for he too had agreed to a meeting. Well, to be more precise, thanks really ought to have gone to an absolute gem of a lady by the name of Suzi, who produced Jonathan's show and who had been extremely helpful in pinning him down – but not in that way.

Come to think of it, I also had to thank my friend Ivor Kayne, whose name, I had discovered, sounded a bit like a mild over-the-counter sedative if you said it quickly enough; it was Ivor who put me in touch with Suzi in the first place.

Anyway, no more thanking for the time being, this wasn't the Golden Globes, which reminds me... Scarlett Johansson.

Carl Fogarty would also be meeting me far sooner than I had thought, so that was a third agreement of the day. On the downside, Thom with a silent 'H' Yorke, lead singer of the group Radiohead, would not be able to meet me, as my friend Aviva, who was friendly with the band's manager, had sent me an email that read:

'I am really sorry but they never do stuff like this, everything is done for charity in a very private way.

As you can imagine, they get an enormous number of requests.'

Not to be too down-hearted, I carried on fighting the good fight by sending another eight letters out to **Daniella Westbrook**, **Nigel Kennedy**, **Sir Clive Sinclair**, **Victoria Wood**, **Jodie Kidd**, **Lennox Lewis**, **Rebecca Loos** and **Shakin' Stevens**.

Thursday January 19th 2006 – Greeting 36
(Neil Kinnock)

I spoke to Gideon today, remember him? The one who took the photo of myself and Sir Ian McKellen several weeks earlier. His breakfast milk had obviously curdled on this day, as he was in a right mood.

To begin with, he described Michael (quite correctly) as 'that lazy s**t whose dining off the fruits of *your* labour whilst sitting on his ar*e doing nothing'. That was fair enough.

Following this potted character assassination, though, he turned his attention to me.

'And as for you... Remind me, why are you going around shaking hands with all these people again?'

'I've told you why, Gideon. No, I'm not a hand fetishist or a... sorry, what did you call it?'

'Palm-o-phile.'

'No, not a palm-o-phile, either.'

'Well, I'll tell you one thing that you are, a right little sycophant. If you'd have done any more sucking up in front of Ian McKellen, Mr Dyson would have tried to patent you.'

Those weren't his exact words, he doesn't have a huge capacity for wit because he's usually too busy working out mathematical formulae on his laptop, but that was the gist of it – that I was some sort of obsequious lick-spittle.

True enough, I had said, 'Pleased to meet you, Sir Ian' and 'Thanks so much for agreeing to this, Sir Ian', but I'm not sure what Gideon had expected me to do (swear at the poor man?).

Anyway, I *do* generally have problems working out how to address titled individuals. I even had a discussion to this effect with Fiona Phillips when I met her. For example, should short members of the royal family be called your *high*ness? Should ambidextrous High Court judges be called the *right* honourable?

In the case of Lord Kinnock, though, my mind was put at rest before I'd even met him.

I was aware that here was a man of substance and good old-fashioned values. A man who ten minutes before our meeting was scheduled, actually called *me* on my mobile phone to apologise and to inform *me* that he'd be several minutes late. And this from a former leader of the Labour Party and EU Commissioner. What impeccable manners.

You see, I like that. Where others would have simply kept me hanging around in some dingy waiting room, leaving me to count the gold embossed fleur-de-lis on the wallpaper, Neil Kinnock kindly put me fully in the picture.

At his offices near Westminster, I introduced myself to the friendly security guard and took the opportunity to ask for some advice.

'So how should I address Neil when he appears? I know he's a Baron but should I call him Baron Kinnock, Lord Kinnock, Mr K, Neil....?'

'M'lud will do.'

I agreed and considered this good practice should I ever get called up before the beak, perhaps for using copyrighted pictures on my website.

I didn't have to wait too long for my photo-opportunity to arrive and the picture was duly taken by the aforementioned helpful security guard. One thing of note was that my usual apparel of brown hooded top wasn't on display this time. I thought I'd make a special effort as I was meeting a Peer of the Realm, for heaven's sake, so I went for an all black ensemble at the risk of being stopped and asked to deliver a box of Milk Tray.

As we made our way up to Lord Kinnock's office to fetch the auctionable gift, with me jabbering away about some pointless topic (I think I was praising the design of the water-jug in the waiting room), I could tell that my host had become somewhat distracted.

This hunch turned out to be correct, since on entering the lift Lord Kinnock turned to me with a friendly smile and said, 'Listen, *do* stop calling me Lord Kinnock. It makes me feel so bloody old, call me Neil,' and with that, I warmed to him even more.

Upstairs, Neil kindly handed me a tie for the auction, I believe in the colours of the University of Wales and following John Motson's similar donation of neckwear accessory, I started thinking about opening up my own branch of Famous Ties-R-Us.

I thanked Neil and, at his request, told him a bit about my professional background.

'Well, I've had a number of jobs to be honest. They keep managing to lose me but I'm currently working in the heady and exciting world of data entry.'

'Oh really? Do you intend to make a career out of that?' he jokingly replied.

'Why Neil, what are you offering? A peerage?'

– laughter –

'Afraid I can't help you there. You'd best speak to the Prime Minister about that.'

After that we had a brief chat about football hooliganism, not because

I was angling for the position of Sports Minister, but because I wanted to inform Neil that I *had* actually been in his presence once before: Wembley Stadium, 1982, Milk Cup Final (Liverpool 3, Spurs 1). My dad and I were cowering in our seats as two thugs were terrorising several rows of the stand with aggressive posturing and the sort of language that would make Bernard Manning blush. Up steps one robust Welshman sitting next to us, who was equally trying to protect his son from the foul tirade, a bit of rough and tumble ensued and before you could say, 'order, ORDER!' the two bullies were sent packing from the Stadium, tails between their legs.

The leader of the Labour party earned himself a slightly bloodied nose in the melée and I recall my dad going up to him at half-time and saying that although this wouldn't affect the way he intended to vote at the next election, he was extremely grateful to Neil for saving the day.

'Yes, that made the papers didn't it?' recalled Neil. 'I remember Glenys being none too impressed about that whole business when I got home.'

So that was it, another meeting chalked off and the two of us left the building together, Neil presumably heading for some important discussion on the British Constitution and myself heading to the Jade Cottage for a duck and rice.

'Oh, say hello to your father again from me,' said Neil with a smile as he walked off into the distance.

Friday January 20th 2006 – Greeting 37 (Chris Martin)

NOT IN MY WILDEST DREAMS could I have expected a vitriolic conversation in a boozer to have resulted in a day like this one.

How do you put into words the fact that one of the most revered musicians anywhere in the world was, on this very afternoon, staring at the 'Tintin & Red Rackham's Treasure' poster on my living room wall?

Chris Martin, the lead singer of Coldplay, one of the hottest acts around and the group whose *X&Y* was the biggest selling album in the world that year, became the 36th individual from my list to shake my hand and the first of them who enabled me to sit around on my a**e while *they* travelled to meet *me*. For the record, he also became the first person I had 'Greeted' to be married to a stunning Hollywood superstar.

I will detail exactly what went on when Julian met Chris in just a few moments, but first please permit me to keep you in suspense for a wee while longer while I rattle off a few other humdrum bits and pieces that I would like to mention.

To begin with, I'd received an email that had pointed out some inaccuracies that I made when I wrote about meeting David Suchet. In the film *Goodfellas*, Henry delivers the silencers to his friend named 'Jimmy' and not to 'Tommy' (who had already been, how you say, whacked?). Second, in the same film, the babysitter was taking a flight to Pittsburgh and not to Philadelphia. So there you go, we can all sleep a bit easier now.

It also appeared that my local newspaper, *The Hampstead and Highgate Express*, had run another piece about my project so I was grateful to them for their continued interest in it and in particular, for not using the photograph of me that looked as though my head had been wedged inside a goldfish bowl.

It appeared as though my illustrious neighbours were starting to rally round me in my hour of need. Chris Martin Friday afternoon, Jonathan Ross the following day and who knows, maybe Jude and Sienna for Sunday lunch at The Hill, but I wouldn't bet on it.

I had waxed lyrical about Chris Martin and Coldplay a number of times since this had all started – long before he agreed to the handshake to be fair – but the fact that he was willing to pop round to my flat to accommodate my request really hammered home just what a gracious young man he must be. He was incredibly down to earth as well: the sort of bloke you could probably nip down to the pub with and chat to about the delight's of Anneka Rice's buttocks, as if he was one of your old buddies.

(Sorry, Gwyneth.)

Gideon would no doubt say that I was once again sucking up to someone, but come on, he was only in the country for a few days, his wife was pregnant yet he still went out of his way to help me.

At this stage I would again like to thank my flatmate Lois and her colleague Paul for facilitating this meeting. Lois told me the previous night that Paul and Chris would pop round to the flat the following lunchtime, since which time I had been rushing round emptying ashtrays, running the old 'J. Edgar' over the carpet and feverishly cleaning the plate next to the sink that had some sort of moussaka cement on it.

Over the previous few days, I had also informed a couple of my workmates that this music legend might be nipping round to my flat and I asked them for advice as to whether I should get a four-pack of Stellas in. The general consensus was that this would be a bad idea since I was told that Chris was an extremely healthy guy who didn't actually drink all that much. I replied that I wasn't really thinking about Chris.

No, it was suggested by the girls at work that I either rustle up a green salad or else buy some macrobiotic tea. After a bit of consideration I decided to do neither, partly because the only thing I can 'rustle' is an empty crisp packet and partly because I don't know what macrobiotic means.

So, there I was that afternoon, lounging on my settee sucking a Chupa Chup and completing *The Evening Standard* cryptic crossword when *Sky News* interrupted their bulletin to broadcast a BREAKING news flash.

(Oh, please don't let this be a story informing me that the world was about to end, or that a meteor was heading for London – I always panic a little when I read BREAKING NEWS. Let me just meet Chris first, if only to learn how to play 'Clocks' on the piano.)

It turned out that I needn't have worried because the rather peculiar story that was breaking was in fact about a whale that was swimming in the Thames somewhere near Albert Bridge. Well, what's so odd about that, I thought to myself, that's where whales usually swim – in water.

However, having watched the pictures for a little while I did have to agree that it was all a little bit too peculiar for me, particularly as I was in a fragile state of mind as it was. Could this be a portent that the end was indeed nigh?

'For lo, it was written that the whales will beach themselves near Costa Coffee on Putney High Street, and the lion will lay down with the aardvark and then eat it and then the world will sort of just explode!'
Kevin 4:20

Fortunately, I didn't have too long to become concerned by this obscure diversion because at that exact moment the door buzzer rang. And there he was, standing outside and looking up at me through my video-entry phone was the unmistakable face of Chris Martin, a man who I'd last seen on TV or in a newspaper or some such form of media and who was now just outside my flat staring at me. He was standing next to Paul and from what I can remember, waiting to be let in.

Well, after a brief '*Rush of Blood to the Head*', I composed myself, opened my front door and greeted them.

First impression, blimey, he's tall. Second impression, excellent, he's slightly unshaven; I don't look out of place. I also remember he had piercing blue eyes. Now don't get me wrong, I'm not a homosexual or anything, not even latently, not that there's anything in the least bit wrong about being gay even if I was, which I am not (OK, I'll shut up now), but I instantly realised how this talented singer, who grew up in sleepy Devon, was ultimately able to end up with one of the most beautiful women in the world by his side. He really had, what I think you could call, presence.

After a brief hello and the offer of a drink (politely declined), and having recently heard that he and the missus were expecting their second child, I offered Chris my congratulations.

'What for?' he replied.

'Oh. Errrm I thought that I just read two days ago that you and Gwyneth had announced that she's pregnant once again. Did I get that wrong?'

'Oh, right. Yeah, that. Thanks.'

I decided to put this brief memory lapse about his second offspring down to the fact that he was busy studying his strange surroundings. After all, he'd come to this dusty, crusty flat, with all it's gauche and tacky ornaments littering the living-room, like some sort of tramp's attic, for no other reason than to shake someone's hand. As I watched him surveying the place, I started to form the opinion that he might just have been starting to get a little bit frightened.

Anyway, as I couldn't really think what to say I soon found myself gesticulating towards the TV and blurting out (incorrectly on two counts) 'Have you heard the news? There's a dolphin in Richmond.'

It suddenly dawned on me though, that to any normal person who *hadn't* heard 'the news', this complete gibberish might sound like the rantings of a psychopath who'd just escaped from Rampton, and in any other circumstance I wouldn't have been that surprised if the two of them had at that point decided to make a polite excuse and get the 'f' out of there. Fortunately, they were aware of the story, Paul mentioned that they'd heard about it on the radio in the car.

So there the three of us were, this giant of the music industry sitting on my very own coffee table (don't worry, it's a low and sturdy pine one), his manager sitting on my settee and myself standing up, as we watched this sickly animal floundering around in the filthy waters of SW1.

Chris quite rightly pointed out that it was really touching and poignant that an incident like this truly bought out the best in people and bought the community together in their attempts to rescue the poor stranded beast and I think I replied by saying:

'Hah! Look at that funny woman's little orange bucket.'

Well, much as I hated to tear everyone away from these tragic events, we thereafter got down to the handshake and photograph. Following this, we briefly chatted about the bet and how I needed a total of 100 handshakes to win it and how even with those that were scheduled I still only had about 50 and how I was therefore destined to lose.

Chris was an absolute star. He said that he was happy to help someone from his 'hood' (he lives nearby I think) and even wrote a message and drew some pictures on a piece of paper that I had spare and which some lucky so-and-so would win at the charity auction. Paul also very kindly said that he would try and pass something else on for the auction.

I was so touched by the generosity of Chris who, let's face it, probably had countless better things to do on one of his four free days back in London, that I really wanted to reciprocate.

As we headed towards the front door, I noticed a pack of Cadbury's Mini Eggs on the worktop in the kitchen and I was very close to giving them to Chris to pass on to baby Apple for a little tea-time treat, but in hindsight I'm so glad I didn't. Potentially lethal: small, hard, pebble-shaped edible things and baby's windpipes are really not designed for one another. Not to worry, I said to myself. I'll let Lois or Paul pass on a small cuddly toy on the arrival of his second child. Gosh, that's nice of me I thought.

That *might* have been the end of it, but it wasn't. Having just shut the front door on the two gentlemen, I suddenly remembered the lack of toilet-paper in my flat. Yes, *that* was the reason that my stomach cramps were by now building up to a bubbling crescendo. I'd been prevented from 'going' all morning because of this fact.

No problem, I could just nip up the road and get some bog roll. Hang on, no I couldn't. Chris and Paul were outside the kitchen window having been cornered by a couple in the street. That was nice of Chris to stand there chatting, but I couldn't walk out past him; he might think I was following him. He'd probably think I was a right weirdo. Yes, walking past him then would just be very bad form.

I knew I'd have to wait a while yet *unbelievably* and in total contrast to Michael's cynical view about how famous individuals such as Chris would absolutely *hate* being bothered in the street, this world-renowned musician carried on chatting to that couple for no less than 25 MINUTES.

By this time, my bowels, or at least one of them, were close to bursting point and I was starting to scour the bedroom for my least favourite article of clothing. Fortunately, following this most protracted of conversations with two randoms outside my flat, Chris and Paul finally walked off. This then enabled me to scurry off in the same direction to buy the toilet paper, which in turn ultimately enabled last night's curry to scurry down my lower intestine and into the London sewerage system.

'How was the meeting?' asked Lois when she got in that evening.

'Yeah, they were really nice,' I replied, in an understated way. 'Shame I couldn't have hung out with them for a bit longer.'

'Really? Well, you probably could have done. Apparently, after they left they just went across the road to the Haverstock Arms and stayed there for much of the afternoon.'

Hmmm, I wonder if they discussed Anneka Rice's buttocks?

Anyway, later that afternoon I recounted the whole day's events to Michael, who wasn't aware of any of what had gone on – the whale story or that Chris was popping over (he'd been sleeping all day, surprise-surprise) – and on learning of these extraordinary occurrences, he asked me whether I'd been standing next to a petrol pump for too long that morning, but what I recounted here is exactly as it happened.

You know what, frankly I didn't care what happened with the bet after all of that, should I turn out to be the winner or the loser when all was said and done. Nope, this day and all of its surreal highlights would live a long, long time in the memory and that was good enough for me.

... So what happened then? Well, after a day as odd as that one, I was seriously looking forward to winning the massive £85 million jackpot on that night's Euro Lottery.

I bought 14 tickets.

Saturday January 21st 2006 – Greeting 38 (Jonathan Ross)

The fact that I'm even writing this book means that I didn't win £85 million on the Euro Lottery the previous night as I expected and I am not currently lying in my mansion in Mauritius (one lucky star and one number if my memory serves me correctly). Nope, the entire '85 long ones' were won by a very lucky Irish lady.

On this Saturday, Jonathan Ross was kind enough to help me out in my quest after Suzi, who produced his TV chat show, had put many a good word in for me once she had learned what I was doing from my friend Ivorcaine.

So there we all were, at lunchtime in a BBC building off Great Portland Street, watching Jonathan through a glass partition as he and his guest, the comedian Omid Djalili, made us and no doubt all of his listeners laugh as they considered the plight of the poor whale in the Thames. Not in a cruel way though, you understand.

After his radio show had ended, Suzi introduced me to the big man and then took the picture of the two of us while I complimented Jonathan on his delightful suit. In fact, the soothing violet sheen emanating from it had a rather calming effect on me. Jonathan informed me that this was one of his more sober outfits.

Once taken, Jonathan suggested that I check to see whether the photo was of useable quality since, as he put it, 'Did you see Suzi when she was taking it? She was shaking more than Hitler in his bunker.'

The picture was fine, once again spoiled only by the fact that I was in it.

So another meeting complete and down in the street, Suzi mentioned that she would try to send me a signed copy of one of Jonathan's scripts from his TV show for the auction and ask a couple more others from my list to meet me. I was delighted by this news and told her that she had now gone down as being the most helpful person I had yet encountered since starting the whole thing.

A name for the Christmas card list in 11 months time.

Sunday January 22nd 2006 – The Morning After

'... If I was two-faced, do you really think I'd have chosen this one?'

I'm just recounting part of a conversation I'd had during a miserable Saturday night, when I bumped into a very hostile ex-girlfriend of mine at someone's birthday. What an aggressive lady.

(Some of my crueller friends used to call her the 'Parrot Keeper' because she'd had a cockatoo in her time.)

So yes, a nightmarish evening and I had to apologise to the birthday boy when I left the restaurant midway through the main course. In fact, the only joy I had all night was reading the graffiti in the toilet cubicle, where some high-brow intellectual had written 'God is dead – Nietzsche' on the wall of the crapper and some little japester had written 'Nietzsche is dead – God' underneath.

Sunday wasn't much better as, to start with, I had overslept. Someone once said that even a stopped clock tells the right time twice a day. That's not true of mine, a 24-hour digital one whose LEDs had become stuck on 88.88 at some stage during the previous night.

On the plus side, I'd received another reply, which I would actually have learned about the day earlier, had I bothered to check my pigeon-hole on the Saturday.

I've mentioned before that I'm certainly no bookworm, but that is largely because I don't have the strength in my arms to read too often. However, I *had* heard of Jilly Cooper and was delighted to receive a letter from Pam her PA, who mentioned that she was:

Sorry to be the augur of bad news, but Jilly is frequently bombarded by requests and she simply can't accede to them all.

231

To Pam's great credit, she certainly seemed to have immersed herself in the details of this strange bet that I was involved in, as she continued,

```
I would be grateful if you could inform Michael that Jilly's
isolation, if indeed it is the case, is due not to her success,
but as an endeavour to try and ensure her continuing success.
She sets a strict schedule to enable herself to write a minimum
of eight hours a day…
```

To Pam's greater credit, she used words like 'augur' and 'accede'.

I duly informed Michael of this latest reply in the negative. He simply shrugged and smiled and said, 'Oh dear, not doing too well are we, dearest?' Michael reads even less than me. Menus are about as far as he gets.

You see, he didn't really have much interest in attending his oddly named school, Quintin Kynaston, which was perhaps why he once said to me, 'You know there are three types of people in this world, those who can count and those who can't.' Although on this occasion, perhaps he was joking.

Monday January 23rd 2006 – Greeting 39 (Andrew Marr)

You know it's cold when you wake up and you can see your breath in your own bedroom (and it wasn't a pretty sight). That's assuming you do not live in an igloo, where I'd assume that *every* morning would be a bit parky.

As I lay in bed on this glacial morning, with a mean wind having travelled all the way from the Urals in order to rock a Land Rover on my street and set off its car-alarm at 5.00 a.m., I thought to myself that one good turn gets all the bedclothes.

Trying to get back to sleep with the automobile equivalent of Kate Bush on helium (metaphor 162a) 20 yards from your head is another matter however.

I lay there considering the logistics of the day, which turned out to be a puzzle more confounding than the riddle of the sphinx. How do I meet Andrew Marr at 10.00 a.m., Bob Holness at noon and get in to work for 9.30 a.m.?

The answer was, I didn't; I turned up late for work (no great crime since, as I have mentioned, I am (un)paid by the hour). After all, how could anyone be expected to work a full shift on what was supposed to be (as three people had already reminded me) 'the most depressing day of the year', even though my most depressing day tends to coincide with my birthday.

In order to try and sound more intelligent to Andrew Marr than what I be, I thought I'd have a glance at the day's papers so that I might be able to pose an interesting question or two to this political guru. The paper had a big story about the now sadly deceased 'Wally the Whale'. It nearly made me blubber.

I've never really trusted the news, to be honest. I remember being confused as a child when I read certain headlines and even in this day and age you can stumble on such pearls of uncertainty as 'Stolen Painting Found by Tree', or 'Grandmother of 8 Shoots Hole in One', or 'Middle Eastern Head Seeks Arms', or 'Coach Fire – Passengers Safely Alight'.

I met Andrew at BBC Broadcasting House at the end of Regent Street and had not one solitary interesting question to ask him or point to make. Nothing about the Liberal Democrats or about Mr Blair's school reforms or British spies in Moscow or the Gorillaz playing at the Brit Awards.

Andrew arrived promptly at 10.00 a.m. in a jovial manner and with chipper efficiency and I scoured the foyer for someone to take the snapshot of us, while an old lady with one of those shopping trolley/upended suitcases on wheels, looked on in bewilderment. I've no idea what she was doing there. Perhaps Broadcasting House has an Asda on the third floor, or she suffered from dementia or something.

Eventually, we approached the friendly-looking security guard who reminded me of a jollier and far more pleasant version of Robert Mugabe.

'Excuse me, do you think you could help me? I'm after a photograph with this gentleman,' I enquired, displaying the camera to him. 'Sure!' he beamed, and bless him, if he didn't go and stand next to Andrew and wait for *me* to take a picture of the two of *them*.

'Ummm, no, I'd like to be in it, if possible. I'll take one of you two later if you like,' but he wasn't fussed and helped us out before proudly resuming his post once more, at the entrance to the elevator lobby.

Andrew kindly presented me with a signed copy of his book before I thanked him heartily and made to depart. I confess I had a bit of trouble leaving the building as, for the first time in my life, I encountered a revolving door that needed a button to be pressed for it to work.

Jolly Robert Mugabe explained how it all worked before giving me a smile and a wink as I almost decapitated myself on my way out.

Monday January 23rd 2006 – Greeting 40 (Bob Holness)

It was then on to my second meeting of the day as I headed to Waterloo.

By some odd quirk of fate, this brunchtime meeting turned out to be my FIFTH one in this curious little pocket of London. I had no idea that Waterloo was so swiftly becoming the new Beverly Hills, but there you have it.

Not only that, but I was back at the National Theatre where I'd met David Suchet just two weeks earlier.

On this occasion I had slightly more time on my hands, so before the meeting I decided to broaden my intellectual horizons by wandering around the Saatchi Gallery and then venturing to the Tate Modern to cast a discerning eye over Rachel Whiteread's 'Unilever Series'.

Actually, I tell a lie, I did none of the above. I ate a full-English in the train station café.

I was supposed to meet TV Presenter Bob Holness, best known I would imagine for his stint as the host of *Blockbusters*, late last year, yet on that occasion circumstances had conspired against us.

This time everything went like clockwork (and unlike the clock by my bed which still stood at 88.88). Just after midday, as I stood outside the bookshop inside the theatre complex, an elegant lady whom I took to be Bob's wife approached and enquired whether I was Jonathan.

'No, I'm Julian.'

'Oh. Do I mean Julian? Yes, I think I do. Sorry, Julian. I'm Bob's wife, he'll be here shortly.'

I assumed that Mrs H had confused me with Jonathan Livingstone Seagull (no relation) and as we waited, we had a fascinating conversation where I discovered that she had been an actress herself back in South Africa. She had even bought along one of the last surviving *Blockbusters* fleece tops, her own in fact, and kindly offered it to me for the auction.

Bob appeared soon afterwards and was as polite and as charming as his wife, handing me a signed photo to go with the fleece.

Mrs Holness then did the honours with Michael's digital Nikon Coolpix 885 and, after studying the photo of Bob and myself, I complemented her artistic flair and announced that we had a budding David Bailey on our hands. I then thanked them again, wished them a pleasant day at the Equity event they were attending and headed off to Blackfriars Bridge to catch my bus to work.

I must say, it's a very interesting walk along that particular part of the Thames bank. Past the OXO Tower restaurant (where I'm sure the gravy is top notch), past a very small patch of grass named Bernie Spain Gardens, and then past Sea Containers House... ? Who on earth would want a crate of seawater in their living room?

And who's Bernie Spain for that matter?

Tuesday 24th January 2006 – Greeting 41 (Carl Fogarty)

It was another day off work (Hurrah!) for no pay (Boooo!), since I had to leave the smog-filled paradise of London to head 'oop' north for two more meetings.

Definitely no rollercoaster rides for me though, as I had finally limped past the 40-meeting mark.

I was speaking to one of my oldest friends last night and said to him, 'You remember when I used to go out with that beautiful German model?' and you know what, he had *completely* forgotten that as a child I used to fly my Airfix Messerschmitt aeroplane in the park every day.

My current German model is a VW Polo 1.4, which, despite being covered in dents and scratches, the poor beast, still managed to get me from London to Burton-on-Trent, Burton-on-Trent to Birmingham and Birmingham back to London without once emitting smoke or a disconcerting noise.

I was due to meet the former four-time World Superbike champion Carl Fogarty, at his Burton HQ at 12.30 p.m. today but I turned up closer to 1.00.

Some unfortunate lorry driver had had a bit of a prang and had spent his entire wad all over a hard shoulder just outside Toddington Services. This meant that much of my journey was spent several inches behind the van of P. O'Brien Heavy Plant Hire – For All Of Your Heavy Plant Needs (presumably full of large flowerpots then).

Once we all got moving again I tried to make up for lost time, and almost ended up in the Shardlow Gravel Pits just on the outskirts of Castle Donington, but I did eventually make it to the Foggy Petronas HQ in one piece where, despite once again having difficulty trying to open the door of the building, (I'm not sure what it is with me and doors), I managed to track down Sue who was my liaison lady for the day, and soon thereafter she introduced me to Carl.

While I'd been in the waiting-room, I tried to swot up by reading the World Superbike 2004 compendium that had been sat on a table next to me, in order to try and impress Carl with my knowledge of his sport. I'd even made a mental note that the number one Foggy Petronas rider was an Aussie called Troy Corser, and so when Carl arrived....

'So Carl, hoping for a good year? Do you think Troy will do the business for your team?'

'Unlikely,' he said with a smile. 'He hasn't ridden for us since 2004.'

'Oh yes, sorry, of course. So now it's...'

'Craig Jones and Steve Martin.'

'Oh yeah that's right, Craig and Steve. Yeah, they're very good, both of them.'

I don't think I got away with it and neither did I help matters by mumbling something about Steve Martin switching from *Planes, Trains and Automobiles* to powerbikes, but this was thankfully ignored.

Sue took a photo of Carl and myself in the team workshop next to three of the most amazing looking bikes I have ever seen and which would no doubt have ripped my shoulders from their sockets had I tried to ride one of them.

Carl's manager Neil then appeared and asked for a photo of his own for the Foggy Petronas website, which I was rather flattered about, before I was handed no less than six signed posters for the auction, two of Carl, two of Steve Martin and two of another rider, Garry McCoy, as well as a signed team shirt. I was delighted with this little bundle of gifts, so I wished them well for this season, asked them for directions to Birmingham, then sped off into the distance.... within the legal limit I should add.

Tuesday 24th January 2006 – Greeting 42
(Joe Pasquale)

Having waved goodbye to Carl Fogarty, I headed down to Birmingham on the A38 - a lovely little route that took me near Uttoxeter, Southwell and various other places I'd only ever seen mentioned in the Racing Post. I was to meet Joe Pasquale at the Birmingham Hippodrome where he was appearing in pantomime.

Everything seemed to be going reasonably well until I got a bit lost around that sprawling collection of motorways on the outskirts of Birmingham, Spaghetti Western or something, but eventually I found my way to the centre of town and parked in the Bullring shopping centre. This is as good a place as any to park, I thought. I'll have no problem finding my way around the City Centre, I thought.

I reckon that they should call the sequel to *Lost in Translation*, 'Lost in Brum'. I'm not talking about the 'why thoy spuyk', an accent which, in all honesty, I quite like, but because the centre of the City is just so damned confusing. So while on one hand I'd been wise enough to print out a map of the city centre before I'd left London, on the other hand, I was soon informed by a friendly local that I was wandering around off the edge of the page.

Eventually, I did find the Birmingham Hippodrome and was welcomed by a door manager in the foyer who, despite not wanting to give me his name for fear that I might mention it on a website or in a book, agreed to show me downstairs to meet Joe as well as Ian (the person who had helped to coordinate the meeting).

'What about me?' said a slightly frenzied looking young guy just behind us as we headed to the elevator. 'I am a good friend of Joe too. He'll remember me, just mention my name', (he gave it).

'Is he expecting you?' enquired my guide.

'I'm a *really* good friend of his,' said oddball with increasing desperation. 'Tell him that we once met in Bromley.'

I almost laughed out loud when I heard him say that, but this slightly menacing character had an unnerving air about him; I decided that I preferred my trachea the way it was.

Joe was a top guy and following on from numerous enquiries that I had had since this meeting took place, I can confirm that 'Yes', he does sound like that in real life. Unless, of course, he was putting the voice on.

Ian took our picture, one where Joe and I looked as though we were old friends, while in reality he probably couldn't wait to get shot of me. My host then nipped back into his dressing room, came back out with a signed photo for my auction and then told the doorman that he was more than happy to go and say Hi to the Bromley stalker upstairs. What a trooper.

Thursday January 26th 2006 – We're Going To Need a Bigger Boat

My throat hurt. This was primarily because I hadn't yet taken the lead of Ai Ai the chimp and was continuing to generously donate a large amount of my loose change to the Mr Benson and Mr Hedges benevolent fund. In other words, lead me not into temptation (because I'm perfectly capable of finding my own way there, thanks).

So why in particular did my windpipe feel as though I'd swallowed a thistle? Why did I feel more exhausted than Rip Van Winkle on Zopiclone. And what's with the odd title mentioned above, as first spoken by Police Chief Brodie in the movie *Jaws* (film reference 32b)?

To be honest, this particular fourth week in January was completely insane. I suppose you could say that it all started with a phone call from a man who worked for the search engine Yahoo! earlier in the week.

By the way, have I mentioned that Yahoo! is, in my humble opinion, the best search engine the world has ever borne witness to? If I haven't, I should have done.

The man at the end of the phone was calling to inform me that my crummy website had somehow won the Yahoo! Website of 2005 award in the 'Celebrity' category, (what, are you nuts? as a stereotyped New York mobster might say). Yes the 'Celebrity' category – sigh –. This was presumably despite my poor grammar and spelling and not because of it.

I told him to pass on my huge thanks to the panel of judges and that I would see to it that their loved ones were duly released.

The man from Yahoo! went on to inform me that I might receive a bit of publicity because of the award and that I might get the odd phone call from a newspaper or radio station. He hoped that I'd oblige anyone who called with a brief interview. With hindsight, I can inform you that he used the word 'might' as in 'hammering a nail through your toe *might* cause pain'.

The last three days had, therefore, seen me complete more radio interviews than bore thinking about, the last of which made me sound like a castrato (I am not) when I heard it played back to me, saw me welcome a *London Tonight* TV crew to my compact and un-bijou flat (whereupon the presenter took the piss out of me off-camera and called me a stalker – how original) and saw Marli's patience wear increasingly thin as I was forced to leave the office every three minutes to recount 'funny anecdotes' to journalists from various national newspapers.

My website had received 300000 hits in three days and had since crashed (hence the above title) and I received almost 400 emails in the same amount of time from all around the globe. And that wasn't even including the 'spam' ones that were trying to sell me Viagra or enquiring whether I wanted to increase my penis size (which was from an ex).

I subsequently watched myself on TV, which I found quite horrific I can assure you. I can safely say that I took to televison like a duck to treacle. For someone of a nervous disposition at the best of times and one not hugely taken by their own image, this was almost enough to push me over the brink and lead me to seek out directions for Beachy Head.

A work colleague found it ironic that this 'social experiment' I had undertaken, where I hoped to shed light on the approachability of famous individuals, had eventually led to my own face being splashed across the papers and on TV and that I'd found this so difficult to handle. Well, that's all very true and I am sure there is a moral in there somewhere.

And what of Laffing Boy? Well, he'd become a complete nightmare, of course. Whereas I'd been totally overwhelmed and not a little embarrassed to give soundbites to the media before my story became the next day's chip-wrapper, Michael was *desperate* to speak to someone, anyone at all, about his take on everything.

The distinct lack of interest in him had made him become rather bloody-minded about everything. He moaned and groaned that the essence of the bet was now totally ruined and that any of the meetings I achieved from there on in would be purely down to the fact that I had appeared in the papers.

I countered that this *still* didn't mean that anyone from my list would benefit in any way by meeting me, for which Michael had no answer, so he carried on eating his chicken drumstick and staring at *Trailer Park Boys* (the TV show I mean) and pretended not to hear me.

Friday 28th January 2006 – The Three That Shouldn't Count (But They Did)

'They asked me to appear on Richard Hammond's *Five O'Clock Show* yesterday, I had to go. Hopefully that'll be the last one now.'

'Oh, that's nice for you.'

'Oh, come on. Don't be like that, Michael.'

'Like what? No, I am fine. I am really glad everyone's hearing *your* side of the story.'

'...Anyway, I got three more handshakes after the show: Richard Hammond, Mel Giedroyc and John Gordon Sinclair. I'm up to 45 now.'

'Umm, no you're not. I don't remember putting any of them on your list. Who the hell is Mel Giedroyc anyway?'

'You know, the Mel from 'Mel and Sue'. She was a co-presenter.'

'Oh right. Well, no, none of them count. Not on the list.'

'Oh come on, Michael. Don't be a *****. I am doing really badly here. You know you're going to win whatever happens and besides, you've included people who live in New Zealand, Spain and the USA on the list.'

I was getting nowhere fast and was just about to give up with my pleading when something astounding happened. Michael rose from the settee, walked to the window and stared into the frosty street below. He continued to stare out of the window and eventually, without turning round simply said, 'OK fair enough. I suppose you *have* put a lot of effort into all of this. Alright, on this occasion I'll let them count,' before raising his hand as if to wave me away.

He didn't actually utter 'Now begone!' but he did then strut out of the room as if he was Caesar and I was a helpless beggar to whom he had just thrown some crumbs of food.

Friday 28th January 2006 – Greeting 46 (George Galloway)

This Friday evening was most relaxing, as for once, I had decided not to usher in the weekend by *paying* to stand around in a *free* house. I'd been watching a fascinating nature programme about lions of the Serengeti, but eventually I got a bit bored with it. I suppose if you've seen *one* lion catch an antelope, you've seen a maul.

I only mention this because on the subject of the cat who got the cream, I also unexpectedly greeted George Galloway on this day.

I had been invited by the producer of Radio 5's *Drivetime* to have a brief conversation with the show's presenters live on air that evening, presumably to discuss whether my project was similar to something that Dave Gorman might do or to ask me whether I was a stalker. In my haste to get this over and done with, I turned up to the BBC's Millbank studios 30 minutes early for my appointment.

A sympathetic receptionist named Alison apologised that the studio wasn't ready and that there was nowhere for me to sit. I asked her what I ought to do, maybe a tap dance in the corridor, to which she laughed and basically told me to just shove off for 20 minutes, although much more politely than that, so I walked up to Parliament Square to read that protesting guy's posters and then walked back again.

I tried my luck at reception for a second time and when Alison saw the shivering little waif in the corner, she took pity and kindly offered me *her* chair, which of course I ungallantly accepted.

Following my brief radio chat, and as I was preparing to leave, who should I see marching around in the marbled foyer in a very dapper navy blue overcoat? None other than the Member of Parliament for Bethnal Green and Bow, who presumably was there to be interviewed about his stint in the *Celebrity Big Brother* house, the house he had just been voted out of two days earlier.

I must say, I have absolutely no intention of discussing politics here or the rights and wrongs of a politician agreeing to appear on reality TV, the only thing on my mind was that George Galloway was on my list of 500, and so I approached him and his cohorts.

I introduced myself, mentioned that I'd written to him at his constituency and asked whether he had received a letter detailing my odd request. He replied in the negative and so to make things easier, or because I simply couldn't be bothered to explain what I was doing, I asked if I could have my photo taken shaking his hand.

To be fair, after everything that had been written about him in the preceding days, he had every right to eye me with a great deal of suspicion and to make a polite excuse and refuse, but to his credit he was happy to oblige and for that I was thankful.

Funnily enough, some time after this episode occurred I remember seeing George being interviewed by a particularly hostile news reader who was castigating him for having appeared on said reality TV show at the expense of his constituents (her words not mine). George was unmoved by the questions and claimed that he didn't regret going on the show for one moment and that very soon after being voted out of the *Big Brother* house, he'd even had people coming up to him wanting to shake his hand.

Just in case he *was* talking about me on that occasion, I would again like to point out that this particular handshake was SOLELY as a means to an end in a bet and should not necessarily be taken as an expression of approval for his feline displays of affection towards Rula Lenska, or indeed his political leanings. My own personal views on those facets of Mr Galloway's character shall remain private.

However, I would like to thank him for introducing me to the word 'scintilla', which I once heard him use in a televised debate. I love it and frequently bandy it about.

That was that; I was slowly but surely (and rather belatedly) creeping up the list of forfeits and only ten more handshakes were now required to prevent me from having to stand for an entire day at Oxford Circus with a bucket and placard. Sorry to all at the RNIB, but that was one that I was particularly keen to avoid.

Saturday January 29th 2006 – Correction Time

My friend Paul, the person who advised me to set up a website in the first place all those months ago, gave me a call to mention that he had recently been glancing at mine and that he gave it his ringing endorsement, although he does actually suffer from mild tinnitus (true) so he may have simply been referring to that.

However, the main purpose of his call was to find out why I'd become the new Walter Mitty and had been lying to the press about every aspect of my life and about my progress in the bet.

Therefore, here are one or two comments that were written about me at the time, which needed just a minor bit of tweaking, lubricating and general fiddling with, in order to make them true:

○ *Julian, a legal publisher* – Jules, who inputs data for a legal publishing company. I say this because I don't wish to be sacked for misrepresenting my job and because I hate the name Julian.

○ *A list of 500 celebrities* – a list of 500 successful British individuals. Not this old chestnut. Hopefully, you know my feelings about the C-word by now.

○ *Zany/crazy/wacky 27-year-old* – nope, sadly I hadn't shed seven years. I was actually 34 at the time and although I am highly neurotic I don't believe this crosses into the wacky or zany realm.

○ *Has six months to meet 500 people* – has six months (extended to seven-and-a-half months) to meet 100 people from a list of 500 drawn up by his friend. It's amazing how difficult a concept this seemed to be for people to understand. I was considering changing the name of the bet to GREETING THE 100 OUT OF 500.

○ *Stalking* – zzzzzzzz...

Jules Segal

O *Has greeted 68 people so far* – would that this were true. Only 46 met with just 16 days left.

I hope that, like an industrial sized tube of Biactol, I have now cleared a number of things up. Thank you.

That last simile was brought to you by the children's television workshop and by the letter 'Z' and the number '10'.

Sunday January 30th 2006 – Mike TV
◇◇

...a character from a Roald Dahl classic, but it could also refer to an irascible slugabed being interviewed on *Sky News*, as so nearly happened on this day.

Just over two weeks were left and 21 people had still not yet been written to because I hadn't been able to find contact details for them. Therefore **Keith Chegwin, John Culshaw, Eddie the Eagle, the Hamiltons, Stephen Hendry, Sam Heuston, James Hewitt, Matthew Kelly, Jay Kay, Nigel Mansell, Malcolm McClaren, Linsey Dawn McKenzie, Colin McRae, Jimi Mistry, Ian Poulter, Claire Rayner, Louise Redknapp, Salman Rushdie, Ricky Tomlinson** and **Anthea Turner** could rest safe in the knowledge that they would not be receive one of my pathetic personal pen letters.

Thankfully, I had almost come to the end of my Yahoo! media obligations as well. I'd promised to do a little piece for *BBC Breakfast News* on the Monday and *Channel 5 News* on the Tuesday, but I thought that would just have to do. After all, familiarity breeds individuals wanting to bottle you over the head.

As for Michael, he was positively drooling about the fact that *Sky News* had asked him to join me for a live interview on this particular morning and was therefore utterly inconsolable when, on our arrival at the studios, the runner that was looking after us announced, 'I am ever so sorry but there's been a breaking story about Saddam Hussein storming out of court just now and so we only really have time to use Julian.'

I suggested that Michael go on the show instead of me but it wouldn't wash with them. So inevitably, on the way home Mr Happiness Personified was spitting out vitriol and bile towards the former Iraqi leader for ruining his big moment of stardom. In fact, he didn't stop there, as blame also fell on George Bush, the presiding judge, and had I not told him to shut up, would no doubt have gone all the way down to the Lithuanian Environmental Secretary.

'By the way,' he said to me as the cab dropped him outside his front door, 'I watched you on TV in the studio reception. Your teeth looked quite orange.'

Touchez!

Monday January 30th 2006 – Can't Cook, Won't Cook, Can Swear

A man by the name of Richard, who was the producer of Radio 1's *Colin and Edith Show*, kindly invited me to take part in one of my slightly unorthodox get-togethers with Edith Bowman later that week. I quite fancied Edith, so Richard, I salute you.

Meanwhile, Sian who works on *Ready, Steady, Cook*, informed me that Ainsley Harriott would also be happy to help. She stated that they had all found my project very amusing and asked whether Michael and I would appear on the show, one of us in the 'tomato' kitchen and one in the 'pepper' kitchen.

I thanked her for her kind offer but had to politely decline. You see I had visions of Ainsley asking my friend live on air, 'So Michael, what are you going to cook for us?' and Michael replying with his usual customary charm, 'What does it look like! It's a f*****g flan of course!'

As for my third reply of the day, I turn to another of the ladies of my boyhood dreams, Michaela Strachan. Not just a delight to behold but with a rapier-like wit too it appears. I quote:

To Julian,

I wish you all the best with your Greeting the 500 project. I'd love to help but considering I now live in South Africa I think it could be a bit further to travel than your budget allows.

I AM filming in Borneo and Kenya if that's easier!!

All the best, Michaela.

She wrote this on a signed photograph which will feature in the auction, the little angel.

I assumed that splitting the difference and meeting in Calais would be out of the question then.

Monday January 30th 2006 – Bifidus on Toast Please

My challenge would soon be over. All I could say was roll-on Valentine's Day (and I'm sure many people did), I'd seriously had enough, particularly bearing in mind days like this one where I was asked to wake up at 6.30 a.m. to conduct a telephone interview from my bed, only for the DJ on Radio Brighton, one Tommy Boyd, to say, 'face it, you're just an attention seeker, aren't you?'

Nice.

My state of mind had not been helped by the fact that I was by now eating at irregular hours and I probably had not been getting enough Bifidus Digestivum. I imagined that my reserves of L. Casei Immunitas were rather depleted as well. I felt a sudden urge to go and eat some sort of dairy product that was 'live'. Meanwhile, Michael was grumbling about his nutrilium and his active retinol and I told him that his 'retinol' would be active if he insisted on eating so much melted cheese.

A lady by the name of Joyce kindly telephoned me in the afternoon to inform me that Sir Ranulph Fiennes, British explorer extraordinaire, would be able to meet me later this week. Our meeting would be taking place in Legoland (obviously).

I had also decided to increase my meetings tally by one, even though I shouldn't really have done so. My second-last television appearance, probably ever, occurred on the *BBC Breakfast News* that morning. I was asked whether the lovely anchor lady, Kate, could take a photo of me shaking hands with anchorman Dermot Murnaghan live on air.

I agreed and so although Dermot didn't actually appear on the list of 500, I unilaterally decided with Michael that this *would* count as one meeting, basically because it was forced on me. So there.

The photo saw me once again looking as though I might have just walked off the set of *Shaun of the Dead*, but I felt better a few hours later, when I opted to sup on a nice tall glass of Ylang-ylang, or beer as I sometimes call it.

My final TV appearance ever, was destined to be a fascinating one, for no other reason than wheezing-boy Michael had been invited to accompany me on *Channel 5 News* the next day and I'd been assured that he *would* get some air-time on this occasion.

I wondered how far into the interview it would be before he uttered his first expletive.

Tuesday January 31st 2006 – Greeting 48 (Tom Baker)

Belated Happy Australia Day to all my Aussie friends. Belated Happy Year of the Dog to all of my Chinese friends. Belated Happy Year of the Person to all of my canine friends, but then again they probably won't be reading this. By the way, I am a pig (1971).

This day heralded, with genuine hope, my last ever appearance on TV, on *Channel 5 News*. Michael was on as well. The big man was in his element, like an excited child on Christmas Eve. Needless to say we were arguing all day. He was jibing me about everything. The fact that I needed to steel myself with a propranolol before going on a TV programme ('Where's your backbone?'), the fact that I had to ask someone whether my coat would be safe if left in the green room ('Yeah right. Someone's going to nick it from here...') and anything and everything I did was criticised by my so-called friend.

I suppose he was just a little too gee-ed up. He knew that one of his biggest heroes, the actor, voice of *Little Britain* and Doctor Who number four, Tom Baker, would be there at the same time. Michael even has a tattoo of a question mark on his bicep in honour of the Timelord.

All went fine apart from when we came off air and Michael shouted to me in a corridor about how upset he was that his chests had looked so large on the TV screen (he had caught a glimpse of himself in a monitor). I told him to pipe down because our helpful runner, Jayne, was walking just in front of us when he'd shouted the words 'MASSIVE BOOBS' and I was worried that she might have got the wrong end of the stick.

The two of us argued some more.

As we were getting ready to leave, Tom Baker appeared by the green room. He was a great sport and more than happy to have his photo taken. Once done, he turned to Michael and asked if he'd like one as well.

Michael got rather flustered and told him not to worry as we'd been told that Tom was in a bit of a rush (and he didn't have his Tardis with him). My moody friend then ended up cursing his own stupidity for missing out on such an opportunity. In fact, he continued to curse all the way to Chinatown where he gorged himself on *char siu bun* in the Joy King Lau and then lamented the size of his tits once more.

Tuesday January 31st 2006 – Greeting 49
(Edith Bowman)

Two 'greetings' for the price of two on this day as having already clasped palms with Tom Baker, the afternoon saw me shake the delightful hand of Edith Bowman.

I elected to take the tube to Oxford Circus, since my meeting was scheduled for the West End and because I was fed up having to stump up for the Congestion Tax. By the way, for anyone who lives their life by the adage 'change is inevitable', try using the vending machine at Tottenham Court Road tube station.

Richard, the producer of Edith's show, welcomed me to the studio just after 4.00p.m. and Edith finished her brief phone call to her friend about 20 minutes later. Once done, she ambled over to me with a broad grin and as she neared, I momentarily forgot where I was, and watching a smiling girl approach me, I almost reverted to default mode and asked for her phone number. Fortunately, I gathered my bearings quickly (I think she'd have probably said no, anyway).

Edith was a real gem, friendly, down to earth and happy to natter away with me. She praised my efforts and we soon got on with the two photos, one a regular handshake and the other, a quick cuddle (hurrah!). I kept my hands to myself, I promise.

Following that, another absolutely amazing gift for the auction was handed over. I was now in possession of one of those metal records inside a glass frame. This one was 'to recognise sales in the UK in excess of 100 000 copies of the album *The Magic Numbers*'. It had Edith's autograph on it and I had a feeling that it would raise a pretty penny for the RNIB.

I wasn't familiar with that album, to be honest, or with The Magic Numbers, but I decided to resist the temptation to smash the frame and listen to it, largely because I didn't fancy hoovering glass up for ages but more importantly, because I don't own a stereo.

Tuesday 31st January 2006 - Hugh Absolute Star

One final message on this day. A real quickie, a metaphorical peck on the cheek behind the bike sheds, as I had to get some shuteye before an early meeting with Sir Ranulph Fiennes the following morning. I received an email from David who represents Hugh Cornwell, the erstwhile lead singer of The Stranglers and a group that happened to have recorded some of my favourite songs of all time. I was informed that Hugh was aware of what I was doing and was keen to help, but sadly he wouldn't be flying in to London from New York until February 15, the day after this challenge was meant to end.

I was going to have to do some serious arm twisting with Michael. Maybe a full Nelson with a double sledge for good measure.

In light of Hugh's willingness to help, I was also going to have to disagree with whoever it was that said there were 'No more heroes any more.'

Oh, it was Hugh himself.

Meanwhile, a friendly young lady named Stephanie, who worked as PA to the football agent Skylet Andrew, called me to say that she might be able arrange a meeting between myself and the young Spurs striker Jermaine Defoe. I asked her to 'Hold on a moment while I pass out.'

For good measure she also mentioned that she was a very, very good friend - nudge, nudge - of Heart 106 DJ, Toby Anstis and that she would see what she could do on that score as well.

CHAPTER 9 – February

Replies received: Gary Bushell.

Meetings achieved: Sir Ranulph Fiennes, Lesley Garrett, Ainsley Harriott, Gary Bushell, Toby Anstis, Jamie Theakston and Hugh Cornwell.

Wednesday February 1st 2006 – Greeting 50
(Sir Ranulph Fiennes)

Among this day's offerings that squeezed into my tight email inbox, was one from an individual of ambiguous gender who referred to themselves as Butterkist - a brand of popcorn that one could munch their way through at the cinema in the 1980s, if I am not mistaken.

He/she wrote '*Michael appears to be your foil...*' and having given it some thought, I wholeheartedly agreed. Foil in the sense that you would often find him wrapped round a piece of roast chicken.

To be fair to the old 'Bubble', I suppose I must thank him for taking all of my flak with relatively good grace. I had known the lad for about 19 years by now and I had to be honest, he could actually be pretty amusing when he wasn't screaming.

Jules Segal

I met the explorer Sir Ranulph Fiennes at Legoland in Windsor this morning, where he was giving a lecture.

Having been told by his agent that time would be of the essence and that I really ought to be at the Legoland Manor House at 7.55 a.m., I was bricking it slightly, if you'll pardon the pun, when the security guard at the main gate refused to let my car through the barrier.

'I'm sorry sir, I really can't let you pass. We weren't informed that you'd be coming. It's more than my job's worth, yadda, yadda...'

Well, praise the sweet Lord that after several hurried phone calls, such creases were ironed out and I was informed that Sir F. was on his way and would be happy to meet me by the barrier.

A bitterly cold and deserted open-air car park in Windsor is no place to spend an early February morning at the best of times, yet, fortunately, I didn't have to stand around for too long wondering whether it was snow or sleet that was falling, as Ranulph appeared out of the gloom and promptly apologised for the rushed nature of the meeting.

Apology graciously accepted, I removed my coat so that the old dog-muck brown hooded top would appear in the photo just as an icy blast sliced across my midriff, leaving me a shivering mess.

At this point, I swear that I was close to saying, 'It's bloody *freezing* today, isn't it, Sir Ranulph'. This, to the man who had single-handedly traversed the Bentley Subglacial Trench in Antarctica, was the first human to reach both the North and the South Poles and had suffered his fair share of frostbite in the past.

I'm glad I didn't mention the cold.

For the auction I was given a signed copy of one of Ranulph's books, *Race to the Pole*, which I would really like to have read, but decided that it was best not to as my fingers tend to be quite smudgy and are often covered in barbecue sauce. I thanked him, wished him luck in his lecture and clambered back into my mint condition car, in other words the Polo, to make the short drive back into London.

Friday February 3rd 2006 – Greeting 51 (Lesley Garrett)

I've been told that when I sing I have the voice of an angel. Well, I say an angel, I mean some croaky cherub that enjoys gargling crushed glass. What I'm trying to say is that the karaoke bar that I go to has recently formed a partnership with the local glaziers.

Lesley Garrett, however, HAS got an amazing voice. Not surprising really, she's the premier opera singer in the country. She had kindly phoned me the previous afternoon, while I was trying to fix my chair at work (it wouldn't recline to the sleeping position) and mentioned that she would be happy to meet me.

So there I was in the foyer of the Classic FM studios the following day, speaking to Frank who works at reception:

'Want to make your way up to their offices on the sixth floor and grab a cup of tea?' he asked.

'Well, I'm not sure. Perhaps I'm meant to wait for Lesley down here.'

'Look do me a favour, mate, and just go upstairs, will you? I don't want to get in trouble for leaving a guest sitting down here in the cold.'

It's all me, me, me with some people.

Up on the sixth floor I walked into an oasis of tranquillity in the middle of the rat race that is Oxford Street: beautiful view, classical music being piped through the sound system (obviously), potted palms, plates of free fruit and lovely furnishings. I wouldn't have minded living there. They even had a piano by the beautifully designed open-plan chrome and pine kitchen. It was all very *Ikea Catalogue*.

Before long, Lesley appeared and made her way over to me.

'Thank you so much for agreeing to this,' I said, which had been my opening gambit ever since the very first 'Greeting'.

I'd been informed by a friend that Lesley was a good old Yorkshire lass and was half expecting her to reply, '...eee pet. Nay problem,' but she didn't.

She was charming. First things first, the gifts were handed over for the auction and it was more amazing stuff. A unique signed T-shirt that Lesley had worn when she ran part of the baton relay for the Commonwealth Games – all the more generous when one considered that this top must have had a special meaning for her.

'How far did you have to run?' I enquired.

'Oh, only about half a mile,' she nonchalantly explained.

'Cor! I'd never have been able to do that. I have trouble running a bath.'

Well, if that wasn't enough, I was also given a signed copy of *Classic FM Magazine* with Lesley's photo on the front and if THAT wasn't enough, the magazine contained a free CD, 'The Best Recordings of 2005' which included Bach's *Keyboard Concerto No.3* , Allegri's *Miserere*, Schubert's *Trout Quintet* and Timmy Mallet's *Itsy Bitsy Teeny Weeny Yellow Polkadot Bikini*. Actually, not the last one.

The photo of myself and Lesley was taken by Suzi at reception and, as you might see, I got another hug, which was starting to become quite a perk of all of this. I enjoyed all the hugs. Perhaps I wasn't held enough as a child.

Once taken, Suzi looked at it and said, 'You know, you're really photogenic,' to Lesley, and 'no offence to you,' to me. Oh well, I have promised not to say anything more about my face looking like a spanked ar*e, so I won't.

There was more good news when I got home as both journalist Gary Bushell and DJ Toby Anstis would be able to meet me the following week. My next target of 55 meetings was looking very do-able. I just needed to find two more subjects between this date and the 14th and I could avoid the whole charity money-raising thing on the streets of Westminster. YES!

I know that might have come across as sounding a bit selfish but come on, as a lazy sod, I think I'd done my bit by now.

Monday February 6th 2006 – Absent Without Leave

For someone who should have been rushing around trying to scratch out two more meetings from somewhere, I had far too sedate a weekend. I spent a large part of it on the settee, watching Tiger Woods win the Dubai Desert Classic at the Emirates Golf Club while fidgeting with my nuts (I was fidgeting with them I mean, Tiger wasn't).

Did you know that the 14th hole of this particular golf course is bordered by the largest bunker in the world.

Yes, It's sometimes known as the Arabian Desert.

– drum crash, cymbal –

Once again, I wasn't at work on this Monday, not because February 6th (or possibly the first Monday in any February) was, so I am told, 'National Sickie' day, where more of us than ever decide to huddle under our duvets rather than faff around on the internet at work, but because Matt and his RNIB colleagues were taking me out for lunch.

Whoever said 'there's no such thing as a free lunch' had obviously never been on remand in one of HM's prisons; neither did they try and have their photo taken while shaking an assortment of hands. I was truly grateful to the RNIB for what I was about to receive – liver and mash I decided to go for. I think the RNIB were quite grateful to me too, so mutual gratification then (which sounds rude for some reason).

It had been decided by all concerned that the 'Celebrity Item Auction' would take place on eBay following the conclusion of the bet, partly because I didn't know where to buy a gavel from and partly because the job lot was quite heavy and I have but the body of a weak and feeble woman (and a VW Polo that doesn't work very well).

As for my poor return of meetings, particularly with members of the fairer sex, this morning my friend Tony told me how and why I'd got my tactics all wrong in trying to shake hands with the likes of Kate Winslet, Kate Beckinsale and Rachel Weisz.

You see, these lovely young sirens might have been more inclined to meet me had I already met individuals of the ilk of Richard Branson or darts player Phil Taylor. Or as Tony put it, 'First you get the money, then you get 'The Power', then you get the women...'

Unbelievable. I throw a 'sickie' just to watch *Scarface...*

Tuesday February 7th 2006 – Greeting 52 (Ainsley Harriott)

What a very arduous day this day was. Much of it had been spent in South London. Those two statements have no correlation, by the way.

Permit me to fill you in, just as if you were some prize turkey and I was holding a handful of chestnuts and sausage meat.

I was forced to undertake a mammoth triangular mission today, much like the one that allegedly put paid to JFK I suppose. I'd taken in almost every borough of London, heading from the Central North of the city, to the South West, across to the South East and then back up North again. I'd basically cut a slew across a huge Dairylea triangle-shaped wedge of the Capital.

My day was supposed to have begun at 8.30 a.m. at Heart FM radio station near Shepherds Bush where I was to meet DJ Toby Anstis. However Steph, my contact, texted me late the previous night to enquire whether wires had been crossed since Toby had been patiently waiting for me YESTERDAY morning.

It seems as though dimwit here had made a stupid error in jotting down details of the meeting. I'd got a bit confused (with the emphasis on the fused, what with the crossed wires and everything). I hoped that another meeting could be arranged.

On the plus side, I had a lie-in.

I was then to meet Ainsley Harriott at a TV Studio in Wandsworth, where an episode of *Ready, Steady, Cook* was being filmed.

The address of the studio was Wandsworth Plain, a name that conjured up images of thousands of bison roaming over Putney Bridge, but I can confirm that I passed no such shaggy animal on my way (although I did spot the odd zebra, crossing).

I arrived slightly early at the studios but was met by Santa's little helper for the day, Amy, who escorted me past the canteen and offered me tea (accepted) and lunch (declined).

While waiting for Ainsley to arrive, my thoughts turned to the poor chef in the canteen who bore responsibility for preparing his lunch. I mean, imagine being a chef and seeing Ainsley or Gordon Ramsey or Gary Rhodes rock up. *That's pressure.*

I was alerted to the arrival of my host by a huge peel of laughter (I know it should be spelled 'peal' but I thought it more appropriate to use a reference to food) coming from the corridor.

It wasn't long before I was whisked (there's another one) onto the set by Emma, the show's producer, who was also kind enough to take the photo(s). I even managed to swallow my pride and pass a message on to this famous chef from my mother.

'Just to let you know, Ainsley, my mum thinks you're lovely.'

'Aaaaah how sweet,' he replied, before continuing, 'Wooooweeee hot mamma...' in an eye-bulging fashion.

'Well, hang on, you haven't seen her yet,' I mumbled. (Just a joke mum.)

After the snaps were taken, I apologised to Emma for not taking up the offer of appearing on the show with Michael, but to be honest my kitchen skills are so poor that I actually burnt a fried egg on the Saturday before this.

I departed clutching lots of great *Ready Steady Cook* stuff for the auction, all signed by the good man himself, in order to cross the vast wastelands of South London for my second meeting of the day.

Tuesday February 7th 2006 – Greeting 53 (Gary Bushell)

Getting from Wandsworth to Sidcup isn't easy. You need to be both a navigator of World Rally Driving standard and also ambidextrous (to turn the pages of the *A to Z*). I went the Tooting-Streatheam-Norbury-Thornton Heath-Elmers End-Beckenham-Bromley-Chiselhurst route, but there was probably a quicker one.

The journey was relatively uneventful. I do, though, remember passing Bird in Hand Lane near Bickley, which I thought quite appropriate as I had two (meetings) in the bush that day.

I also happened to pass extremely close to the home of yet another former squeeze of mine, Clare with fair hair, who hailed from Bromley (possibly somewhere near Joe Pasquale's friend). It wasn't a problem, there was no restraining order or anything, but I decided not to pop in and say 'Surprise!' to her parents, anyway.

Lovely girl, Clare, although I guess I threw a minor spanner into the works when I told her one week into our five-month relationship, 'Y'know this relationship is ultimately doomed. We may as well just carry on seeing each other until we find someone better.'

Inevitably, she did first.

As I approached Sidcup, I phoned Gary to let him know I was on my way and he suggested that I pop round to his home, so he joined Sir Patrick Moore, Sir Tim Rice and Jeffrey Archer on a new list of 'famous people's homes I'd been in' (not including Scarlett Johansson's, since she wasn't aware of it at the time).

Gary's pretty companion took the photo, although I'm not entirely sure why I was directed to stand in a particular spot beneath a shield of St George on the wall, possibly because Mr Bushell was a staunch patriot and wanted the shield to appear in the photo, or maybe it was simply because the colour of the wallpaper masked my sickly pale complexion. Anyway, once snapped, and following some general chit-chat where I discussed with them what exactly my mission entailed, I was kindly given a signed copy of Gary's book.

I then let my host get back to watching *EastEnders,* but not before he had given me directions up towards the Blackwall Tunnel.

It turns out that I'd have been better off walking home since I soon encountered the Great-Aunt of all traffic jams on the A20 by the Longlands Flamingo Park.

Total time spent in a car today, three hours 14 minutes; distance travelled. about 30 miles.

Thursday February 9th 2006 – Greetings 54 and 55 (Toby Anstis and Jamie Theakston)

◇◇

Only five more days to go, only 46 more meetings needed, only a miracle could save me now.

So what if I was to lose. Fine, I'd have to buy Michael a pay-per-view Sky football season ticket. I would have to sporadically clean his toilet, the bowl of which usually looks like The Somme after a particularly muddy battle. I may even have had to stand at Oxford Circus for one entire day trying to get people to donate to the RNIB (lunchbreak allowed, by the way). The question was, had it all been worth it? Someone once said that 'Time is a great teacher, but unfortunately it kills all of its students,' and I suppose if I had had my time again, perhaps I wouldn't have taken part in this crazy folly, but it certainly had its moments.

Back to this day and it was off to Heart 106.2 FM to greet two DJs, greetings numbers 54 and 55, respectively.

On driving to Latimer Road, I was deciding whether or not to spill my thoughts out to Toby Anstis when I met him. You see, I'd been considering asking my latest willing listee for advice on affairs of the heart (he does work for that radio station after all).

Basically, I had a dinner date the night before which had turned out to be... well, just dinner. I wasn't upset by the non-responsive attitude of the young woman in question, unfortunately she was 'a little *confused at the moment*'. In other words, confused about how to get out of the awkward situation of being sat opposite someone she didn't fancy.

Well, again, I'm deviating a little here but I decided not to burden Toby into giving me relationship advice because where would it all end? I might end up confessing that I was having a mini nervous breakdown because of my recently blocked toilet. I wasn't sure how it got blocked, the only things I'd been flushing down were toilet paper, an old manuscript of mine and someone else's body parts.

Back to this morning and I got to the correct road but could not for the life of me find the Chrysalis Building and it was then that something really strange happened. While your average man, woman and child in the London street tends to storm up and down the pavement without a cursory thought for those around them, and usually while wearing a frown, on this occasion, every single person I encountered seemed to be unbelievably altruistic.

I'm not sure why, possibly because the sun was shining. Or maybe they'd heard the old proverb: 'Be nice to other people – they outnumber you 5.5 billion to one.'

Cabbies and van drivers let me turn in front of them at will, a toddler waved at me from a bus (surely she wasn't watching me on Sky News?), an eastern European man in a newsagents actually offered to walk me to the building and a young Irish lady at a bus stop literally showed me to the door. All of this put me in a really good mood and made me love this brave new city of ours even more.

After the crossed wires of earlier in the week, there were no mistakes today. I arrived early and Jane behind reception made the appropriate calls upstairs after first embarrassing me by saying, 'I think what you're doing is sooo funny.'

Toby appeared soon afterwards and really was as nice as 3.1415926... etc. (Don't blame me if you don't understand that. You should have paid attention during double maths instead of scratching your name into the desk with a compass).

Jane took the photo and I was then invited into the canteen to sip coffee but the bean doesn't agree with me early in the morning so I politely declined and bid Toby farewell and good luck with his show at 9.00 a.m.

Fast-forward 25 minutes and Jamie Theakston appeared, his show ending as Toby's started. He too was as sound as a quid and was happy to have the photo taken. He also presented me with the gift, a Heart T-shirt signed by himself and Toby, as well as a couple of other DJ's, Emma B and Greg Jones.

So that was it, two more down, one or possibly two more to go. I did hope that the Spurs striker Jermaine Defoe might have time to meet me within the following few days. You never know, he might even turn up at my house, slap me on the back and say, 'Hey, how's it going, you old tosser!'

Well, he's always been a little forward.

Sunday February 12th 2006 – Will to Win

I had just got home from a bracing constitutional across Primrose Hill. I do like long walks (particularly when they are taken by people who annoy me) and now with this dreary night closing in, I had the perfect opportunity to unblock my toilet with sulphuric acid and to stuff my oven and subsequently my gullet with Mini Kievs.

Let me cut to the chase. Theoretically, I had 52 hours left until the bell rang and 'Time, gentlemen' was called on my bet with Michael. An appropriate analogy really, seeing as how this whole foolish experience started following a heated discussion in the Cricklewood Crown.

I was also quite clearly going to lose the bet, though, and lose it heavily. In fact, the last time a wager of mine went so awry was when I put £10 on Roll A Joint in the 1990 Grand National. The poor horse not only fell at the Canal Turn, it also died there.

No, I was quite clearly not going to reach my target of 100 meetings before the Tuesday night since I still had 46 to go, yet when all was said and done, after 227 days of rushing round the country, vying for supremacy over Michael, we were not left with a *total* anticlimax. We did still have something of a cliffhanger, albeit in this instance a rather unimpressive rocky outcrop, of say, 8 ft in height.

In order that I would not be forced to undergo Forfeit 3, that is to say, freezing my chestnuts off on a street corner for eight hours, I needed one more handshake in what was left of my time.

At this point I ought to remind you of a reply that I received way back on August 1st from a lady called Kirsten:

On behalf of Mr Hague, I would like to thank you for your letter of 4th July concerning the challenge you have accepted.

Mr Hague would be happy to meet you though, now that the House is in recess, I am afraid that it will not be possible to make any arrangements until the autumn. However, if you would not mind, I will make a note to contact you then in order to agree a suitable time to meet.

I therefore jotted down a meeting with The Rt Hon as being one that was in the bag, like a ready-cook cod in parsley sauce. I had subsequently spoken to Kirsten a couple of times, yet despite being an eternal optimist, I now finally had to resign myself to the fact that Mr Hague *was* probably too busy to accommodate me after all.

Either that, or else perhaps he never returned from his summer holiday in Magaluf. I would, however, not wish the MP for Richmond to spend a restless night tossing away, asking himself how he could have let me down so badly and so I say to him, 'William, it was really nothing.'

Meanwhile, despite the young Steph's best endeavours, it also seemed unlikely that I would have time to meet Jermaine Defoe within the next two days and so I turned my attention to another hero of mine, former *Stranglers* frontman Hugh Cornwell.

We did have a bit of a quandary, however, since although Hugh had now announced that he would be popping over to mine, to help out for the greater good, in other words 'me', he couldn't actually make it until the 15th, a day too late, as he was in America until the Tuesday night.

It was with that in mind that I recently approached Michael and played, what I came to call 'the Jimmy Hill card' to try and seek a final 12-hour extension.

As you may recall, back on January 15th, I journeyed all the way to Isleworth to meet Jimmy who, prior to the meeting, had agreed to go through the motions with me, yet on that day, despite kindly leaving me a signed card for the auction at reception, was unable to leave the studio to give me some skin.

The fact that I made the effort to drive to the depths of West London at 8.30 a.m. on a Sunday morning, saw Michael mumble something about my probable crossing of the Intenational Date Line over the last seven and a half months and so, as Mr Fogg before me, I was thankfully given a final 24 hours. He didn't really care, anyway. As far as he was concerned, he'd proved me wrong weeks ago.

Notwithstanding that fact, for ensuring that I would now meet one of my favourite musicians of all time, I will eternally be in Micky's debt and would even consider bowing down at his feet (while *facing* him I mean, you sickos) but only if he had his shoes on.

Tuesday February 14th 2006 – My Bloody Valentine

◇◇

...and now, the end is near, and so I face blah, blah, blah.

Today, a day which had, for much of the last few months, been scheduled as the final day of this ridiculous long-haul bet that had taken over my life for the last 229 days, was now actually T-minus 1 (milk, no sugar please).

I spent much of it brushing up on the 'last post' and by that, I don't mean I was learning how to play the bugle, I mean that I would be slapping the concluding entry onto my website at some stage over the next 24 hours.

But for now it was Valentine's Day. Oh, joy.

I would have broken into song (because I couldn't find the key) but it had never really been my favourite day of the year. I had, once upon a time, even split up with someone on this so-called romantic day. She was a beautiful girl, she got her good looks from her father (a plastic surgeon), but she threw the towel in and threw me out when I failed to plan anything special for Valentine's night 1995.

Meanwhile, for any particularly smug couples who tend to feel all starry-eyed and lovey-dovey on this day, here are some statistics for you:

○ 1 in 7 people have been unfaithful to their current partners;

○ in 2004 there were 167 116 divorces in the UK; this is one of the highest rates in the world;

○ in 2000 there were 340 million new cases of STDs worldwide;

○ it is estimated that 47 000 different books are published every year that deal with the subject of stressful marriages;

○ train attacks soar by 43 per cent.

I am aware that the last one was a little off the subject but I read it in my paper the same morning and just thought I would let everyone know.

So there we have it. Apologies for urinating on the parade of many happy couples, it's just that I was rather jealous you see... and I was also just about to lose a bet.

Happy VD, anyway (Valentine's Day I mean).

Tuesday Febru… Oh whatever — Greeting 56 (Hugh Cornwell)

Peaches, Strange Little Girl, Nice 'n' Sleazy...

Actually, before I carry on, I'd like to point out that the text above is in no way a reference to the daughter of Sir Bob Geldof. They just happened to be the titles of some of my favourite songs composed by one of my favourite groups of all time, a.k.a. The Stranglers.

Well, as it came to pass, my door buzzer rang at lunchtime on this final FINAL day of my bet and lo, I was happy.

There I was, slumped asleep on the black plastic sofa in my living-room (that I sometimes try to pass off as genuine panther leather), drool no doubt dripping onto the cushion, when I was awoken by the doorbell.

Now I have to say, I don't think that I will ever get my head around the fact that some of my favourite musicians of all time had, over the course of these few weeks, popped around to my home for afternoon tea, minus the tea, but as was the case with Chris Martin several weeks earlier, I once again found the whole experience both exhilarating and surreal in equal measures.

Hugh was a total star in every sense of the word and you know what, the whole experience could quite easily have blown my head clean off since he informed me that he was scheduled to have dinner with the delectable Debbie Harry (Blondie) in London that evening and had her flight not been stuck in New York because of the snow, I suppose she too might have been standing before me on my coffee-stained rug.

Effing snow.

I rather embarrassingly told Hugh to 'send my best to her when you see her tonight,' as if I were some former childhood sweetheart of hers. I have no idea why I said that; she wouldn't know me from a pork chop but my guest said he would pass on my best wishes nonetheless.

As my final 'Greetee' had turned up without David (his manager who had kindly set the whole thing up), the final one of my 56 'greetings' would also become the first one in which the photo was taken by yours truly at arm's length.

Once taken, we both agreed that the snap had turned out fine (apart from my face being in it and my Tintin picture not quite being in it) and Hugh remarked that I looked a little bit like Sil Wilcox.

'Sid errr who?' I enquired.

'SiL Wilcox, the manager of The Stranglers,' Hugh explained, and so once again I humiliated myself, this time displaying breathtaking ignorance and a complete lack of knowledge about a group that I claim to be one of my favourites of all time.

I was then handed a gift for the auction that again turned out to be an item that I would dearly loved to have kept – an extremely rare, limited and signed CD of Stranglers songs that Hugh had made recently in the USA.

Just before he left, I simply had to ask him a question that had been bugging me for many years and one that I thought I might already know the answer to, having supposedly been informed of said answer by a good friend of mine.

'By the way. Who the hell's the 'Great Elmyra' you sing about in *No More Heroes*? Wasn't he some famous art forger or something?'

You know what, my mate was right.

How unbelievably poetic and ironic then, that on this final day of the bet, a bet made by my good friend who was so often wrong when screaming about his certainty of something, Michael had been proved right twice in one day!

GAME OVER

Crack open the champagne! Crack open the poppers (of a party variety)! Stop all the clocks. Cut off the telephone. You might as well prevent the wife from barking with a juicy bone, too...

(My apologies to W.H. Auden.)

IT WAS OVER – THE BET WAS FINISHED – IT WAS DONE – MY TIME WAS UP – NO MORE – THIS WAS AN EX-CHALLENGE.

I apologise to De La Soul but in *this* particular case, following my mammoth effort over the preceding 32.43 weeks, where I had tried to shake hands with as many famous Brits as I could from a list of 500 that had been compiled by my friend, I discovered that it wasn't three but it was actually 56, *that* was the magic number.

You will soon read the conclusions that I had reached through undertaking this lengthy and preposterous... how shall I put it... 'social experiment'.

Had my views about certain people changed? Who was I most upset about not meeting? How smug was Michael? Had I managed to unblock my lavatory's U-bend? Some of these totally unimportant questions and more will be answered.

In due course I would no doubt be forced to wear a pinny as I retched while cleaning my friend's disgraceful toilet, pocked-marked with excrement as it was, such was Michael's scatter-gun approach to using the porcelain, but for now that was it. *C'est suffit.*

I shall temporarily leave you with one of the most important lessons that I had learned through carrying out this whole seven and a half month, country-spanning, marrow-sapping exercise: if you can keep your head, when all about you are losing theirs and blaming it on you, you're doing better than Marie Antoinette.

TO THE WINNER – THE SPOILS

(To the Loser – the Soiled)

So I had come up short! Like a... actually, let's leave the metaphor on this occasion.

As a result, and even before my time limit had elapsed, that is to say at about 5.00 p.m. on Wednesday February 15 2006, 90 minutes or so after I'd seen Hugh Cornwell off with a wave and a 'Goodbye Hugh. Enjoy your dinner with Debbie you lucky, lucky man,' my telephone rang.

On picking up the phone, it didn't take me long to realize that any lingering hope or belief that Michael would take the winning of this bet with the slightest scintilla of humility or shred of good grace was instantly dashed.

'You got my money yet, loser?'

'Wow, you don't waste much time do you? What money?'

'For the football thing, don't act all forgetful. I've already rung Sky, loser. There's a couple of decent pay-per-view games coming up this weekend. It'll be something like £30 quid to buy the whole package till the end of the season, so seeing as you're the moron who believed that

A lovely toilet that I was forced to clean on
numerous occasions for losing the bet.

loads of important people would have time to meet you and seeing as
how they didn't and how you were proved spectacularly wrong, I want
MY ****ing MONEY, LOSER!.'

'Yeah alright, alright. I'll drop it round this evening.'

'OK, nice one, loser. Then we've got to get you started on some domestic
chores. How much do you reckon some Marigolds, a few clothes pegs
and a nice little frilly pink apron will cost?'

'Very funny. Anyway, what d'you mean by 'a few clothes pegs'? I'm not
going to have start hanging out your washing as well, am I?'

'No mate, you're going to be cleaning my toilet, remember? Just a little
word to the wise, it doesn't exactly smell like a bed of roses in there.'

'Oh right, so presumably you mean a - pheeeew - clothes pegs then.'

'Precisely. Look, you've only got yourself to blame. No-one held a gun
to your head, although perhaps you'll be wishing that someone did
when you see the little gift that Purdey's left for you under the bed in
the spare room.'

– laughter –

'Maybe you'll listen to Uncle Mike next time. Remember, he always
knows best.'

I cleaned more crockery than Josiah Wedgewood's wife.

Purdey was his cat and so as it turned out, I would soon be cleaning up the faecal matter of both pet and master.

I dropped the money round to Michael's that night, £30 to be spent on upgrading his satellite TV package, although for all I knew he would simply end up buying 23 tubes of Pringles to be gorged in one binge-sitting, but then again, that was entirely his prerogative and his health concern.

As it happened, he *did* actually spend the money in the correctly assigned manner, I should know, I ended up watching most of the matches round at his place, while on each occasion nervously scanning his litter-filled living room to see what chores of delight I had in store for the following fortnight.

This frequent cleaning of Michael's flat did truly turn out to be a living hell. With hindsight, I would have gladly swapped places with Hercules. There is no way on earth that all of the Augean cattle, at their coprophilic worst, could have soiled their stable as badly as Michael had this small flat in Child's Hill.

I'm no Mrs Mop and neither did I look particularly fetching in a pinny, but rules were rules and Michael saw to it that I completed my chores suitably attired every two weeks. He assured me that he gained absolutely no sexual gratification in seeing me dressed up in such clobber (neither did I in wearing it and yes, I did have clothes on underneath), but he just wanted to see me suitably demeaned and made to look like a prat. So much so, in fact, that on most occasions he invited mutual friends of ours round to his flat to coincide with my cleaning detail.

Many was the time that I would be washing – or as necessity dictated, throwing away – the chilli-encrusted crockery in his kitchen, all the while having to listen to the laughter that bellowed around the living room, before the inevitable, 'How you getting on, Mavis? Nearly finished? Bring us all a cuppa, would you?'

'Oh, **** off. That's not part of my remit. How can making you all tea be categorised as cleaning the flat?'

'Alright Mavis. Keep your rollers in. You don't want your angina playing up, do you!'

– more raucous laughter from the living room –

The very first time that I was required to give this flat the once-over was perhaps the most horrendous experience of them all. His toilet bowl looked as though it hadn't been cleaned since the Hope Diamond was just a lump of coal, and I'd forgotten to bring my flame-thrower and pneumatic drill.

'Michael, I am going to be sick.'

'Oh, SHUT UP.'

'No, I am not joking, I *really* am going to be sick.'

'Don't be such a WIMP, the bleach has got some of it off, just use the toilet brush.'

'I AM, Michael. It's not coming off . What the hell have you been eating anyway, pistachio nuts and superglue?'

'Look, I don't know, just boil some water in the kettle.'

While I didn't orally egest my lunch that day, it was a close run thing. My gag reflex was in overdrive. More gags than at *An Audience with Tommy Cooper*, in fact, and so I spent much of that afternoon with the bitter taste of bile swilling around my mouth.

As for the spare room, Purdey had indeed left a small turd under the bed, but at least this one was dry and in compact pellet form.

'Haven't you heard of a litter tray, Michael?'

'*I* have, there's one in the corner; apparently Purdey hasn't.'

After this there were soup can-cum-ashtrays to be disposed of, gravy puddles to be mopped off carpets, crockery mountains that resembled the north face of the Eiger to be cleaned, vast quantities of hairs to be untangled from dust-busters, snot-filled Kleenexes to be detached from rugs; the list was endless.

And so it went on like this, as month followed month, as watery sunlit Spring became World Cup disappointing Summer and then Polonium-210 discussing Autumn, regular as clockwork I would be vacuuming and wiping down and ventilating and bed-making and completing a multitude of other tasks until one day, just short of Christmas 2006 and with only two months left to carry out these most onerous of duties, Michael simply said, 'Why don't you just pay for me to get a cleaner twice a month.'

So I did.

REFLECTIONS

'Celebrities' eh? A word that strikes fear into the hearts and minds of pseudo-intellectuals and *Times* readers up and down the country, not surprising really if you look what we've had to put up with recently. We've had *Celebrity Big Brother*, *I am a Celebrity Get Me Out of Here*, *Celebrity Farm*, *Celebrity Love Island*, *Cirque de Celebrité*, *Celebrity Weakest Link*, *Celebrity Fit Club*, *Celebrity Fight Club*, *Celebrity Wife Swap*, *'Celebrity' You Are What You Eat* (i.e. a tub of lard as one of my friends cruelly put it after watching the famous young chubster in question), *Celebrity Who Wants to Be A Millionaire*, *Celebrities on Ice*, *Celebrity Stars in Their Eyes* and *Celebrity Wind in Their Hair* (OK, not the last one).

We've also watched famous people ballroom dancing, wrestling, playing golf, driving really badly, playing football, driving really quickly, singing, playing poker, pummelling each other in a boxing ring, living with each other's spouses and playing darts. I was going to say that the only thing we have yet to see is a porn star baking a cake and then I remembered *Hell's Kitchen*.

Yes, in this day and age, one can make the front pages of the tabloids by having no discernible talent whatsoever but merely by being married to Aston Villa's centre forward, and once a year, for a couple of weeks, the most talked about person in the land is someone who has lived in a house in Elstree with 12 other people while making a complete tit of themselves.

Shortly after the bet that you have just read about had ended, a good friend of mine asked my opinion on the Arctic Monkeys. I replied with uncertainty and asked whether they were being driven towards extinction, at which point I was corrected and informed that they were in fact the latest in a long line of 'Great New Musical Sensations' that *everyone* was talking about.

At about the same time, a young lady from Wickford in Essex by the name of Chantelle, emerged blinking into the moonlight having just been crowned winner of *Celebrity Big Brother 4* yet ironically enough, she was the ONLY ONE of the 11 housemates to be described as a 'non-celebrity' when she entered the house.

Wars start, holes in the atmosphere grow, planets become declassified, yet the conveyor belt of fame, or indeed infamy, rumbles ever onwards, churning out new heroes and villains; new names for us to digest every day. Once these names are locked into the subconscious, recent new examples might include Lily Allen, Alexander Litvinenko or David Banda Mwale Ciccone Ritchie, there they might remain forever. They may remain even where we forget the name of the first girl we ever kissed at the 4th form social while dancing to *Belouis Some*.

I suppose that how impressed, obsessed or full of admiration we are for those who are well-known invariably depends on us as individuals. Whether we would like to meet them, or sleep with them, or sit next to them and bore them on a flight to Miami, may well depend on where we find ourselves in our own humdrum existences.

Not that I am decrying this whole ethos of idol-worshipping. Why would I want to take the moral high-ground and promote a celebrity counter-culture ideal, particularly when I hadn't done too badly myself off the backs of Jonathan Ross, Nicky Clarke, *et al.*, thank you very much (well I didn't write this for free).

I am no Dennis Pennis; neither am I a 'One-Question Lady' or a squirter of water through fake microphones. I wouldn't want to pretend to be part of the 'Staines Massive' and ridicule the high and mighty or indeed in any way want to embarrass, harass, stalk, take down a peg or name and shame any high-profile personality who by hard work or sheer luck has made it to the top of their profession.

Why not? Because who the frigging hell am I to do so? Where on earth are my great achievements that entitle me to pour scorn on people of whom I am jealous? When did I last split the atom, or find a cure for syphilis, or do anything to promote world peace?

I might be excellent at barbecuing chicken but that does not give me a right to pick faults with Jo Wiley, Russell Brand, Tim Lovejoy or Paris

Hilton. I mean, no-one's flawless, are they?

The only thing that I can say with any certainty is that these 'Individuals of Note in their Professions', these 'Celebrities' are as manifold and varied in their personalities as the rest of us. That is not rocket science either, and therefore, despite losing this bet, I still cannot agree with Michael's preposterous generalisation.

He assumed that we would be able to draw conclusions from our findings; we would be able to tell what it was that made famous people tick (apart from swallowing hand grenades obviously) and whether these individuals were generally salt-of-the-earth, feet-on-the ground, run-of-the-mill types, types like you and I.

Do they also have trouble opening a tin of corned beef with one of those little keys? Or hold their partner's head under the duvet after breaking wind in bed? Or complain in the Post Office when the customer in front of them natters away with the cashier for ages?

Well, as Will Self completely correctly pointed out to me in his letter, and something that I very quickly came to realize having started my challenge, was that sending out 500 letters to such people to see how many would meet me for no reason, would prove absolutely nothing about them. I might as well have written to 500 successful pilots or gym instructors.

No, this 'Social experiment' as I embarrassingly called it for the first few weeks, was no experiment at all and quite patently had no merit or scientific worth whatsoever. It would not and should not be referred to in any social treatise written on the 'Cult of Personality' and any statistics gleaned from it were about as useful as a marshmallow crash helmet.

I honestly believe that the reason that over 300 people from my list of 500 never replied to my letter was due to the fact that over 300 people on my list probably never even saw it or had any knowledge of it.

Maybe some that *did* see it but chose not to meet me only took this course of action through fear that I was a weirdo, or because they were abroad, or because they were unwell, or in rehab, or going through a divorce, or were just about to give birth. None of the individuals that failed to get back to me are bad people as Michael had suggested. This was no witch hunt, it was an exercise that was flawed from the outset.

The coverage that this stupid project received in the media, while simultaneously being both daunting and flattering, also led me to the quite obvious conclusion that as a public, we continue to be fascinated by hearing snippets of information about those who appear nightly on the Idiot's Lantern in the corner of the living room, or on the silver screen, or over the airwaves.

I worked out that over the 32 weeks course of my bet, I received almost 5000 emails from total strangers sending me good luck messages in my attempt to try and make my best friend look foolish with his cynical view of man(and woman)kind.

People from as far afield as Australia, Germany, India, Brazil, France, Denmark, Holland, Hong Kong, Pakistan, South Africa, Spain, Malaysia, Argentina, Israel, USA, New Zealand, Poland, The Czech Republic, Kenya, Dubai, Japan, Croatia, Jordan, Ireland, Canada, Sweden, Romania and Stoke took an interest in my bet. (Just a few more countries and we could have had a mini World Cup tournament.)

I remain baffled to this day as to how and why the details of a conversation I had with a friend in a pub in North London managed to spread around the globe. Such is the power of cyberspace, I guess. Or perhaps there are countries other than England where people get bored at work and look for something strange to read about on the internet.

I'm certainly no socio-anthropologist and despite what Michael and I set out to explore, I am aware that none of the anecdotes that you have just read will have provided you with the slightest insight into the psyche of famous British individuals. I'm no Jean-Paul Sartre, but then again my book is cheaper than his and besides, I'm sure that you're less interested in his theories on whether humanity can reach a perpetual state of fulfilment, and are more interested in what George Galloway's coat was like.

I would be the first to admit that what I have written is hardly likely to win the Booker Prize; neither will my findings be as remotely useful as those of Kimberly Allen in *Celebrity Culture, Performing Arts Pedagogy and Female Individualisation* which I recently stumbled across on the internet. Nevertheless, I hope that if you *have* managed to finish this book before you lost the will to live, you'd feel as though you have just been transported on a proverbial 'rip-roaring rollercoaster of a ride'. And not just because you feel like vomiting at the end of it.

I shall now leave you with that oft-quoted Groucho Marx line, one that a good friend of mine kindly reminded me of just the other day: *'From the moment I picked up your book until the moment I put it down, I was convulsed with laughter... One day I intend to read it.'*

BECAUSE I WILL NEVER
WIN AN OSCAR

To everyone who donated money to the RNIB on my sponsorship website, I salute you. Roger, I don't know you, but you obviously have the generous nature and the deep pockets of Mother Theresa wearing a clown's suit.

To the several thousand people who took the time to email me their support, either on my website or directly, I thank you equally.

I had better thank my friends and family as well (especially Michael), since although none of them had the basic good grace to garner me a 'Meeting' with Paul McCartney, I suppose they *were* quite supportive (once they'd finished laughing).

Obviously, I'm indebted to everyone at the RNIB, particularly Matt, as well as to any of the agents who DID actually pass my letters on. Special mention to Gaye, Suzi, David, Neil, Steph, my flatmate Lois and her colleague Paul and Ros who all went over and above the call of duty and who managed to collar me Fiona Phillips and Lorraine Kelly, Jonathan Ross, Hugh Cornwell, Carl Fogarty, Toby Anstis, Chris Martin and Bob Holness, respectively. I'd also like to thank my own agent, James (yes, unbelievably I, too, have one now) as well as everyone at The Friday Project, especially Clare W, for ensuring that one or two more people could read about my ludicrous bet in book form.

Jules Segal

Finally, my eternal, overwhelming gratitude and love to the most important 56 people of all, the 'Individuals of Note in Their Profession' who were willing to shake the hand of a random, five ft 9 inch, 10½ stone, pasty-skinned, salt-n-pepper haired member of the public.

I couldn't have done it without them and I'm not just saying that.

DVD EXTRAS*

◇◇

APPENDIX A

◇◇◇◇◇◇◇◇◇◇◇◇◇◇◇◇◇◇◇◇◇◇◇◇◇◇◇◇◇◇◇◇◇◇◇◇◇

A Message From The Truculent One – (From my website on Feb 15th 2005)

All hail the Winner!

'Here I stand, basking in the glory of being right yet again and also soon to be lounging in my clean flat whilst watching Pay-per-view football.

Jules lost the bet so he will soon be greeting my 500 dirty dishes and my 500 carpet stains and I don't think he'll need a list this time. Yes, he's been brave but on this occasion, fortune favoured the fool.

After the mammoth effort made by my good mate I think the next challenge will be even more fiendish (NO! never again, Michael, – Jules). Maybe I'll get him to try and make the newspapers that this story featured in, print the correct one and to include a photo of ME for once.

Anyway, congratulations to myself.

Love you all. Mick the Greek.'

---

*'Dis Very Diary.

278

◇◇

The Auctionable gifts

A number of the gifts that you see below were sold on eBay in May 2006. The ones that were not will be auctioned in a similar manner soon after this book is first published. It is therefore impossible to give you an exact figure as to how much money was raised for the RNIB right now, although it's already into the thousands, so basically, a massive thanks to everyone who gave me a gift (no Ferraris or pieces of fluff after all of that) and thanks to everyone who bought one.

LISA RODGERS – one grey jump suit, one grey bodice (I think that is what they are called), one cream jacket with fur-lined hood, all as worn in the TV show *Scrapheap Challenge.*

LORRAINE KELLY – one pink dress as worn on GMTV; one signed photo; one signed sticker.

FIONA PHILLIPS – one GMTV Goody Bag (pen, keyring, T-shirt, travel mug); one signed sticker.

JASON QUEALLY – one red/blue cycling jersey.

ALAN TITCHMARSH – one signed photo. Various Kew Gardens pamphlets and entrance ticket (used) thrown in by me (and signed by me for what it's worth...).

RICHARD WILSON – one signed photo.

FIONA BRUCE – one signed sticker.

NICK ROSS – one signed sticker.

NICHOLAS PARSONS – one Nicholas Parsons quizbook; two signed Nicholas Parsons CDs – *Fantasy*; one signed sticker.

IAIN BANKS – one signed hardback copy of *The Algebraist.*

LAWRENCE DALLAGLIO – one signed sticker.

DAVID GOWER – one signed N-Power T-shirt.

JOHN FRANCOME – one signed *Jockey Club Rule Book*; one entry badge (used) and betting slips (losing) thrown in by me (both with message from me).

JIM MCGRATH – one Timeform Chase Season 2005/6 book; one signed sticker.

ANN WIDDECOMBE MP – one signed copy of *The Clematis Tree*; one signed sticker.

SIR TIM RICE – one signed autobiography (to me, although it says Jason(?) not Julian) *Oh what a Circus*; one CD *Aida*; one signed sticker.

CHERIE BLAIR – one signed copy of *The Goldfish Bowl*.

CHARLES KENNEDY MP – one signed photograph.

JEREMY CLARKSON – one signed photograph.

LESLEY GARRETT – one unique signed T-shirt worn by Lesley when taking part in the baton relay for the 2002 Commonwealth Games; one signed copy of *Classic FM Magazine* with Lesley's photo on the front +free CD attached. +

BRUCE FORSYTH – one signed photograph with amusing message.

BILL KENWRIGHT – two complimentary tickets to the theatre (*Blood Brothers*); one signed sticker.

CLARE BALDING – one signed Windsor racecard; one entry badge (used) and betting slip (losing obviously) thrown in by me (both with message from me).

DAVID SUCHET – one *Poirot Casebook*; two signed photos; one autograph of David's on a Hercule Poirot letterheaded notepaper.

CHRIS TARRANT – four VIP tickets to recording of *Who Wants to be a Millionaire*.

MIKE LEIGH – one signed photograph.

JIMMY CARR – one Xfm wall hanging; three Xfm badges

JOHN MOTSON – one tie (one of his favourites).

JEFFREY ARCHER – one signed copy of *Heaven*; one signed sticker.

TONY HAWKS – one HB pencil (with genuine teethmarks as Michael pointed out); one signed authenticity sticker.

SIR PATRICK MOORE – one *Atlas of the Universe*; one signed sticker.

JONATHAN EDWARDS – one signed photo.

DERREN BROWN – one limited edition print of an original Derren Brown painting of Sir Anthony Hopkins.

BRUCE OLDFIELD – one signed copy of *Rootless* (with Bruce Oldfield boutique carrier bag).

JIMMY HILL – one signed photograph.

BOB HOLNESS – one pink *Blockbusters* fleece top; one signed photograph.

NEIL KINNOCK – one signed tie (University of Wales); one signed sticker.

CHRIS MARTIN – one personal note including small amount or artwork; one Coldplay postcard signed by the band.

JONATHAN ROSS – one calendar of scantily clad men with Jonathan's face superimposed over each one (as featured on Jonathan's chat show); one fluffy tie embossed with small metallic trinkets; one autographed T-shirt with a male face on it (currently un-identified but possibly Lawrence Llewellyn Bowen).

ANDREW MARR – one signed copy of *My Trade*.

CARL FOGARTY – six selected signed posters (2×Fogarty, 2×McCoy, 2×Martin); one signed Foggy Petronas-Racing shirt.

JOE PASQUALE – one signed photo.

EDITH BOWMAN – one of those metal records inside a glass frame (autographed by Edith). This one is 'to recognise sales in the UK in excess of 100 000 copies of the album *The Magic Numbers*.

SIR RANULPH FIENNES – one signed copy of *Race to the Pole*.

AINSLEY HARRIOTT – one signed *Ready Steady Cook* apron, carrier bag, table mat and photo.

GARY BUSHELL – one signed copy of *Two Faced*.

TOBY ANSTIS/JAMIE THEAKSTON – one signed Heart 106.2 FM T-shirt (also includes autographs of Emma B and Greg Burns).

MICHAELA STRACHAN – one signed photo ('To Julian' (me) although you can always get your name changed by deed poll) with amusing message.

HUGH CORNWELL – one signed copy of exclusive CD – *Hugh Cornwell Live: Live It And Breathe It* (not available in shops).

You might notice that not everyone who met me is named in the list above. It's not that I've *kept* any of the gifts for myself, I promise, it's just that a number of those I met were not aware that they had been invited to bring something along for me. So don't have a go at them, have a go at me or their agents for not making it clearer to them. Actually yes, have a go at their agents.

APPENDIX C

◇◇

Michael's attempt to '…write better than Kafka'

'Self-control means wanting to be effective at some random point in the infinite radiations of my spiritual existence.' **Kafka**

*'If a tree falls in the forest and there's no-one to hear it, does it make a sound? Of course it ******* does!'* **Michael**